Francis Francis

Wild Rose

a tale of the Mexican frontier

Francis Francis

Wild Rose
a tale of the Mexican frontier

ISBN/EAN: 9783743324381

Manufactured in Europe, USA, Canada, Australia, Japa

Cover: Foto ©ninafisch / pixelio.de

Manufactured and distributed by brebook publishing software (www.brebook.com)

Francis Francis

Wild Rose

WILD ROSE

A TALE OF THE MEXICAN FRONTIER

BY

FRANCIS FRANCIS

AUTHOR OF "MOSQUITO," "SADDLE AND MOCCASIN,"
"IN A LONDON SUBURB," ETC.

New York
MACMILLAN AND CO.
AND LONDON
1895

All rights reserved

WILD ROSE.

A TALE OF THE MEXICAN FRONTIER.

CHAPTER I.

"ALL of you for outside?" asked Ned Chase, from the box-seat of the Duckville and Dogtown stage-coach.

In the chorus that came from the roof behind him, there was not one reply in the negative.

"Then I'll take two to one we upset before we make Willow Springs," said the driver, grimly.

His passengers, however, were full of confidence, and greeted the prophecy with derision.

"That'll be all right," he pursued carelessly. "But I've seen top-heavy coaches on tracks like this before to-day. However, suit yourselves; I ain't kicking a particle. All aboard?"

"Which of you gentlemen is going to offer me a seat on the box?"

The speaker (a brunette of two or three and twenty — tall, slight, and dressed in a style that Duckville ladies might occasionally have pictured in their dreams, but knew not otherwise) had just issued from the stage-coach office, and stood on the little corduroy platform before it, awaiting a reply with quiet self-possession.

Ned Chase glanced at the reins in his hand, and then

at his neighbour — a black-browed, black-bearded, unprepossessing miner, who did not seem inclined to respond to the invitation.

"The lady's speaking to you," he said after a moment's pause; "I reckon you don't want *me* to climb down."

"Wal, *I* spoke for the box-seat before —"

"Oh, pshaw! Don't preach on it, anyway. The lady spoke for it *afterwards*, that's all."

A murmur from those behind indicated that the sense of the company was with the driver, and opposed to the occupant of the seat beside him. The latter hesitated a moment, as though still half disposed not to move. Then, with a muttered curse, he jerked himself out of his place and descended to the interior of the coach, while the new-comer calmly appropriated his vacated seat.

"Vy! ef it ain't Vild Rose," exclaimed Solomon Poheim, a well-known mining speculator of obvious extraction, whose fat form was perched on the very summit of the coach.

Proceeding deliberately to arrange herself, the young lady he had recognised glanced aside at him with a slight elevation of the eyebrows.

"Some mistake, I think," she said coolly.

"Not much! I known Vild Rose ven I seen her!"

"Yes, but Doc Peters told me two years ago in New York that you had been killed up in Butte City, for beating some fellow out of a mine, and — one doesn't expect to see a man about again — so soon, that is — after dying —"

"*Ach, was!*"

"It's a little indecent —"

"But I vasn't dead!"

"Well, all I know is, that it was told me by a doctor, and a doctor ought to know when a man's dead."

"But—"

"Oh, pshaw! you're dead, Sol! Quit talking in your sleep," cried the others, laughingly.

"*Ach, was!* Der vas some liddle trobles — shootings and dot, but dey don't amount to nozzings. De shentleman vot done it, he 'pologise afterwards. I cou'n't beat no one out of anyzings — dey beat me, ride along! But how you come on, Rose?— vot you doin' here, enyvay? vhere you from? vhere you goin' to?"

"To play and sing at the Mint Saloon, in Dogtown."

"Der new piano player, vat?"

She nodded.

"You don't say! But — but Dave Kellon vas trying to sell out von der 'Mint' dey say —"

"Well, I reckon whoever takes the Mint on will take me on too."

"Dat's so; you bet dey don't led you go once dey god you."

The coach was already well under way. At first the team had seemed disposed to do everything but go in harness, and go together. But Ned Chase knew his business. A little coaxing here, a rating there by name, elsewhere a couple of stingers, skilfully applied under the splinter bars, had brought the troubled quartette of tossing crests into something like order. Only the nearside leader's traces were slack; the rest had begun to go together and go well up into their bridles.

Meanwhile the young lady and Poheim had exchanged news, and with the utmost *sang-froid* she had critically inspected her fellow-passengers, most of whom Sol had introduced to her, giving her name to them as "Miss Rose Carlin." With an eye of approval she now began to watch Ned's driving, and—a finished whip and horsewoman herself—she saw that he did not keep that dead benumbing strain on his horses' mouths which the poor brutes usually suffer from in America, where such training as they do receive tends to make them go the harder the harder one pulls, and to slacken speed when the reins are dropped.[1]

The pace began to improve, and the coach, since all the weight was on its roof, for there happened to be very little baggage below to balance it, swayed bodily at every turn and rut in the rough track. Some of the passengers remarked more or less jocularly that "the old coach swung good and free"; that "she bowed like a Frenchman," and so forth. But Ned drove on in imperturbable silence, a course which affected these gentlemen far more than would have any overt endeavour on his part to alarm them. Gradually some of the passengers grew less talkative.

A short stretch of really bad road lay in front, wherein big rocks and big mud-holes occurred without any uniformity or order.

"Hold on, Miss Carlin," counselled Ned, *sotto voce*.

Bump, jump, bang, dip—and once more d——ip! The men on the roof were tossed one against another in the wildest confusion.

"Crimson Crimes! vat a ride ve are heffing!" ejaculated Sol, his rich and infectious laugh testifying to the fact that he, at any rate, was not nervous.

---

[1] Possibly this originated in a particular style formed for driving trotters. It may be the custom to throw the weight of the sulky on the trotter's mouth in order to give freer play to its shoulders.

"Sol Poheim," gravely observed Colonel Dodge, a handsome old mine owner with a twinkle of dry humour in his eye, "it doesn't look over and above well for you to steady yourself on the diamond pin in my bosom every time we hit a rock or a chuck hole. The pin don't afford any holt wuth speaking of, and if we was to happen to upset, it might come away altogether."

"— In Sol's hand," suggested Dan Birchfield, amidst a good deal of laughter.

"Sol'd take the best kind of care of it, Colonel," remarked Judge Maddox, reassuringly; "you wouldn't have any cause for further anxiety."

But at this point, one of the division whose fears had reduced them to silence declared that "he didn't believe the old coach cared a cuss whether she upset or not, and he reckoned he'd go below."

A Government surveyor, and a whiskey drummer, whose habit of consuming even his own samples, when on the road, had shattered his nerves, decided to follow his example; and the weight being thus more evenly distributed, the coach proceeded steadily enough.

"Who's the lady, Sol?" asked Judge Maddox, who occupied the seat beside him.

In an undertone Sol briefly gave him her history.

It appeared from this that " she came of good family, but at the age of sixteen had run away from school, in Oakland (a suburb of San Francisco), with Bob Hannaford, a gambler, whom she had married and accompanied to most of the mining towns and camps in the Northwest. Bob had treated her badly, and when one day she had discovered that he had another wife living, she had left him. Then — well, then she had been a piano girl for a while; and finally Jim Tritton, an old mining man, had adopted her as his daughter, but he had been killed by accident soon afterwards in a row in a gambling house. However, he had lived long enough to will his pile to her — $50,000 or thereabouts — and shortly afterwards she had disappeared — gone to Europe so Sol had been told. As for herself, she was a roulette fiend, bright as a new dollar and straight as a string, high-strung and hot-tempered — could handle a six-shooter, too, with any tough on the frontier, but was good-natured from her boots to her bonnet, — so long as you didn't try to monkey with her. If you did — well, you soon learnt that she wasn't afraid of anything on God's earth, and claimed to be treated like a lady.

"I reckon," concluded Sol, reflectively, "dat's 'bout all vat any von can tell you 'bout her — dat's de outsides von Vild Rose, anyvay. But she's — vell, I tell you, shentlemen, she's got whole tracts of feelings and opinions vat she kips fenced in like."

"— Which a man's just got to go'n' explore for himself," volunteered cheery old Dan Birchfield, who had bent an attentive ear to Sol's story.

"Dan —" commenced Colonel Dodge gravely, and then he paused. "How old are you, Dan?"

"Fifty-two, Colonel."

"Well (persuasively), ain't it pretty near time for you to quit tearing the veil of virgin modesty from these sacred feminine treasures of character and things?"

"Why, Colonel, fact is, I jest keep all on a-tearing, and don't stop to do no reckoning."

Wild Rose, the unconscious subject of conversation, considered the prospect of rolling prairie about them, looked at Ned once or twice, and once or twice addressed him. But although the son of wealthy people "back East," an educated man, and a regular dare-devil when moved to action, he was not easily drawn out.

Ned Chase was about seven and twenty, and with his sunburnt olive skin, black hair and little pencilled moustache, his level brows and quiet mouth, grey eyes and clean-cut features, was a man at whom most people would look twice. Although spare and of not more than middle height, he was very square-shouldered and muscular; and his face wore an expression of reserve and determination that was well in keeping with his strong frame. As a rule he was reticent, particularly with strangers; he often appeared therefore cold. But with those he liked he was frank and generous to a fault, and they soon learnt that, spite of all his apparent indifference, he was extremely sensitive.

"That near-side leader breaks up the team," observed Rose at length.

"Yep."

"He's too sulky to live; he's worse than a mule."

Ned nodded.

"Get in there, you plug!" and he sent the lash out to him with a vicious cut.

"I guess I'll earmark him once, and see how it works," remarked Rose, producing a little "Smith & Wesson" six-shooter from her hand-bag.

"Go ahead," rejoined Ned, imperturbably, watching her out of the corner of his eye.

She levelled the weapon and fired.

At the same time Chase laid the whip across his wheelers, touched the off-side leader, and the team was off at a gallop. The passengers behind and inside were caught with the excitement of the moment. Six-shooters were produced on all sides, and a score of shots fired into the air, the passengers warwhooping like red Indians. The coach itself rocked and bounded along like a band-box. But fortunately it was on a stretch of good road, and before bad ground was reached again Ned had steadied the team, the near-side leader bearing a little red mark in the point of one ear, going well into the collar now.

The incident was curious for the instinctive confidence in each other which it proved Ned and his passenger to possess. If Rose had done what she had done, it was because she had recognised Ned's capacity to deal with any emergency which might occur in the handling of his team. A similar feeling of confidence in her, on Ned's part, explained his having allowed her to shoot, notwithstanding the fact that he had never seen her fire a shot before. He would have taken the revolver away from any other woman, and from most men.

The coach swept on. Willow Springs soon came into view, and a short stop at the wayside store — the only house there — gave the nags a rest before continuing the journey to the mining village of Bantry, where a change of horses was in readiness.

The party on the outside of the coach was a cheery one, and as they approached to the horizon of hills many a good story was told of life in that yet wild quarter of the Southwest.

"Who was the first judge in Dogtown?" echoed Colonel Dodge, a discussion having arisen upon the point. "Why, Wiggy Thompson, of course. I remember their electing him. The night before, there'd been seventeen fights in town, on — on general principles.

Quite a number of the combatants needed burying next day. The influence of the law-abiding citizens was at a discount. So they concluded to have a judge, and they chose old Wiggy, who kept a store, 'cause the miners didn't have any time to spare, and they allowed that as Wiggy gave pretty fair weight in his own scales, he wouldn't be liable to stint customers when he came to handle the scales of justice."

"And how did old Wiggy take to it?"

"Wal, Wiggy he took to it quite naturally. He bought him a pair of spectacles to add dignity to his appearance. He couldn't see *through* 'em, but that didn't matter; sometimes he looked over and sometimes under them, and his verdicts ran a good deal in that same fashion, too. I remember there was a fellow called Dancing Joe in Dogtown those days, and somehow Joe'd come to be a sort of scapegoat of the town. When no one else could be found to take the blame for anything that had been done, they just had up Dancing Joe and fined him. Happened one day that some lumber belonging to a sluice was stolen. No one knew who'd taken it, but still justice had to pursue its course. So they had up Joe for trial. There wasn't a particle of evidence against him of any kind. However, Wiggy, he heard the case out gravely, and then, putting on his specs, he looks at Joe. 'Well, Joe,' he said, 'the evidence against you don't 'pear to be very clear in this case — not so clear as I *have* known it, but in the interests of justice the court will have to punish you all the same. You're fined fifty dollars. If you're guilty, its dog-gone lenient; and if you're innocent, why, it's just enough to be a lesson to the son of a gun who ought to be standing in your place!'"

"Do you remember his trying Joe Grant for shooting a Chinaman?" asked Birchfield, when the laughter had subsided.

"No; what was that?"

"Why, Joe and Wiggy were interested in some mine together. Joe ran the mine, and shot his Chinaman cook for hard-boiling the eggs, or suthin'. Nat'rally, first time he come in town for a bill of goods he was brought up before Wiggy. Wal, Wiggy consulted his law books for a long time before he chipped. Finally he says: 'The court decides in this here case that the pris'ner's discharged. There ain't nothing in them books about shooting a Chinaman. If you was to shoot 'em often enough, and in sufficient quantities, I reckon the Federal Government 'd hev t' allow Chiney to say suthin' diplomatic about it; but such international matters as that is beyond the jurisdiction of this court.'"

Rose and the driver were a little outside the eddy of conversation. Now and then Ned was appealed to, or caught the subject of their mirth, and threw in a crisp word or two that added to it. But for the most part he was silent.

Rose, too, gradually let her attention drift from the talkers, and fell to contemplating the scenery abstractedly. Stretches of sparse woodland had succeeded the prairies as they drew nearer to the hills. She shivered slightly, and speaking half-absently, said:

"I wonder why the earth always looks so sad?"

Ned was silent while his glance swept the landscape before him. Like all untouched nature after the hour of dawn, it certainly had an air of melancholy, bathed though the scene was at present in the glow of a sunset that shone like a conflagration of old-world jewels upon the summits of the distant hills.

"You mean the prairie, forest, hills?"

"Yes; when they're quiet they look so old, so wise, so impenetrable — so utterly hopeless."

"I guess, half the time, the look of things depends more on our own moods than on theirs," he said thoughtfully.

"Perhaps — how I hate that!" she exclaimed, almost savagely. "One can never get away even in thought from one's poor, miserable self. We think we feel something — half the time it's only pictured in our own imagination. And all that one *does* see or think about is dipped, steeped, saturated in our own personality — dyed the coarse colour of our mental eyes, dressed in the ragged clothing of our moods, begotten halt and blind of our crippled powers of reason. What we *see* is never what actually *is*, only a lying reflection of it."

There was a pause, during which the girl's face lost its momentary sternness and grew soft again. Ned was musing.

"I guess you're right," he said at length. "Come to think of it, we're sort of chained up all the time and fighting shadows."

"But don't you ever get tired of it all — tired of yourself? Don't you ever feel a contempt for yourself and hate yourself? — as one might hate a person one was married to and had grown to despise;" and she glanced at the clean-cut face turned from her to the horses. "Don't you ever feel that you would like to get right away from yourself — yourself with your same old, worn-out arguments, and borrowed, poverty-stricken tracks of thought, that seem ashamed even of themselves for pretending to lead anywhere — Don't you long sometimes for a new idea? Oneself is such a little circle, and *such* a failure."

Ned laughed curtly. "Yes, I know something of all that, too."

"One's thoughts are like good old domestic animals, — that have been domesticated for thousands of years, — and have never yet taken anybody more than a few miles away from their old farmyard of civilisation, and never, never, never will. Oh, dear! After all, what does it matter!" and she laughed shortly. "Let's be good, and nice, and love the Lord, and not care. It'll be all the same some day. Is that Dogtown?" and she pointed to some houses ahead of them.

Ned replied in the affirmative, and a moment later Rose was laughing and talking to the men behind her.

"Sol, how are you fixed about now?" she asked.

"Financially?"

"Financially — you know what I mean."

"How much you vant?" asked Solomon.

"Oh, I'd just like you to loan me a few hundreds till the luck changes."

"De money vas yours," replied Sol, promptly, and taking out his pocket-book, he handed her three $100 notes. "Shentlemen," he observed to the others, "I vant you to understand right here dat Miss Carlin's a young lady vat you kin bet your last tollar on. She never go back on you. Ve're olt-time frients from Montana und Vashington Territory. I take her word sooner as mos' men's bond. Vat she say goes! See?"

Rose laughed. "Sol thinks he's selling a mine," she said, and she handed him back his notes. "I don't want them, Sol — not this time. I still have a few left. I only wanted to find out whether you were changed. But it's the same old Sol, I see."

And as she spoke the coach drew up before the verandah of the Mountain Pride hotel.

CHAPTER II.

In the plain suit of dark clothes in which he returned to the hotel to supper, Ned Chase looked a very different being from the broad-sombreroed, flannel-shirted, dust-begrimed driver who had brought the coach there an hour before. A knot of miners standing under the lamp in the verandah greeted him cordially as he approached.

"Well, Joe, what's the best word? How does the mine come on?" he asked of a fair-moustached, handsome young giant who was lounging in the group.

Joe Johnstone was Ned's partner in the "Fresh Start" mine, and Joe ran the mine while Ned drove the coach, paying a substitute to work in his place until the property should be sufficiently developed for them to begin shipping ore.

"Ned, she's a dandy!" cried Joe, gleefully, and as he spoke he grasped Ned's hand, and swung him about playfully as though he had been a boy. "She's the boss. I put in a blast this morning which uncovered a body of ore that'll go $4000 to the ton. Here, sample that!" and he produced a specimen of ore from his pocket, and held it in the lamp for Ned to see. "How's that for high? Look at the coarse gold in it!"

"Gosh! Joe," said Ned, turning the ore sample over carefully, "you've struck it this time, and no mistake!"

"I should smile! Why, it'll go it in gold alone, to say nothing of the silver!"

"Can I take a look at your rock, or don't you care to show it?" asked the man who had had to surrender his seat to Rose Carlin that afternoon, and who now happened to be standing near them.

"Why, cer'nly," replied Joe. "Let the gentleman see it, Ned."

Chase looked his late passenger over coldly, and then handed him the specimen rather ungraciously. He was guided a good deal by impressions in his estimates of men, and was not prepossessed in the stranger's favour.

"What mine 'd you say it came from?" asked this latter.

"*Didn't* say," returned Ned, dryly.

"Oh, pshaw, Ned! The 'Fresh Start' of course — our mine," said Joe, good-humouredly. "And she's going to be the boss mine in this camp, Sirree."

"You don't say! Why, the owners is in luck then," observed the stranger with an odd look, as he handed back the sample.

"Well, Joe, so you're still bent on getting married to-morrow?" said Ned, changing his tone and turning his back on the speaker.

"That's what I am — to-morrow evening. The boys are giving us a dance here to-night as a send-off."

"Is that so?"

"'So'? Why, blame your old skin, you're the prime mover in it — you set it afoot! The boys gave you dead away when they came to me about it this morning. If you ain't the triflingest old fraud! There! come right in and let's take a drink before supper."

They passed indoors to the bar, and thence to the dining-room, where most of the tables were already filled. Ned and Joe took seats at one occupied by Judge Maddox and Colonel Dodge, ministering to whose wants was a neat little waitress of medium size but very shapely — bright and cheerful, light-haired and blue-eyed, with the fairest of skins, freely freckled, a sunny smile, pearly teeth, a dimpled chin, and a fresh, wholesome, "early-morning" look about her that was good to see.

"Miss Hunter tells me that she's going to be good enough to marry you to-morrow, Joe," said the Colonel, gravely, with a glance aside at the trim waitress as she went off to bring the new-comers their suppers.

"Ah, Colonel, you can't keep a secret!" cried the girl, looking back with an arch smile. "How 'd you know I wasn't going to keep Joe on the anxious seat till to-morrow?"

"Yes," said Joe, with honest pride and modesty combined — the pride for Kitty Hunter, the modesty for himself; "Kitty's allowed she'll take pity on me at last. You bet I'm playing in luck, Colonel."

"The biggest kind of luck, Joe. The best luck a square man can play in is to marry a good woman."

"— And have the Colonel give him a handsome wedding present," added Judge Maddox, slyly.

"Why, it does look that way, don't it," responded Joe, with mock gravity. "Darned if I see how he'll be able to get around it after declaring himself like that. But there! guess I'll have to let him off, I wouldn't know what to ask for. It just seems as though I'd got everything in the world."

"When a man feels like that," observed the Colonel,

parasol her toilet was so exquisitely neat and finished, so totally unlike anything that he had seen since he had left his own home in New York.

She laughed once when he was surveying her thus, and without turning her head said:

"Mr. Chase!"

"Well?"

"Do you think a woman doesn't know when she is being looked at?"

"But it's such a long while since I've seen — any one like you," he explained, apologetically.

"And you used to once?"

"Yes."

"You weren't born to — this sort of thing?" and she waved her hand towards the houses about them, as she turned and looked at him.

"No."

"I knew it, of course. Let's be friends then, and when we're together be — as we used to be. It'll be a relief."

They sealed the compact with a glance.

"Where are you taking me to first?"

"To the Mint — and here it is."

They turned into a large saloon, on one side of which was a bar, bedecked with large mirrors, great show of glass, and nickel-plated fittings. Seats were arranged round the room; in the middle of it were a large stove and a couple of billiard tables. Big Frank, one of the bartenders, a good-natured-looking, burly giant of about six feet four, leant over the bar discussing a specimen of ore with a couple of prospectors in blue shirts, blue canvas overalls, and black slouch hats. Upon seeing Rose, he bowed with the deepest deference, and when Ned had explained to him the position that she was about to occupy in the house, he literally beamed as he stretched out a brawny hand to her in welcome.

"Mighty glad to make your acquaintance, Miss — your name's well known to me, anyhow. Dave's inside," he said to Ned. "They had a late session last night — only jest broke up. Some of the boys came on here after the ball."

They passed through the swinging doors into the gambling-room within. Upon one side of it were two faro tables, at one of which a little desultory play was still proceeding; on the other a roulette table, and a horseshoe table for stud-horse poker, both of which were deserted. The end of the room was occupied by a raised platform with a rail round it, within which stood a semi-grand piano.

There had been some heavy play in the last twelve hours, and Dave Kellon had not yet gone to bed. He had relinquished his seat at the faro table, however, and was on the point of leaving when Ned entered and presented him to Miss Carlin.

"I guess we've met before, Miss Carlin," said Dave, genially. "Anyway, I seen you up in Helena, four years ago. Your name was familiar to me just as soon as you wrote, only I couldn't place you. One moment, please," and he went to the swinging doors.

A minute later Big Frank appeared with an open bottle of champagne and some glasses on a tray, on which lay also the specimen of ore he had been examining.

"Them men as was here when you passed wanted for you to have this specimen, Miss Carlin. It's a dandy, too. There's a chunk of gold in it as big as a $10 piece. It ain't no good refusing. They're gone and I d' know who they were — they didn't want no thanks, anyhow."

The champagne was the greatest compliment that Kellon knew how to offer to his new employée, and although champagne at ten o'clock in the morning was rather a trial to Rose, unused as she had become to the vagaries of the frontier, she, nevertheless, took a glass without flinching.

If there be anything in chivalrously acting up to the spirit of certain ideals and a certain code, in being true, no matter at what cost, to the best lights that circumstances have enabled one to possess, in being scrupulously straight in all dealings, brave to the very core, good-natured to a fault, charitable in regard to the faults of others, and void entirely of little weaknesses and meannesses, then Dave Kellon, though a gambler and a man of but little education, was a gentleman. He was tall, as thin as a hurdle, fastidiously neat and cleanly in person; and his impassive physiognomy was chiefly remarkable for a voluminous brown moustache, and fine but unutterably mournful eyes — the eyes of a bloodhound less their characteristic bloodshot feature.

"Miss Carlin," said he, looking rather embarrassed, and stepping a little aside with her, "your — your money will begin from to-day, of course; but I should like for you to take a day or two off and look around you a bit before you start in to work, so I reckon it 'd be a good idea if you was to take this $50 bill on account. No? Well, that's as you say, of course. But if there's anything you stand in need of, you just come right to me, every time. You're going to do the best you can by us, and I'd like to keep even with you.

By the way, you'll want rooms,—well, here's Billy Murray"—he pointed to the dealer at the faro table he had just quitted—"he and his wife have a cottage with spare room in it— But"—and here he hesitated, "I don't know as I'd altogether advise you to go there— Billy gets on a tear sometimes, and— You'd best take time, and stay a day or so at the hotel till we can fix you nicely. It's rough here, of course, but we'll do our level best to make you comfortable."

Rose refused the proffer of a few days' rest, and undertook to begin work that evening. She sat down to the piano and ran her fingers over the keys to see whether it was in tune.

"I had a man come up from Las Casas to fix that in good shape for you," said Dave; "but if it ain't right yet, why, we'll have some other fellow to work on it. It'll do, eh? Well, that's good. Then I guess I'll get along home and lie down awhile. I shall be around here in the evening. If there's anything you want meanwhile, you send right here for one of the boys to come to you. See you later. S' long, Ned."

"How 'd you come out on the night, Dave?" asked the latter.

"Away behind. Sol Poheim beat the game out of $1480, and the Colonel he piked in and pulled out close on five hundred."

The spirit of the old gambler drew Rose towards the roulette table, where she gave the wheel a little spin with the tip of her parasol.

"Set the ball rolling," she said to a croupier, who had immediately taken his station behind the table to "give her a game."

He continued to spin for her, but she did not offer to

play, only guessed once or twice at the figures before the ball fell.

"I made some nice winnings last year at this game at Monte Carlo," she said to Ned; "eighty-six, sixty-seven, forty-seven, and twenty-eight thousand francs, besides some smaller sums."

"Beat the game, eh?—but did you quit winner?"

"Oh, I lost most of it back, of course, but I left 'away ahead of the town'— That was my first visit. Afterwards I went back and had a bad time. Come, let's go, or I shall begin to play, and I'd sooner go for a walk. Ah! there's my lucky number turning up—ten! Spin once more. I'm betting $20 on it this time for a repeater," she said to the croupier.

"It's above the limit, Miss, but we'll let it go this time if you say so."

"Then let it go, for Heaven's sake, for I do say so—most earnestly," she said, with feigned entreaty.

The ball fell in zero.

She threw down a $20 gold piece.

"Two nights' pay for the piano girl," and she laughed mockingly. "Come! let's go," and they left the house. "Let's have a few hours' holiday in the open air, and try to forget who we are, and think we're nice, good, happy people. Take me for a walk — anywhere — somewhere up there'll do," and she pointed to the hills above the town—"somewhere where we can sit down before a view, and shan't see a single specimen of humanity. Poor humanity!—nothing but men and women! And to think that one has to endure them all one's life! Was there ever such a wretched institution as humanity? Do you really think it does its work well in the world—whatever it may be? Say? does it? *Can* it? What miserable and abominable work it must be if it does!"

Ned laughed.

"You're out of tune this morning, and you won't soothe your nerves by being bitter."

She looked at him curiously, and as they strolled on up the hillside slowly, Rose, lapsing almost into silence, began to pick the wild flowers she saw. Once she reached out and touched Ned's arm with the tip of her parasol. He looked round inquiringly.

"Go on," said she, with a smile. "It's nice, though, to be able to touch some one, — to feel that somebody's there, — when one's nerves are all ajar. Do you understand? — you do," and her great, luminous, black eyes seemed to read his thoughts. "No, don't talk or make me talk. I'll just reach out and touch you when I want to," and she laughed a little, softly.

Occasionally Ned added one to her bouquet of flowers as they went on. As a rule she took what he gave her in silence, or at most with a smile of pleasure. They said very little.

"Are there any flower gardens to any of the cottages here?" she asked once.

"Not one. You're fond of flowers?"

She nodded.

"I can bring them up for you on the stage from down below. The Mexicans on the Rio Grande have plenty, — Mexicans are fond of flowers."

But she did not seem to hear what he was saying.

They reached a spot where, from beneath the shade of a juniper tree, there was a fine view of the Rio Grande valley, and here, without preparation or remark, she sat down.

Ned stood near, rolling a cigarette, and presently sat down himself.

"You haven't touched me lately," said he.

"I feel better now;" but as she spoke she did stretch out her hand to him and touch his lightly with one finger.

With his hat tilted over his eyes, he lay on his side smoking, caressing his little Spanish-woman's moustache unconsciously, as he watched his companion arranging and rearranging the flowers in her lap. She failed to devise a combination that pleased her, however, and finally, with a wilful gesture, cast them all away.

"Heigh-ho!" and she leant lazily against a boulder beside her. "It's very strange about one's moods, isn't it — the gayety and sadness, moroseness and fear, that come upon us for no reason whatever, and leave us without warning? Whence do they come? Are they real, or only imaginary? Is a fit of gayety, for instance, anything that could be measured by length or weight, — not by us, of course, but by one of the invisible some ones?"

"Oh, I suppose some one does measure things for us," said Ned, lazily; "but look at those poor flowers in the sun there — butchered to make a woman's holiday!"

"We haven't many," said Rose, softly.

"How can you bear the gaze of their coloured eyes as they fade and grow dim, and reproach you?" he proceeded, mock-seriously. "Can't you almost hear them whisper —"

"Can eyes 'whisper'?" murmured Rose, as, sinking lower down, and nestling her cheek comfortably in the hollow of her arm, she looked out through half-closed lids on the scene spread before her.

He laughed.

"Some eyes can do 'most anything, I guess."

There was a pause.

"These old mountains want re-covering and re-stuffing; they look so ragged and worn out," said Rose, dreamily.

"They ought to be pulled down and rebuilt altogether — furnished with elevators, too."

"H'm," she assented.

There was another little pause.

"Mr. Chase!"

"Yes?"

"Pick them up, won't you? You've made them look so reproachful — and made me feel so heartless;" and a note or two of soft laughter fell from Rose's lips.

"The mountains?"

"No — flowers."

Ned proceeded to do as he was bidden.

"Every single one — don't desert any," she said softly.

When he had finished, he turned to present them to her again. But he hesitated; her eyes were closed, and taking off his coat instead, he spread it over her feet.

She had fallen asleep with her flushed face resting on her arm.

Once as he sat smoking beside her in silence, she uttered a sound as of a child in distress, and, turning, he saw that her lips were quivering. A moment later, and a few great tears welled forth amidst her thick lashes, and fell upon her cheeks. But her dream, whatever it was, soon passed away.

It was afternoon before she awoke — with a slight movement and a sigh at first, and then, just as she began to lift her arms in unconscious abandon, she became aware of where she was, and suddenly sat up and looked about her — looked at Ned, and saw his coat over her feet. She lifted it up and gave it to him.

"Thank you," she said simply. "It's late, isn't it? How good of you to let me sleep like that!" (Not every man would have ignored *himself* to that extent, and she knew it.) "I don't sleep well at night — " she was saying, when her hands went to her eyes, which were still wet. "Was I — did I speak — was I crying in my sleep? — I was dreaming, and — "

"Didn't utter a sound that I heard," answered Ned, lying good-naturedly.

She looked at him doubtfully for a moment, but let it pass.

"Where are my flowers?" she asked, rising from the ground, and, as he gave them to her, they started home.

The following day Rose took two rooms in Billy Murray's cottage, an arrangement which came about by chance. Passing by the house when she was out walking, she caught sight of a child playing in the verandah with a dog. The child was aged about three or thereabouts, as pretty as a flower, but sadly dirty; the dog a half-starved setter. Devoted to children and dogs, Rose stopped to look at the couple, and whilst doing so a placard in one of the windows announcing " rooms to let" caught her eye. She entered the verandah.

"Whose pet are you, sweetheart?" she cried, picking the child up in her arms.

The child shook its head. Rose knocked at the door.

"Well, what's your name then?"

"None of 'our biz'n's."

At that moment the door was answered by a pretty little woman with soft manners, and a small, thin voice.

"You have some rooms to let?"

"Yes, Miss."

"My name's Carlin. I'm the new piano girl at the Mint."

"Oh, indeed! My husband, Mr. Murray, works there, too."

"Ah! — Mr. Murray — " echoed Rose, rather dubiously. "Is this your child?"

"Yes," sighed Mrs. Murray, "it's mine. Naughty little thing, you're all mussed up again!"

"Pshaw! Why, it hasn't been washed for a week," said Rose, frankly. "See here, I'll take your rooms, but for mercy's sake wash this poor child."

"Won't you come in and see the rooms?" asked the woman, colouring.

"No — bedroom and sitting-room I suppose!".

"Yes."

"They'll do, then, I reckon — only wash the child, and for Heaven's sake give that poor dog something to eat. I'll pay for it. What's the child's name?"

"Bee's her name. Come to your mother, deary, you'll tire the lady."

But Bee, not to be wooed by honeyed accents the value of which she probably knew from experience, strenuously objected to exchange the protection of her new friend for the more legitimate shelter of her mother's arms, and it was not without difficulty that Rose got rid of her.

"Then I'll send my things over right away, Mrs. Murray, and come back myself after lunch," said Rose, as she turned to go. "Good-bye, Bee; whose pet are you going to be?"

"'Ours," said Bee, still studying the stranger with wide open, but yet scarcely innocent eyes.

Before evening Rose was installed in her new quarters, and had already gained the full confidence of the child and the half-starved setter.

CHAPTER IV.

WILD ROSE soon justified her nickname. The mood in which Ned had so far known her did not last. Indeed, when he saw her that same night in the Mint Saloon, the champagne bottles supplied by her admirers covering the top of the piano, and she herself, amid shouts of uproarious laughter, returning jest for jest, sally for sally, in the cross-fire of banter maintained by the men collected round her, he found some difficulty in reconciling this Bacchante-like damsel with the fastidious and nervous woman of the morning.

Ned's grey eyes looked black by night; his clean-cut, rather cold face was easily distinguishable amid the crowd of blurred and drink-inflamed visages about him. Rose discovered him, therefore, at once, and lifting a glass to her lips, glanced over the bubbles at its edge and pledged him with a look. Then, sweeping the men around her aside with a gesture of both hands, she dashed into some Hungarian dance music, and crashed through its wild strains with a fire that inspired the whole assemblage with enthusiasm.

Music was no mere talent with her, to be called into service at any moment — it was an instinct, a mood, under the influence of which she forgot herself and played as naturally as in other moods she laughed or grew angry. At such times there was something actually magnetic in the strains she produced; but, on the other hand, her performance was as remarkable for its poverty of feeling and lack of brilliancy when she played reluctantly.

Shouts of applause greeted her now. The reckless spirit she had engendered ran high. Amid the nervous and excitable crowd with which she had to deal, the subtle force of her magnetism was a real power, though it affected her audience unconsciously. Play grew more reckless, drink flowed more freely; men hummed her music upon all sides, and felt, for the time being, equal to any folly or extravagance.

Caressing his big, brown moustache, Dave Kellon watched the game beneath him from the look-out chair behind one of the faro tables, and keenly surveyed the seething and excited crowd beyond it. Nothing escaped him. To be cool and observant was his business, and he was probably the only unmoved man in the room.

"She's a dandy," said old Boger the barkeeper, who had just brought a tray of drinks to the table, and stood for a minute at Kellon's elbow, watching the game. "How she has got the boys ginned up!"

"Yep," responded Dave, imperturbably. "The wust cur in the room 'd begin a fight to-night."

"Looks like she was a pretty good Mascot, too, Dave."

"Best in the world. Haven't hardly lost a bet since she's been in the room."

"That's good. Just look at them stacks!" Boger was referring to the pyramids of counters staked on the faro table. "If luck went dead against you when they was betting 'em like that, you'd soon have to go down into your pocket and dig up. Whip-sawed again! Jake, you can't make no hand of it to-night," he said to a man whose face was one of the livid ring of red masks crushed together round the table. "Durned if that queen didn't lose every time."

The hours sped swiftly by — swiftly even for Rose herself; since, for the time being, she was filled with the same wild spirit with which she inspired the others. She was not employed in counting the moments any more than they were. But her performance was nearly over when, above the tumult which she had been mainly instrumental in fostering, her voice ran clear and strong with the opening note of her last song: —

> "Wine! Wine! One more cup of red wine!
> One more draught of oblivion divine!
> Drink deep! Curse the sunlight! Be mine
> But the light that glows deep in red wine.
> Ah, wine, blessed soother of care!
> Friend of joy, and arch foe of despair!
> With thy sleep and thy passion whate'er
> Be the future, that future we'll dare.
> Drink! drink! drink deep and drink hearty!
> Drink every man of you all,
> As 'twere the last bumper to start ye,
> Down grade! and whoo—oop as you fall."

No creature who had any afterthought for effect could have delivered that mad drinking song with the wild élan that characterised her rendering of it. The passion she threw into it was the passion of despair, and might have revealed to some a glimpse of the mental hell that gave birth to it. But there was none there to seek or question feelings below the surface. As the verses followed one another, the coolest of those present was swept away by them. The chorus was taken up by all, and threatened to lift the roof. Old timers at the gambling-tables doubled their bets, recognised cowards stood boldly up beside well-known "bad men," and looked them in the eye defiantly; whiskey soakers called recklessly for champagne to toast Rose in. A regular madness possessed them.

But it was her last song; for twelve o'clock had struck, and she had been sitting at the piano for four hours.

"You've done great work for us to-night, Miss Carlin," said Kellon, approaching her. "Would you like for one of the boys to walk you home now?"

"Not yet, Mr. Kellon. I'm going to buck against the tiger a little, myself, before I go."

"Hadn't you better keep off from that? We don't want to run *you* in debt," whispered Dave, with good-natured solicitude.

She laughed.

"Mr. Kellon, it's run in my name, this show," and she tapped her own breast lightly, as she spoke, "but I don't control it — or I shouldn't be here at all. Anyhow this is my night — I feel it — and I shall win — you'll see! Give me $100 worth of checks," she said, throwing down a note, when they had made room for her at the roulette table.

She staked on and all round her lucky number, 10, and lost. Again she trusted it, and lost once more. Another unlucky coup would have exhausted her checks; but the next time she won something on a number adjoining ten, and backing it to repeat (which it did), she won a big coup. Luck now favoured her. In a very short time she had won over $1500. Then, as her fortune began to waver again, she cashed in her checks, and left off, a winner of over $1100.

"Dan," said Mike Brannigan to Birchfield, who was

sitting next to him at the roulette table, betting in half-dollars, and who had seen Rose's play, "why can't you and me wipe 'em up in that shape?"

"Ain't got the sand," declared Dan, frankly. "She's blooded; she's a pigeon-winged race-horse! You and me ain't on'y fit to class as one-card keno players alongside of her when it comes to snap. Was you there that day she earmarked the nigh leader coming into Willow Springs?"

"No; it was Ned druv the coach that day."

"So it was — we was playing in big luck, too. Ef it'd been you, you'd have upset us, and so'd 'most any other — Here! Drop that money! That don't belong to you!"

"The hell it don't," retorted the man addressed, his hand still grasping Dan's checks. "I set it there, anyway."

"I'll be — — if you did! Ask Jim."

"Mr. Birchfield's bet, John," said the croupier thus appealed to.

"But I staked —"

"No, sir, you didn't — not on that number," said Dan, removing his two half-dollar chips from the other's hand, and ready to fight for them in another moment if necessary.

"Your mistake, John. Take a drink on it," said the croupier, beckoning to a darkey waiter. "What's your pizen, Dan?"

"Whiskey sour."

"John?"

"Wal, if I couldn't get away with the gentleman's bet, I'll have his drink, anyhow. Bring me a whiskey sour, too."

comically, "best leave him right alone. If you interrupted him, forcing benefits on him, and loading him down with presents, you might change his luck."

"If there're any presents running loose, send 'em right here, Colonel," said Kitty Hunter, laughingly, as she set the dishes she had brought before Joe and Ned. "I'll undertake to say they don't put any hoodoo [1] on me."

"Well, a man and his wife are one," commenced the Colonel, deliberately, "and —"

"And that one's the wife,'" pursued Kitty, gayly.

"More times than folks think," assented old Dodge. "Still, as Joe says he's got the whole world anyway, it'd be just foolishness to try and add to his responsibilities."

Wild Rose came in at that moment, and sat down at a table by herself, where Kitty's alert eye discovered her at once.

"Came in on the stage with you, didn't she?" she asked in an undertone.

Ned nodded. "She's the new piano girl at the Mint."

"Why, Ned, she's perfectly beautiful!" declared Kitty, enthusiastically, adding, after a moment's pause, "only — her face makes you kind o' sorry for her, all the same."

"How's that?"

"It looks — so — so tired — so indifferent, and yet so proud too. I'll go and see after her."

A minute later she was to be seen smiling brightly and pleasantly, as she discussed the supper order with Rose. Curious was the contrast between their two faces! The two girls were about the same age. Only the one face was fair, the other dark as a creole; the one

---

[1] "Hoodoo": *spell of bad fortune.*

fresh, radiant, ingenuous, and happy; the other — the face of Wild Rose.

Supper over, the room was cleared rapidly for the ball. The floor, already dressed in the afternoon, was swept and powdered once more with wax; and scarcely were the preparations completed when the guests began to troop in from the village and the neighbouring mines and ranches. The ball was given by a few of Joe Johnstone's friends to celebrate his approaching wedding. Apart therefore from the fact that Kitty Hunter seemed an established favourite, as for her sweet temper and good nature she deserved to be, on this occasion she was the guest of the evening in virtue of her position, and women vied with men in paying her attention. She herself revelled in the scene, dancing and enjoying herself with her whole heart, as she was accustomed to do everything, — as, indeed, she loved her handsome, gallant Joe Johnstone.

As for Joe, although, as he frequently had occasion to say, "Dancing was not his strong suit," he kept pace with her, and did his devoirs with admirable spirit and good humour.

Waltz followed polka and polka waltz, a Virginia reel varying the programme occasionally. Very little jewelry might be seen among the dancers, and not much finery. Here and there there was an evening dress, here and there a dress-coat. For the most part, however, the guests wore ordinary "store clothes." But there was a life and go about the wearers, for the absence of which no amount of fashionable display could have compensated. The buzz of laughter and of conversation was unceasing, and the guests danced well, as Americans of all classes always do.

"Sol," said Dan Birchfield, with much ceremony, to Poheim, "let me present you to a young lady whose father is one of the prominent ranchers in this neighbourhood. Mr. Spicker owns 'cattle on a thousand hills,' and his cheque is good for $50,000 any minute in the day that he's a mind to draw it."

"He ain't of that mind very often," remarked the young lady to whom Poheim was being introduced. "Paw's ter'ble slow at parting."

"You don't say! The old tough! He's got no shame to him," laughed Dan. "Why, ef I only had a daughter like you to spend 'em, I'd just write cheques till they littered the ranch."

"You bed!" said Sol, fervently; "me, too. I couldn't 'ride 'em fast enough."

"Wal, I'll be a daughter to the pair of you," said Miss Spicker, readily.

"Why, that'd suit me — down to the ground," said Dan, "on'y I ain't got no pile to draw on. Here's Sol, though, he's rich. Miss Eunice Spicker, I want yer to know this man — he's an old-time friend of mine. They do say," pursued Dan, with a ferociously confidential wink, "that ef Sol 'd stayed back in Europe he'd have been called a Sheeny.[1] But he come over here, and so it's all right. Sol's American; Sol goes."

Introductions in the far West often take longer to accomplish than do criminal trials involving questions of life and death, and with the solemnity of Presbyterian prayer combine an impertinence of biographical detail which only an American newspaper reporter could properly relish.

Such matters, however, disturbed not Mr. Poheim.

[1] A Jew.

"Vat name?" he asked, gravely turning to Dan.

"Miss Spicker — Miss Eunice Spicker."

"Miss Spicker," he repeated impressively, as though committing the name eternally to memory. "Delighted, Miss Spicker, to hef de honour to meed you;" and the ceremony over, he dismissed all gravity, and laughed gayly.

Miss Spicker, who had ruddy hair and was a head and shoulders taller than Solomon, laughed too. "Guess you are — got to say so, anyhow," said she, good-humouredly. "Ain't more 'n met me half-way yet, have you?" and she looked down at Poheim quizzically.

"Ve meed pelow now," replied Sol in the same vein. "Py'n py, led's hope ve meed above. But ve are vasting precious time. Don't you tanz, Miss Spicker?"

"Why, cert! that's what I'm here for. Catch a-holt on me, and try."

Poor, fat, turtle-shaped little Solomon did try. But he was no match in wind or limb for Miss Spicker, who danced him nearly into a fit of apoplexy without turning a hair.

The ball was progressing merrily; but outside in the verandah Wild Rose was seated by herself. She had danced once or twice with old friends that she had encountered, but somehow — Perhaps her frame of mind were best expressed in her own thoughts, as she mused there alone in the shadows: "I suppose I know now how it must feel to be old — to have learnt that you're a failure, and to have realised that there is no chance of your ever changing the verdict. It has been the same all along, though, only — I'm losing pluck and interest now — 'losing my grip.' What wonder!"

And yet as she sat there she looked young — scarce

even her age of two and twenty — and, for all the recklessness revealed in the expression of her features, wonderfully beautiful. Beautiful with the dark, strong beauty of the Spanish gipsy, which strikes like a revelation rather than wins slowly; but yet had, in this instance, a wonderful depth of charm and interest beneath its mere outline and colouring. For, despite her armour of defiance, there was so much that was sweet, so much that was womanly and true about her, the reflection of which was constantly betrayed in some look, some tone, some transient expression; and a gleam of passionate regret, that she could never quite extinguish, lived always in the depths of her dark eyes.

She laughed to herself once. What a long lifetime she seemed to have lived in the past five or six years! What scenes she had passed through! What curious vicissitudes of fortune! What wealth of passionate feeling, and nervous force and longing she had expended — and wasted. Sol Poheim's story of her had been true enough. On the frontier she adopted the frontier spirit and language as though to the manner born; but she had not forgotten the forms and tone of the class that she had been born into, and at any moment she could revert to her original character. As Poheim had stated, she was a lady by birth.

There may be many exceptions, but as a rule Americans are unwise parents. Even when really interested in the welfare of their children, it is generally with the exclusively material side of it — with the side which has reference to money or position. They train them for employments, cultivate them for show. But in such cases it is the material side of the question which is the artificial one, after all. Health and character —

health of mind and body are of greater moment as regards the happiness of a human being than either accomplishments or wealth. Little pains are taken to secure the former in America. In the vast majority of cases these matters are left to chance. Not because parents are more indulgent in America than parents elsewhere, but because they are less alive to the sense of paternal responsibility and its meaning; because they are apt to regard their children as toys, and to think far more of the amusement to be got out of them than of the duties they owe to them; because they are too selfishly absorbed in their own pursuits to devote personal study and attention to their offspring. To be left to follow his own occupation in peace, the American father will often pay, and pay well. Much of his boasted generosity is due to this reason. Instead of earning the affection and respect of his children by self-sacrifice, personal attention and thought, he buys the semblance of them with indulgence, money, and that which it affords. And how gladly he shirks responsibility, and shields himself behind a flimsy precedent the moment he is able to do so! How few rich American fathers break through the so-called "custom in America" in such case, and provide during their own lives in proportion to their wealth for their children when these latter come of age or marry! When allowances are made them at all in such cases, they are generally paltry. As a rule, after having, to compensate for their own shortcomings, brought their children up in habits of reckless extravagance and luxury,—totally unfitted them, in fact, for economy or work,—they turn them practically adrift. To the girl the father says: "Let your husband support you;" to the boy: "At your age I earnt my own living; it's time you did the same," forgetting that he himself and his wife were probably trained to work and economy in the school of want from earliest growth, while to avoid trouble and spare themselves a little self-control, they have trained their sons in dissipation and their daughters in extravagance.

Rose Carlin's parents had not been among the exceptions from the rule referred to. A girl with magnificent possibilities in point of character, they had cultivated her like an animal for show, encouraged her in her wildest extravagances, been proud of her most headstrong follies, enjoyed the vulgar applause which these had won her from the crowd. In view of her more showy qualities they had lost sight of everything else.

At the age of sixteen she had eloped from school with Bob Hannaford, a handsome but unprincipled scoundrel. Looking upon themselves as injured instead of to blame, from that day forward her parents had disowned her, nor had they ever made the slightest endeavour to assist her. As for Rose, she had awakened slowly to the fact that the ideal being, into whom with girlish enthusiasm she had transformed Hannaford in her imagination, was as different from the real man as white from black. Possibly in the whole range of human disaster no wreck occurs so piteous as that which attends this awakening, no anguish keener or more hopeless than that which accompanies it. One day Rose had learnt that Hannaford had been married to another woman before she herself had met him, and that his wife was still alive. Her own marriage had therefore been a mockery. She left him immediately then, and for a time supported herself as a piano girl. But Hannaford had followed her, scheming always to deprive her of her situations, and finally reducing her to absolute want in his endeavours to regain possession of her. At this point, an old miner named Jim Tritton had come to her assistance. Being a man of some means, in the off-hand spirit of his class he had adopted her as his daughter, and with him she had gone to San Antonio in Texas, where, soon after their arrival, he had been shot by accident in a disturbance in a gambling saloon. He had lived long enough, however, to bequeath what he possessed to her, and some months later, when the estate had been realised, she had started East. High play at Monte Carlo, a summer's yachting and travelling, one glorious season with the best packs in Leicestershire and Warwickshire had dissipated her little fortune. And so, actuated by that subtle magnetism of custom which draws so many back to old associations, she had drifted back to that rough but hospitable shore, the frontier.

How sordid, squalid, and unkempt the country, people, everything, looked to her after the luxury in which she had been living lately.

She laughed. Did any of them remember her in North Warwickshire, she wondered? One man did, she was sure; and probably some of the hunting women recollected the stranger who rode four-hundred-guinea hunters, and stopped at nothing.

But the current of her thoughts was changed by the sound of a voice she knew. Two men, unconscious of her presence, were talking near where she was seated in the shadow.

"You've been to Las Casas and looked up the register?"

"Yep — stopped there on my way up."

"And how does it read?"

"Ain't a flaw in it. The mine stands in Tom's name, and Tom's name only."

"Don't mention no partners?"

"Not one."

"H'm, I reckon that as they were up in Colorado when he denounced it, it was easier to take out papers in his own name, and wait till they all got together here before they fixed matters up in proper business shape."

"Like enough; but they never fixed nothing, all the same. He died before they got as far as that."

"And what's your idea now?"

"Why, as Tom's legal heir the whole mine belongs to me."

"A third share in it does. You may lay your claim to the rest, but you'll never make it stick in court."

"Court! we can buy up any court that stands in the way."

"Maybe; that ain't everything, though. You've got to consider that the partnership was generally known; the men are popular here, and the sense of the community'd be with 'em. Even if you got your case, you'd still be away off getting your mine."

"Oh, pshaw! they'd quit — they'd have to."

"Not much, they wouldn't. You couldn't run any bluff on Ned Chase, or Joe Johnstone. They're fighters, these men. They'd hold that mine down with shot-guns. And you ain't known in this camp. Of course if you feel equal to carrying the thing through on your own hook, why, sail in. If you want me to take a hand in it, you'll have to give me a third interest in the mine.

I'm acquainted here. I've got money, and — well, no man that's lived has ever made me back down. If it comes —"

"You're a liar, Bob Hannaford!" came a voice from out the shadow. "Jim Tritton made you take water — and you took it, too, like a duck!"

"Wild Rose, by God!"

"You've guessed it. You keep away from me, too."

"Oh, pshaw! Let's be friends now, Rose."

"No, sir; no friendship can ever exist between us again. Say! Mr. Chase!" — at that moment Ned had appeared in the light of the doorway — "Mr. Chase, these two men are plotting to get your mine away from you. That man who came up on the stage with us claims the whole of it."

"What's your name?" asked Ned, swinging round on him.

"Tom Dutton."

"Dick Dutton's brother?"

"That's what I am."

"Why didn't you come right out and say so, then, when you saw that rock? Dick was a partner with Joe Johnstone and me — and a square man, too — no squarer ever passed in his checks. What's you are needs proving. But I'll tell you one thing, and tell it you right now; that mine belonged to the three of us equally, and we can prove it, though it did happen to stand in Dick's name when he died. Joe Johnstone and I are prepared to surrender Dick's heirs a third interest in it, as we took steps to advise them the moment Dick died. If you want more than that, you've got to take it. And you won't take it quietly, you bet! There'll be trouble first — bad trouble, too, by God!"

There was a look in Ned's face which boded ill for the man who quarrelled with him. Its expression of unflinching determination was utterly relentless. As Hannaford had said, he did not look like a man who could be bluffed.

"Hadn't you better wait for a quarrel until some claim's made on you?" asked Dutton, sullenly.

"That'll be all right. Folks ain't so infernally liable to quarrel when they know just how far they can go, and right where they've got to stop," rejoined Ned, savagely. "As for you, Bob Hannaford, you'd best keep away from what don't concern you."

"You needn't trouble for me, Ned. I can take care of myself," replied Hannaford.

"And, d——n you, you'll want to, if you go to monkeying with that mine, take my word for it!"

The music struck up again inside, and Ned was turning contemptuously away when he stopped.

"Miss Carlin," said he, "I'm much obliged to you for speaking. Give me this waltz."

"With pleasure," she answered; and as she passed Bob Hannaford she looked him full in the eyes with an insolent smile.

"Well," said Hannaford, interrupting Dutton in a string of curses as they descended the steps from the verandah, "how's it to be?—cursing won't help you—am I in with you on this deal or not?"

"You're in. I'll run 'em out of that mine if it costs me the mine itself in expenses, and I get full of lead doing it. I don't take no bluff any more 'n Ned Chase does, and I'm in his debt already for this afternoon."

CHAPTER III.

When Ned came down to the hotel to breakfast next morning, Rose was already at table. He asked if he might sit with her, and she, with an air of comical relief, immediately handed him the menu she had been studying.

"By all means," said she, "and then you can order my breakfast for me."

"Have you no choice?"

"What choice can you have when you've no appetite and don't like any of the food, and eat solely from a sense of duty? And duty to whom? Oh, dear!" and she laughed a little harshly, "I feel desperately vague this morning. Nothing seems to be of the least importance."

"You didn't sleep well?" said he, glancing at her.

She shook her head. "I didn't sleep at all."

Most men would nevertheless have appealed to her to confirm what they ordered. But Ned took the menu, and promptly ordered breakfast for both without further reference to her; while she, with idle eyes, noted his crisp, decisive manner, and recognised that here was a man who, whatever the difficulty, would take his own course through it without hesitation and without swerving. Not until he had finished giving his orders did Ned hand Rose the menu again, and then with a twinkle of mischief in his grey eye he said:

"Don't you want to countermand it all now, and order for yourself?"

She laughed.

"No satirical reflections on the ways of my sex, or I'll countermand nothing and grumble at it all."

"— Cry over each dish, and say I'm a brute."

"Exactly!" and she laughed amusedly; "that's what I will do. Have you ever been married, that you possess such a knowledge of our resources?"

Breakfast passed without incident, save for the few trivial accidents and frivolous remarks that occasioned their mutual laughter. And yet it was a pleasant meal. It passed so easily. Instinctively Rose and Ned felt that they could be perfectly natural one with the other without risk of misinterpretation; and that sense of security, especially when it is a new acquaintance who assures it, has a greater charm than the most brilliant conversation.

Towards the close of breakfast Rose grew distrait, as it became no longer possible to ignore the prospect of a whole day among strangers.

"How is it that you are not driving the stage to-day?" she asked.

"I only drive every other day — turn and turn about with Mike Brannigan. This is my day off. Say! why don't you make use of me to-day?" There was a tinge of red in his sunburnt cheek for a moment — "Let me show you around the town."

She had been leaning back listlessly in her chair before he spoke. She sat up now, interestedly.

"Will you? It won't be taking you from anything you wanted to do?"

"Not at all."

"Then I gladly accept your offer; you see, Mr. Chase, you know these people, and can tell me about them — give me a few 'pointers,' eh?" and she smiled. "Of course I'm familiar enough with the life; I'm an old timer in mining camps — so it seems to *me*, anyway. But I've been away from it all in Europe, and — and — well, the frontier makes you shudder when you first come back to it." She glanced round her as she spoke, evidently comparing the present picture with her memory of what she had been accustomed to lately.

"Brace up!" said Ned, cheerily. "You don't want to look back or stop to think here. You must live all the time in the present — live in the flying moment, and do, and do, and do!"

"'For in a sieve I'll thither sail,
And like a rat without a tail,
I'll do, I'll do, I'll do,'"

she quoted, smilingly. "I wonder how a rat without a tail feels."

"You can bet one thing, and that is, he don't waste much time *looking back*," responded Chase, laughing.

"I guess you're right," said she, lifting her long lashes and glancing at him curiously. "How old are you?"

"Twenty-seven."

"Is that all?" and something in her look, more even than in the tone of her voice and what she said, made him feel boyish beside her. "Tell me about the Mint."

"You'll be all right there. It's the best house in town. Old Boger runs the bar, and he's a square man. And Dave Kellon, Clint Morris, and Jimmy Dillon run the gambling saloon. Clint and Jimmy only have a small interest in the concern; Dave owns most of it, and Dave's one of nature's gentlemen — straight as a line and true as steel. Morris is tricky; besides, he thinks that every girl — well, he's a dude, and goes a heap on his own shape; but he hasn't any force to him. Jimmy's a good boy, who'll do anything you ask him."

As he spoke Ned could look at his companion as much as he pleased, for her lids were lowered while she listened to him. Exquisitely beautiful were her pale and regular features, notwithstanding the fact that every trace of feeling seemed to have faded out of them, and that for the time being they were as cold and impassive as stone. But when she lifted her glorious eyes to Ned's as he finished speaking, the look of indescribable pathos in them sent a thrill through him which seemed to touch every feeling within him that could add strength to compassion or devotion.

"Well," she said, rousing herself, "then you are going to be my cicerone, eh? — and take me up to the Mint, and introduce me to the boys, and help me to find lodgings, and — oh, do lots of *little* things for me. It's the little things that make the mountains in one's life. The constant drop of little things will wear away one's soul."

"Just shift them on to me. I'm at your service entirely."

She nodded her thanks prettily, and went off to put on her hat.

When she came down again Chase was in the verandah, and the Duckville coach was on the point of starting. Ned introduced to her two or three of the men who were present, and they all stood chatting together until, with the cry, "all aboard!" and a few pistol-like cracks of his whip, Mike Brannigan put his team in motion. Then they set out up the rugged hillside street which comprised the greater part of Dogtown.

The white stare of the morning sun was on the straggling wooden houses, the store windows and their gaudy signs, the unwashed loafers on the occasionally boarded pathways, the red, juniper-spotted hills in the background; and it brought into strong relief the beauty or unloveliness of everything that it touched.

"What is there over there — beyond the pass?" asked Rose, pointing to a notch in the hills above them, where the road disappeared.

Ned shook his head.

"It's a little like the Hill of Life, this Dogtown main street of yours, then — short and steep, and rocky, and beyond — ?" She shook her head as Chase had done, only in a sad little way of her own — "Beyond, no one knows what — the 'Never-Never Land,' perhaps."

"Let's go and see," said Ned, smiling.

"Yes — not to-day, but later on, certainly. I love long days in the open country on horseback."

"You don't — "

"I don't look like it?"

"No."

"Oh, I'm tough," and she laughed curtly. "Ask Sol Poheim."

She did not appear "tough." There was nothing robust or sturdy about her — nothing to promise endurance, unless it were her thoroughbred symmetry and look of dauntless courage. Truth to tell, she seemed terribly out of place in Dogtown, and as they walked along Ned could not help turning occasionally to glance at her. From her pretty feet to her large cloud-of-lace

Dan laughed.

"No offence, pard, *had* to call your attention, though."

"That's all right," said the man, "go right along, sirree. I'm a winner, anyhow," and the incident closed with a laugh, though it might easily have ended very differently.

A few days later, for a bet of $100, Rose undertook to ride a bucking broncho that had unseated most of the ambitious horsemen in the neighbourhood. The bet was made during the mad hours that she spent in the saloon, and when the man with whom she had made it recollected it next morning, he begged to be allowed to pay forfeit rather than let her run any risk. But Rose vowed that she would ride the broncho whether or no, and she had her way.

Lassoed and led into town, it was saddled, after a severe struggle, in front of the Mint. Then one of its forelegs was lifted, and two men held its ears while Rose was helped into the saddle. It bucked from the Mint to the Mountain Pride Hotel, a distance of over two hundred yards, followed closely the while by a crowd of men and boys. But Rose, who was a splendid horsewoman, and utterly fearless, sat her mount faultlessly. At the hotel she managed to turn him, and galloped him back to the Mint. Arrived there, however, she slipped from the saddle, tottered a few yards and fainted, the blood trickling from her mouth with the severity of the punishment she had undergone.

Nevertheless she appeared on duty that evening as usual, although she looked like a corpse, nor was it until Kellon locked the piano and threatened to put out the lights and close the saloon, that she could be persuaded to return home.

E

For the next few days they forced her to take a holiday.

Chancing one day when she was out walking to pass a corral in which a teamster was trying vainly to lasso a young horse, she stopped to watch him.

"What are you going to do with him?" she asked.

"Halter-break the yaller-skinned, one-eyed, lop-eared son-of-a-gun."

"He's never been handled yet?"

"Can't yer see he hasn't! I just druv him in from the hills to gentle him a bit, but — — his or'nary soul, he won't have me lass' him!"

"Let me come in there, and you get out — you don't know how to treat a horse, anyhow. I'll put a head-stall on him without any lasso."

"Oh, pshaw! Don't I tell yer he hasn't never been handled!"

"So much the better; if he had been, I couldn't do anything with him. See here! here's five dollars; let me work on him for an hour. If I haven't got a head-stall on him in that time, you shall have another five."

Dollars appealed to the teamster's sense of chivalry, and he "reckoned that ef she wanted to monkey awhile with the horse she could."

"Get me a whip," said Rose, "and a stick about the same length as the whip-stock. I shall want a bit of old sacking, too, and the headstall."

Armed with these articles she entered the corral, and, with the exception of the whip, threw them down in the centre of it. The gate was closed behind her. The colt stood snorting as he watched her.

For a little she eyed him carefully, talked to him, and finally approached him. But their acquaintance was too young as yet to be improved upon, and he immediately began to trot round the corral, which, fortunately for Rose's purpose, was a very small one, although high enough to defy all his attempts to jump out of it. Rose cracked her whip, touched the nag's heels with it, stopped and turned him, stopped him again. Talking to him all the while, sometimes sharply, sometimes encouragingly, as occasion demanded, she repeated these manœuvres until the horse began to understand that there was a certain point in the corral where she wished him to stay, and would stop there for a little quietly. When he had learnt this, his lesson was already well under way. She had caught his attention, and he would stand, the picture of expectation, studying her intelligently; he would even advance a step or two towards her, or let her do the same to him. Not the first, nor the second, nor the third time that she tried it, did he allow her to touch his muzzle with the end of her whip-stock. But she succeeded in doing so eventually. And, bringing him back time after time to the same spot, from touching his muzzle she came at length to stroke his cheek and neck and shoulders with the whip.

She now picked up the other stick, and went through the same performance with them both at once, — stroking, caressing, steadying him with them, gradually advancing all the time, until the handle of the whip, and finally the hand which held it, touched his cheek. At length she could drop her sticks altogether, and approach and handle her new friend all over. Confidence was thoroughly established between them, and this without the slightest exertion of strength or lapse into roughness on Rose's part. Of course this result was not obtained without patience. Time after time the colt broke away from her. But time after time she brought him back to the same spot, never losing heart or temper for a second. Occasionally she slipped the loop formed by the whip-lash over his head, and let him feel a slight restraint.

Her next step was to pick up the old sack on the points of her whip and stick, and, having faced the horse and steadied him, offer it for his inspection. After smelling at it timidly at first, he soon allowed this also to be passed over his head and neck. It only remained to accustom him to the headstall in the same way. Little by little this was done, and finally patience conquered. The horse allowed the headstall to be put on him, and it was adroitly buckled. Then, fetching the lasso, Rose attached one end of it to the ring of the headstall, and handed her pupil over to its owner.

"Well, by gosh! ef that ain't the prettiest I ever did see! Ef I hadn't have seen it, you couldn't have made me believe it," said he. "Here! take back your money; you've put twenty dollars on the value of that horse. I couldn't have done that much with him working on him a week. Where 'd ye ever learn that, anyhow?"

"Way back in California, when I was a girl. An old Irishman on a ranch I used to stay at fooled them like that."

"You don't say! Wal, that's a hell of a game, sure! You'd best go gentling colts right away; darned ef it ain't your nat'ral-born lay-out."

The escapade of the bucking broncho took place without Ned's knowledge, or, failing other means of preventing it, he would probably have shot the broncho. From the first he had, unostentatiously, cast the ægis of his protection over Rose, and in the large chapter of her admirers (which included half the male population of Dogtown) was on a somewhat different footing with her from the rest. Ned was no squire of dames. It was popularly supposed that he did not care for the society of the weaker sex. Certain it is, at any rate, that he had never frequented that of the better class of Dogtown's dames and damsels. At the same time the influence of former associations, together with a vein of natural refinement in his nature, kept him entirely aloof from that constellation of which, unlike the Pleiades, not one, but every sister, was lost. The only woman with whom he had been at all on terms of intimacy hitherto had been Kitty Hunter; but then Kitty's relations with his partner had forced them together. Moreover, she had a charm and freshness, and a straightforward frankness, before which the coldest reserve must have yielded.

Rose Carlin was a different being — as different as the wild hawk is from the song-bird. Nevertheless, she and Ned had become close friends. He rarely approached her when she was in the saloon, but he often called on her and sat with her in the verandah of the cottage she inhabited. They went for walks and drives together. Once they had made an excursion to Fallen-star Lake, which lay within reach of Dogtown, to picnic and fish for trout. When he was away with the coach, she sometimes used a buggy that he had placed at her disposal, and drove herself out with her now inseparable little friend Bee.

Dogtown said that Ned Chase was Rose's lover. That is to say, many people, to whom to be sure of their company was of more importance than to be sure of their facts, made the assertion without contradiction.

But the suggestion was not universally accepted. Indeed, there were a good many men before whom it had never even been mentioned, and before whom it would have been particularly unfortunate if that or anything else disparaging to Rose Carlin had been even remotely hinted. Particularly prejudicial to peace would it have been had any rumour of such gossip reached Ned's own ears.

"But ef he ain't her lover," argued Dogtown's chatterboxes, "what for's he always freightin' her up sich truck as books 'n' flowers? — flowers, by gosh! — every trip as he makes to Duckville — gets 'em sent up from Las Casas. And what in 'nation do they find to talk about all them hours, as they walks and goes buggy riding and horseback riding and sits out on piazza together? 'Tain't in nature for 'em to talk good horse sense all the time — not much!"

"Good horse sense" they may have deflected from occasionally; as a matter of fact, they did do so constantly, for they were often very frivolous. But each seemed to encourage the best side of the other's character, and so they felt happy together. Life and its problems furnished them with a rich field for discussion; for Rose was fond of analysis, and both were given to questioning and deciding beliefs for themselves. Then each of them liked books, and, somehow, to Ned Rose could "gossip," in the pleasanter sense of the word. She would talk to him of her trip to Europe, occasionally refer to her childhood, draw from him with the greatest interest all that pertained to Joe and Kitty's courtship, marriage, and housekeeping; and tell him all the thousand and one little harmless bits of news that reached her through her already extensive acquaintance in the country. After all, Ned was a gentleman by birth and education, she a lady. What more natural than that they should drift together for companionship in the rough community in which they found themselves, insensibly drop frontier slang and mannerisms, and revert with relief to earlier habits? The one subject they never touched upon, even ever so remotely, was that very one which erring Dogtown felt convinced was all their theme. There was in that curious unfathomable glance, half critical and sceptical, half sad, which Ned found sometimes in the eyes of his companion, a something that made him feel so young in experience of feeling beside her, and made her seem so hopelessly beyond his power ever to influence in that way, that, whatever *might* have happened had it been otherwise, no note of love was ever struck in their conversation.

They were good friends, that was all. Ned was the sort of man that women like sometimes to make a friend of. They rarely grasp the full depth of such characters, nor do they often love them, but they find a sense of rest and safety in their strength which is grateful to them. Ned was strong both mentally and physically, never in doubt, never flurried or put out. Beneath his strength there was much thoughtfulness and kindness, beneath his even temper a lurking devil that only needed rousing, and Rose knew it. But that rather lent him an attraction for her. They were good friends; for they, at any rate, could fathom one another's characters, and recognise in them qualities that the world at large did not suspect. And the mutual consciousness of this knowledge, like the possession of a mutual secret, naturally brought them closer together, and bred a feeling of confidence between them. They were good friends, no more.

Rose often saw Hannaford, and Hannaford always spoke to her as though no quarrel existed between them. Sometimes she let him do so, and though her answers might be taunting and sarcastic, yet she answered him. But more often she merely stared at him with open-eyed insolence, or turned her back on him completely.

On one occasion he refused to be thus ignored. She was seated at the piano in the saloon, and Hannaford, who was slightly under the influence of drink, persisted in treating her to champagne. In obedience to his order, a darkey waiter had brought a bottle and some glasses; but at a word from Rose was about to return with them, when Hannaford took the tray from his hands and set it upon the piano. It was during an interval between her songs. Without the quiver of an eyelid, Rose continued talking with those about her while she finished the prelude that she had been improvising. Then, leaning forward quietly, she lifted one edge of the tray and scattered its contents upon the floor.

"Bob Hannaford," said she, with a little hard laugh, and her fingers returned to the keyboard as she looked him full in the eyes, "do you think that you dare fool with me? If so, try it!"

But, with the intuitive watchfulness that long practice had made second nature with him, Dave Kellon from his lookout seat had scented discord in the air almost as soon as Hannaford had approached the piano, and was already at his elbow.

"That's enough, Bob," said he, in an undertone. "I'm

protecting that young lady against any annoyance. That's all right; talk don't go," he insisted, cutting short Hannaford's explanations. "What's happened's of no consequence. Quit, right now."

"Curse you! do you want to make trouble?" cried Hannaford, savagely.

"I'm here," was all that Kellon answered.

But in the usually mournful eyes of the gambler, despite his unmoved demeanour and subdued tones, there was a cold, clear gleam as unflinching as sunshine, which left no sort of doubt as to his meaning.

Fortunately, at this point friends of both parties intervened, and partly coaxed, partly hustled Hannaford away.

"Dave'll fight, you pet!" said Sol Poheim, when he heard of the scene afterwards. "Py golly, efen ven I vas looking for a fight, you see me go arount Dave Kellon like I go arount a mud-holes."

CHAPTER V.

AFTER remaining a few days at Dogtown, Dutton had left without approaching either Ned or Joe, or in any way declaring his intentions with regard to the mine. Indeed, he had not yet avowed his connection with it at all, except to Ned and Hannaford. Since neither of these had mentioned the subject to any one, the fact that there was trouble in store for the ostensible owners of the "Fresh Start" was not as yet generally known. Even Joe himself was ignorant of that fact; for, arguing that trouble, if it were coming, would come quite soon enough, Ned had not deemed it worth while, under the circumstances of his partner's recent marriage, to mar his happiness by telling him the ill news so long as this could be avoided.

Kitty — her married dignity almost three weeks old — was now fully installed in Joe's cabin on the hillside near the mine. Here she did all the housework herself; for there were no servants but Chinamen to be had in Dogtown, and she strongly objected to having one "anywhere round her house."

"I'd feel ter'ble mean if I couldn't fix things to beat any Chinaman that ever toddled," said she. "Beside, Joe, dear, a Chinaman would cost us forty dollars a month! and we must remember our great scheme. We shall want all the money we can save for that."

So Kitty had her way, and, born housewife that she was, scrubbed and swept, and cooked and washed, and dusted and tidied up, singing all the while, and as happy as it was possible to be. For she loved Joe dearly, whilst Joe had no thought that, directly or indirectly, did not come home to Kitty, and she knew it.

Their cabin was only a board shanty of two rooms. But a nice woman — a womanly woman — lends a charm to everything she comes in contact with, and can make the roughest quarters take the comfortable guise of home.

"What a wonderful thing this being in love is!" said Kitty to herself once, as she stood surveying the effect of some rearrangement of furniture that she was essaying in the room in which the couple lived. "It makes you quite clever! *I* think it gives you more taste, too, in — fixing things," and she cast a look in the glass, and touched her fair, wavy hair here and there. There was a slight alteration in the arrangement of this also.

If Kitty had not model features, and was not regularly beautiful, she was wonderfully pretty nevertheless. Her skin was white as milk, the tiny freckles that powdered it only enhancing its fairness. Her great blue eyes — eyes so frank and true that no one could ever doubt their owner's sincerity — were lovely, and if her mouth *was* almost a large mouth, it had the sweetest expression in the world, and, with the smile which revealed her dazzling white teeth, was simply adorable. There was something so soft in the swimming beauty of the contour of the girl's face, that it almost seemed to be seen through a haze of sunshine or a veil of dreamy shadow, according as its moods were gay or grave. Hers was a beauty that allures and wins,— gently, unconsciously perhaps; but the spells of such beauty are chains, once riveted never to be entirely shaken off again.

Kitty Johnstone's history was very similar to her husband's. Both were of English parentage; both had been brought to the States in childhood; both stood alone there now. "Back in the old country" they had relatives living,—uncles and aunts and cousins; —and the "great scheme" referred to by Kitty, when she refused the luxury of a Chinese chêf, was a promise Joe had made to take her back to England as soon as they were rich enough to buy the old farm homestead near Godalming which had once belonged to her father, and live in it without being entirely dependent upon "crops and seasons." Kitty had long ago begun to save up with this object, and since Joe, despite his American training, was still at heart an Englishman, she had found no difficulty in imbuing him as thoroughly with the idea as she herself was possessed with it. Their aspiration, therefore, was to develop the mine, sell out their interest in it, and return to England.

Joe's cabin commanded a full view of the mining camp, which lay in an amphitheatre formed by two spurs dipping towards a level plain that reached out to the Rio Grande, seventy miles away, and further still until blue hills in Texas met it. The red and white hillside on which the camp was situated was dotted with juniper and fir trees, interspersed by straggling brush and sparse grass. At intervals which marked the various claims were the board cabins of the miners, the ore-sorting houses, the "whips" for hoisting ore up the shafts, the grey "dumps" of "waste." Here and there there was a "bunk house" for those who had not yet built accommodation for themselves at their own mines, or were unable to find it at the mines where they chanced to be employed. Elsewhere stood a camp restaurant, kept by Chinamen. Down below, on the Scottish Chief mine, was the engine house of a steam hoister — the only one in the camp as yet, whose rattle and snorting destroyed a vast amount of quiet. From time to time could be heard the muffled, underground explosion of a blast "put off" in one of the neighbouring mines.

Stray horses, released from their task of hoisting at the "whips," wandered about haphazard, and nibbled the grass here and there. On the shoulder of the spur to the left a few steers were grazing among the rocks. There seemed to be quite a population of sadder-but-wiser-looking dogs, and sleek self-satisfied cats; the former pursuing a spiritless quest for fragments, the latter proceeding about their business in a deliberate and decided fashion, almost suggestive of afternoon calls.

Dogtown, itself, was hidden from sight, down below, behind the spur on the right. But all the afternoon men on horseback passed to and fro alone or in couples. For there was not a man in Dogtown but was interested in some mine or other, whatever his legitimate business might be; and the calls of that once satisfied, most of these speculators snatched an hour "in the shank of the afternoon," to ride up to the camp and "see how things were shaping" in regard to their own particular ventures. To be sure, it was not often that the "shape" things were assuming repaid them for their trouble; but the exercise was healthy, whilst the excitement of expectation kept their minds alert. Since the road between town and the main part of the camp lay directly across the "Fresh Start" claim, many a visitor stopped at Kitty's door, and many a little present in kind was unostentatiously left there. Her marriage had met with popular approval, and Dogtown was as apt to be free-handed in testifying its satisfaction, as under other circumstances it could be free-voiced and impertinent in signifying its disapproval, sometimes even when the matter in question did not in the least concern it. But this absence of restraint is characteristic of the States, where, whatever may be the freedom of the masses, the freedom of the individual, even in the most trivial affairs — affairs which concern only himself — does not by any means of necessity receive consideration. Might is right in America, and no man there is justified in differing from his neighbours.

Ned was working in the mine to-day. It was not often that he did so — not that he was afraid of work; when needful, he could handle a shovel or drill as well as any man. But his mind was too active for any kind of employment that did not occupy it to satisfy him. Thus he preferred to pay a substitute whilst he himself drove the coach or concerned himself in other matters. Besides the "Fresh Start" he and his partner had an interest in other mining ventures in Colorado, where they had worked before coming to Dogtown. But the money derived from those undertakings had scarcely sufficed to pay the expenses connected with their present property, and the ready coin which Ned was able occasionally to bring into the Dogtown enterprise was of immense service to them.

Sworn friends though they were, there was a marked difference in character between the two men. As a mining expert, Ned was far superior to Joe; not only was his practical experience wider, but he possessed a great deal of theoretical, geological, mineralogical, and mining information which he had gathered from books. Ned read everything that he could lay his hands on, and would go any distance to see a new mine. Joe never opened a book, nor was he ever very curious about any mine but his own. Joe never touched a card; Ned was a born gambler — a bold and dashing, although shrewd, gambler. Faro dealers knew that when Ned Chase opened a vein of good luck, they were sure to have a lively deal or two. The news would bring men in from the drinking bar and road to watch him. With all the money that he was allowed to stake in constant play upon the table, rolling up and accumulating, or vanishing as the case might be, he would back his luck to its utmost limit. If fortune favoured him, he was worth thousands of dollars for a time. If it failed him, he accepted defeat with a smile and a pleasant word or two, all the more effective coming as they did from one of his usually reserved demeanour. He never surrendered his aim in anything that he had undertaken, as long as there was any difficulty or opposition to encounter. But when opposition ceased, he would sometimes, in a spirit of "pure cussedness," abandon the fruits of his labour for lack of interest to complete the trifling exertion that would have secured them. Joe was less dependent upon external influences. He never went out of his way to court opposition, but neither did he ever diverge from his path to avoid it. Men were of far less moment to him than objects or measures. If he strove for anything, it was because he knew his own mind, and had determined that he wanted it. Difficulties and opposition, therefore, added no especial zest to his pursuit of it, nor when they were removed did they leave him one whit the less intent upon accomplishing his original object. Which, it may be remarked, sooner or later he usually did. In his affections he was like a big dog. Once they were given, he could not waver or be false. For the rest he was as honest as the day, had the full courage of his few opinions, and possessed a temper that it took a great deal to rouse, but required, when roused, even more to allay. Ned was far more apt to act upon impulse and to be governed by impressions. He took strong likes and dislikes, the latter sometimes unjustly. His somewhat cold reserve hid extremely sensitive feelings and a highly nervous organisation; at heart he was intensely proud, but pride, notwithstanding it may be accounted one of the deadly sins, is accountable for much of the chivalry and virtue that keep alive one's faith in humanity.

As already stated, Ned was working at the mine to-day; for Joe, ignorant of the possibility of trouble ahead of them, was anxious to forward a shipment to the smelting works of the rich ore that he had struck a couple of weeks before. A boy led the horse to and fro from the derrick, hoisting bucket after bucket full of ore. At the shaft's mouth Ned received it, emptied it into a barrow, and wheeled this to the sorting house. Down below, in the mine, Joe and a couple of helpers were engaged in bringing the ore to the foot of the shaft and filling the buckets.

Ned more than suspected that the work was work

thrown away, for every day he apprehended an order from the district court of Las Casas, forbidding them to ship ore until the question of title was settled, or placing a distringas upon the proceeds at the smelting works should any already have been shipped. But Joe and Kitty were so happy, so full of castles in the air that were dependent entirely upon the mine for realisation, that he had not the heart to arouse their fears.

At the door of the cabin stood Kitty herself, looking prettier than ever as she leant her fair head against the door-post, and with an aspect of perfect happiness gazed on the prospect before her. Brit, Joe's old half-breed bulldog, sat on the step below her, and with the tip of one shoe she was stroking his rugged head.

It was just the beginning of that hour when there is gold up in the heavens, there are ruddy hues upon the hills, and a purple haze, soft but inexpressibly beautiful, is filling the valleys, stealing out upon the plains, and gradually enveloping everything in its swimming atmosphere. Here and there in the silent sky, as it deepened from grey to greyish blue aloft, floated a few isolated shreds of silvery cloud stained on the nether side with a tinge of rose. Far away off upon the plains flashed the gleam of a few pools of the Rio Grande, where it wound its sinuous course betwixt New Mexico and Texas.

Kitty watched for a little while Ned working at the shaft's mouth, and finally strolled towards him.

"Say! isn't it 'bout time for you boys to quit work? —ain't you tired, Ned?"

Ned thrust back his broad cowboy hat, and brushed the beads from his brow.

"Stand right there, Kitty! A man couldn't get tired with you around, you look so cool and fresh."

F

"You go work down the shaft, then, and send Joe up here to look at me," she answered, with a laugh. "Aren't you cruel to keep my poor Joe down there all day! Oh, Joe!" she called down the shaft, "Oh, Joe! don't you want me to come down and help you out a little? I've done fixed all the housework."

"Last load!" shouted Joe.

The last load had come up, then, one by one, the men who had been working with Joe, and lastly Joe himself, with one foot in the bucket and his arm round the rope, looking so big, and strong, and reliable, and contented, that Kitty felt quite proud of him, and had to say as much.

They turned towards the cabin, not, however, until having smoothed back with both hands her clean dress from the muddy miner, Kitty had tiptoed up and kissed him lightly.

"Dear, old, grimy face! I could grow lettuce on it!"

"Grimy! You don't want to say a word against that dirt. That's what's going to pay for that farm of yours back in the old country," said Joe, with a wise smile.

The words went to Ned's heart. He followed in their steps, watching them, as he might have watched two children — half envyingly, half compassionately. He envied them their contentment, their fresh power of enjoyment, and though he foresaw the disappointment in store for them, even envied them the fact that the mine should mean so much to them. He wondered whether he would ever take as keen a delight in anything as they took in this mine? To him it meant so little. However well it might turn out, it would be nothing more to him than a "raise," a "starter," the means, merely, of extending his field of operations. He knew that whatever he got out of it would be risked again and again before ever he reached a footing of financial security — if, indeed, he ever attained that condition. Not that he was particularly ambitious, nor in the least degree avaricious, only he would never be contented. He was too restless and energetic, too fond of excitement. Nothing less than speculation that involved the whole of his available capital would ever satisfy his craving for a stimulus. Most men are born to be the ordinary warp and woof of humanity, and take the world as they find it. At rare intervals a man is found with force to fashion things to his own liking. And not a few there are — and Ned was one of them — who, if events required and occasion were to find them, would give proof of unsuspected greatness. Like fine tools for which there is no use, they lie unnoticed, or at most merely re-excite curiosity that so much that is good and strong in the world should apparently be created only to be wasted.

Half an hour later Ned and Joe, washed and clean-shirted, sat on the steps of the shanty waiting for Kitty to summon them to supper. Joe was smoking. Ned seldom smoked; indeed, in his habits he was wonderfully abstemious, a circumstance by no means as unusual on the frontier as might be thought.

The sun had set, and there was a mysterious stillness on the hillside, a richness and sweet softness in the air, that almost thrilled with its beauty. A man on a grey pony was coming slowly up the track from town.

"Why, it's Nate Frost, the new sheriff," said Joe, who had been watching him. "Who's he after, I wonder?"

Ned had already recognised him, but had said nothing. He said nothing now, for he suspected the nature of Frost's errand.

"Boys, how 're you making it?" cried Frost, pulling up before the door and cocking one leg over the pommel of his Mexican saddle.

He was a small, wiry, plain-faced, rather insignificant man in appearance; but he had a pleasant voice, and two brilliant blue-grey eyes that seemed as though they could focus on a needle point, so keen and piercing was their regard.

"Get off, Nate, and come inside," said Joe.

"Why, no, I reckon I won't get off, Joe. I've got to get away back to Bantry 'fore morning, and put out after that Mexican whelp 't shot the deputy yesterday." He paused for a moment, then resumed abruptly: "Look at here, boys, there's trouble about the title to this mine of yours,—maybe you've heard of it."

"Not a dog-gone word," returned Joe, looking from Frost to Ned in surprise.

"Wal, it's like this,—Mrs. Johnstone"—Kitty had appeared in the doorway at this point—"I haven't had the chance to say my congratulations to you since you was married. Here's wishing you luck—all the world and a little brass fence round it. On'y wish I'd brought you better news right now. Boys, it's this way: Seems as this here mine stands in the name of your partner what died awhile back, and his heirs has got an injunction from court to prevent your shipping ore until this question of title is fixed up. Now, I've got to see that injunction carried out, and if you insist on shipping, my duty'll be to set a guard over the mine."

"You can't set it too quick then," exclaimed Joe, savagely. "But, by God, you'd best set your men away back from this mine, if you want to find 'em again. Ned, have you heard anything of this?"

"Yep — I saw Tom Dutton. He claims the whole outfit."

"And you didn't tell me?"

"What was the good? — and you just married."

"You're right," muttered Joe, and his face grew pale. For the moment he had forgotten the responsibility this fact entailed. He was no longer entitled to risk his own life at will.

"See here, Joe," pursued Frost, kindly, "I reckon it's only a question of knocking off work for a few weeks. It looks like, to me, as you'd got a cast-iron holt on the mine. The facts are all known. You three men were partners. You staked Dick Dutton to come down here prospecting, whiles you and Ned stayed up in Colorado, looking to the claims as you all three was a-working there. Dick found this mine and denounced it in his own name, 'cause you wasn't either of you here at the time. The fact as you didn't fix up the title right away when you come here wasn't only miners' keerlessness. The fellows 'll be with you, and you'll get all the witnesses to speak for you as you've a mind to. It ain't anyways likely the court 'll give it agin you. Anyway, it ain't no sort o' good making a kick yet awhile; it'd on'y prejudice your case. Sit back a bit, and see how things is going to shape."

"Nate's right," said Ned, curtly.

"By God! if Tom Dutton hogs the whole of this mine, he won't live to work it," swore Joe.

Ned laughed — a little, hard, sinister laugh that was very unpleasant. "You keep your hair on, Joe. I'll look after Dutton; you've got Kitty to think about."

Poor Kitty! She knew the nature of the men she had to deal with, and visions of bloodshed in the future already filled her with terror. She was as white as a ghost.

"Well, boys, how's it to be?" asked the sheriff.

"We won't ship," said Ned.

"You give me your word on it?"

"Yes."

"That's all I want. So long, then! Mrs. Johnstone, I hate the worst kind to bring you this sort of news, but I reckon you'll understand that there's no gettin' around it. It lies in the nature of my business, worse luck," and he turned the grey pony's head towards town. "Do you take the stage down to-morrow, Ned?"

"Yep."

"May see you in Duckville, then. So long."

"So long."

For a few minutes after he had gone Kitty had a hard struggle with her tears. All her palaces in the air seemed wrecked. But she silenced her regrets, took her own line, and stuck to it gallantly; and before supper was over and Ned had left them, her cheerfulness had partly won Joe, at any rate, from the fit of savage temper into which Frost's news had thrown him.

"Tell me, Joe —" she whispered, as they watched Ned going off towards town in the early moonlight — "won't you tell me that, as long as you have me, you won't care what becomes of the mine?"

"Why, no, in one way of course I don't care. You're more to me than all the mines or riches in the world, a thousand times," and he looked up proudly at the little figure that sat on the step above him. "But still a man don't want to lie down, and let every dog-durned thief roll him that has a mind to — not much!"

"But you don't have to, Joe. Joe, dear, listen — listen to me: I don't *want* you to get into any shooting scrape. Ah, Joe, think! Ah, Joe!" and Kitty's arms went round Joe's neck, and she bent down and set her sweet little face close to his. "If anything should happen to you, what *would* I do? Think! And even if *you*, Joe, *you* hurt any one! No, no, I couldn't bear it! For your sake, darling, and mine, and — and all that may be dear to us by and by, there must never be any stain on your hands, Joe. Promise me — promise me that."

"Why, no, not if I can help it. God knows! I love you too much to get into any scrape of that kind if it can be avoided. But a man's got to hold his own in this world, and make other folks respect it. Yes, I'll go slow — the thought of you'll make me go slow enough, you bet."

CHAPTER VI.

It had become a custom with Rose to take little Bee Murray for a walk before the heat of the day, or rather to allow herself to be so taken by the child, since it was Bee who commanded during those expeditions. At any rate, she commanded while the outward voyage lasted, steering a course that touched at all the ports — to be more exact, the shops where articles of juvenile interest were to be found. Having completed a tolerably extensive cargo of these, for which she was indebted to Rose's good nature, she promptly professed to have grown tired, and surrendered her command, allowing Rose to convoy her home as best she might. It was characteristic of the spirit in which in America children are regarded, that people should see no more in this than the fact that she had a "level head." The level was certainly not a high one, but such as it was, it was undeniable. Rose's advent had undoubtedly been a fortunate event for the child; for she supplied her almost entirely with clothing, cared for her, kept her from the gutter, and tried, albeit in vain, to awaken some generous instincts in her arid little nature.

Strolling up from breakfast at the Mountain Pride one morning, Ned encountered the two together.

"Little things amuse little minds, they say," said Rose, smiling as she stopped. "Is that why Bee amuses me so?"

"No; it's because she's fond of flowers, isn't it Bee?" exclaimed Ned, gayly, catching the child up in his arms.

"'Umps,'" replied Bee, who had already attained to a full appreciation of compliments. Under ordinary circumstances she would have added, "I'se a f'ower, ain't I?" But she had a mind's eye that never lost sight of business, and she hastened to say, therefore, "Oo tarry me home — say! — or I'll t'y." And she would have cried, too, had he not acceded to her request; for she had long ago gauged the water-power of tears, and knew when and where they would prove effective.

So Ned started to carry her home, Rose walking beside him.

"You were playing out of luck last night — I came down and looked at you once," she remarked.

He nodded, smiling.

"Yep; somebody 'd put a 'hoodoo'[1] on me. Couldn't win a bet, could I, little one?" and he danced the child up in his arms.

"R—r—r!" squealed Bee. "Oo tumble my f'oc!"

"Kiss me."

"Smoof my f'oc, then."

Ned did as he was bidden, and Bee paid him for it with a little, hard kiss, like the peck of a bird.

"I hear Dutton has got an injunction to stop your shipping ore from the mine?"

"'Umps,'" replied Ned, imitating Bee, laughingly. "Oh, well, luck comes and goes in streaks. We sold a claim up in Colorado the other day, but haven't got the money yet. I shouldn't wonder if something were to go wrong with that, too. We're hoodooed just now, that's a fact."

[1] An evil spell.

But there was no trace of irritation in his voice; the anger was in Rose's eyes, as she said: "Why aren't you mad about it — about the mine, I mean? I should be."

"Eh? why?" and he glanced from the child to the beautiful face beside him, and half turned away, and then looked again. "Why, of course I'm mad — when I think about it. Only, after all, it seems such a little matter, by comparison. All life's a gamble, and some of it — well, some of it's very pleasant. I'm sorry for poor old Joe and Mrs. Joe, 'tis for them I'm sorry."

"Joe Johnstone?"

"Yes. You see, they were scheming to get back to the old country to live, and they reckoned to do it with the money they pulled out of this mine."

"I'm sorry for them, too — very sorry for her. Every one speaks so nicely of her, and a mining camp's no place for a nice woman. It may come out all right, though, yet."

"Oh, yes. Dutton has the power to waste time for us, but I don't see how he's going to win his case."

"Who you torry for — me?" asked Bee.

"No, dear, not just at present. Say! Mr. Chase! Have you heard whether this man is taking any part with Dutton in the matter?" and she glanced at Bob Hannaford, who was approaching them in the road.

At the sight of him Ned's face changed.

"Dat Misl Hanelfo'," whispered Bee in his ear. "My mamma tiss Misl Hanelfo'."

But Ned was too preoccupied to notice this interesting statement, and the light it threw upon Mrs. Murray's character.

"From what you overheard that night, it seems quite likely. It'd be just the mean kind of game he deals in, to find the money, and rib Dutton up to try and get away with us. I've been waiting for him to make some break about it, but he won't. I wish to Heaven he would!" said Ned, savagely.

As Hannaford passed, he avoided Chase's eye, but took off his hat to Rose as though they were friends; and Rose returned the bow.

Ned glanced at her queerly.

"It seems you had some trouble with him the other night. I wasn't there, worse luck!"

An expression of dumb revolt lived for a moment in her eyes.

"Does he — does he trouble you at all — that I don't know of? — tell me."

"Ah, the brute!" ejaculated Rose, with loathing.

"He does?"

"No, no; he doesn't trouble me."

"Why don't oo talk 'o me?" asked Bee, who began to feel neglected, and who put her arms round Ned's neck, and kissed him — very sweetly this time.

"Presently, dear."

"No; now."

"How is it you bow to him?"

"Oh, well — I do, sometimes."

She did not tell him that she had done so in this instance merely because she did not desire to see him and Ned flying at one another's throats on her account.

They had reached the cottage gate, and Ned had put down Bee (who had gone off in high dudgeon), and was standing straight in front of Rose.

"You have known him a long while?"

"Ah! — you don't know?"

"Know what?"

"It was he who took me away from school, and — and — " and the colour rushed into her cheeks.

Ned's eyes flashed, and his dark face grew duskier still with the hot blood that burnt there. Somehow the knowledge had escaped him — possibly owing to the fact that he pried so little into, and so little encouraged gossip about, the affairs of others. He had, however, heard some story of a girl — a lady by birth — whom Hannaford had carried off in the past, and now it all recurred to him. Until that moment he had forgotten it, and certainly it had never occurred to him to connect the incident in any way with Rose.

"Yes, I know him," she pursued defiantly. "I ought to. And he knows me. He won't trouble me much! No; I don't want you to interfere — I won't have it. I'm not in the least afraid of him, and I don't want anything to happen to him on my account. Look at what my life is, and think what it might have been! Oh, I've too great a score against that man to wish him free of life. Let him live! — life's the worst misery there is."

But the truth was, that Rose had a curious feeling with regard to the man who had ruined her whole career. Much as she detested him, and notwithstanding the fact that, under the influence of passing anger, she might have found some fleeting gratification in seeing him suffer on her account, in her calmer moments she did not wish to take revenge on him. She had loved, and she had been betrayed; she would not sully her cause by reprisals. She had given all, surrendered everything for him, freely and frankly, without receiving anything in return. And therein lay the one solace that her heart found in the matter. Had she one benefit, one disinterested kindness to thank him for, or had she ever taken steps to avenge the wrong he had done her, and so cancel the debt, it would have deprived her of the sole feeling, that of the sacrifice of alone bearing the punishment for her connection with Hannaford, whilst he, the more guilty party, went free, that preserved in her any of her self-respect or pride. It was only a half-superstitious and fanciful feeling after all, perhaps, but it was all she had, and she clung to it.

"Won't you come in?" she asked. "Come in and see the lovely flowers you sent me last night. I haven't had time to arrange them yet."

He followed her into her sitting-room, where a large bowl of flowers stood in the centre of the table, containing roses and oleanders, carnations and pinks, dark purple pansies and forget-me-nots, with others of various kinds, all thrust into the water haphazard.

"Ouf! it's warm in here," said Rose, throwing down her hat and parasol. "Let's take the flowers with us, and sit out on the piazza."

And, followed by Ned, she went out again to the steps of the verandah, and sat down at one end of them in the shade.

For a while they talked about the Johnstones, about the mine, and the prospects of the action which Dutton would probably bring for the ejection of its existing possessors. Meanwhile, Rose played idly with the flowers in the bowl beside her, sometimes holding one of them at arm's length for inspection.

"See! I'm going to illustrate the story of my life with these flowers," she said presently.

"How can you do that?"

"In colours — I'll tell the tale in colours with these flowers," — and then her fancy changed suddenly.

"Pshaw! what's the use! Let me tell you of a painting that I saw once over in Europe. It was by a man named Benlluri, and it told the tale of a woman's life just in the sort of way I mean. It was painted on a palette, and so looked as if the artist, tired of work, and sitting back from his easel to rest, had begun to play with his colours, and, getting interested in the story he was telling, had gone on with it to the end. Beginning close to his thumb, he had sketched all round the edge of the palette, and finished in the middle of it.

"At first there was a child's face nestled among a few rose leaves — all of the faintest and most delicate tints. As you proceeded, and the face was repeated again and again, it grew older and more of the figure was shown. At length you saw the form of a beautiful girl. All the time the colours about her had been strengthening like the tones of growing day, and soon you saw a suggestion of danger in a line or two of startling red that did not harmonise with the other tints. The dark figure of a man was introduced, watching the girl, his shadow falling across her pathway like that of an evil genius. Next, the two were seen walking together. You saw them sitting side by side. The colours glowed warm and rich, golden and ruddy — deeper still, though gradually disturbed. The man and the girl — no longer a young girl now, but a woman — stand facing one another, finally, amidst hues that are lurid and discordant. And the woman goes on alone; but the dark figure of the man — only a shadow now — follows her all the time. Her gay dresses vanish, and she gets to look weary and ragged. The colours about her fade until they become dreary, and sullen, and cold. But the black shadow of the man is always strong; that never leaves her. At last you see the woman dead; and away off you see her white spirit winging its way above the mists towards the sunrise. And still across the poor little trail of light it leaves behind it lies the shadow of her evil genius, and — it makes you frightened for her still."

Ned was silent, but the effect of her story was visible in the expression of his face when she looked up at him.

"I can't describe all the suggestions of joy and tenderness, and passion, and trouble, and pain that were in the sketch; but there was true genius in it — at least I thought so. Isn't it strange," she resumed, musingly, after a pause, during which she had quietly continued arranging the flowers with which her hands were occupied, "isn't it strange, love is the only thing that makes life worth the living, and yet if we yield to it we die — ah, die a thousand deaths. Love gives us wings to soar above the earth — away from all its sordid cares and wretchedness into a glorious sunshine. Suddenly, without any warning"— Rose snapped her fingers lightly — "the wings are broken, and we fall back to earth to drag them along crippled and useless, for the rest of life. Wouldn't it have been better never to have had them at all?"

"No," replied Ned, with a queer flash in his eyes. "No! Love doesn't always end like that. And even when it does, it must be worth while to pay the recompense for what you've had. If you've never loved and loved well, you've never lived, — you don't know what life is, or rather what it can be. True love ennobles all who feel it. To love, and love worthily, is the best religion that man or woman can have."

She looked at him with that curious, far-away, yet

searching glance of hers, and Ned met it fairly. Had he his story, too, she wondered.

"Yes," she said wearily, "that's true. If there's anything strong or noble in a woman, love will discover it — it will betray her, too, if she is only weak. But" — and she almost shuddered — "from love and all such tenderness good Lord defend us."

"You would be afraid to love now?"

"Horribly! Honestly, I'd sooner die."

She knew that she had never loved as a woman can love. She knew that the first love of a young girl is, as a rule, little more than involuntary exuberance of feeling — love for the joy of loving without much reference to its object — a blossom that may, but will by no means of necessity mature. And though this love was all that her experience had taught her, it had enabled her to understand the rest. "Ah, no! ah, no! What have I to do with love?" she mused sometimes. "Love should have a lodging white as snow; to love now would only make me loathe myself the more."

Her voice had trembled as she had spoken to Chase, and her black eyes had filled suddenly with tears. She looked up at him, and smiled as she brushed them away.

"How the boys would laugh to see these from me — from Wild Rose! But you don't laugh."

"Do you think a woman's tears are something to laugh at?"

She lifted her shoulders. "Oh, well, I'm glad that you don't, anyhow. Come! To have seen them may change your luck — don't they say that's so sometimes? Go and try it. Good-bye," and she rose to go indoors.

CHAPTER VII.

IN the Mint Saloon only one table was in play. This one had never been closed during the two years and a half that the saloon had been open, but had been kept open continually, by relays of dealers, throughout the twenty-four hours. Play did not begin at the second table until evening, when the rooms became crowded.

It was in the "shank of the afternoon," and ten or a dozen men sat or stood round the board of green cloth; some playing in a desultory just-to-pass-the-time fashion, others merely taking part in the conversation.

Jimmy Dillon (a little Irishman of somewhat Jewish colouring and features, whose physique was about equal to that of a well-grown girl of fourteen) was dealing, while "Mississip'," one of the paid dealers, was resting in the lookout chair. Unless high play set in, in which case either Kellon or Morris was summoned, Dillon ran the establishment during the day, his partners taking charge of it during the heavier business in the evening. The Chinaman who owned the adjoining restaurant, was keeping the cases, and gambling boldly with the yellow counters provided for the exclusive use of his countrymen in order to obviate international disputes. Mike Brannigan; Nix, a poker-playing, card-sharping carpenter, who supplemented his legitimate business by lending small sums of money at enormous rates of interest; "Cow" Comers, or "Cucumber," as he was often called, a cattle man and "quarter-horse" owner of readier wit than money; and a loafer who "worked in" with Cow in some of his transactions, and whose family name of Dinklespiel was by universal consent curtailed to "Dinkey"; these were some of the players. The rest were men from the adjoining mining camp.

"And so Big Alice stood you off, Dinkey"—Big Alice, be it known, was the proprietress of an establishment in the town of unmarried ladies of sociable natures, but sadly irregular habits—"Big Alice stood you off yesterday when you made a break to get Goldie back, eh?" said Jimmy, completing the shuffle, and introducing the pack of cards once more into the dealing box preparatory to the commencement of a fresh deal.

Dinkey clucked to himself sardonically, and removing the stump of a cigar from his ample mouth, signed to Mississip' to pass him a match from a holder attached to the wall near the lookout chair. Without altering his position of nonchalant ease by one inch, the gambler lifted an arm and tossed a couple of matches on to the table among the counters there for Dinkey to gather up.

"Why, it was like this—" began Dinkey, drawing in vain at the sodden end of his cigar—"I'll take a cigar, Colonel," he interrupted, *par parenthese*, throwing the stump of his own away finally.

"You will? Well, Dinkey, there ain't any strings on you that I know of," replied the Colonel, judicially. "It's a free country. The freedom of the masses to—"

"With *you*, I mean—I'll take a cigar with you."

"O-h! but why wait for me, Dinkey? Ask some one else to join you. Somebody give Dinkey a cigar—give him a box of them. Don't let a good man like Dinkey die for want of a little bad tobacco."

But no one responded to the appeal.

Dinkey sighed with pathetic resignation.

"It's a hard world — hardest I ever knew."

"Ged on mit der story von Goldie," interpolated Nix, ignoring Dinkey's private feelings.

"Well, it was like this —"

"'It happened like this, there were three of us,'" interjected a miner, gravely.

"— It was like this," proceeded Dinkey, imperturbably, "I came home 'loaded' the other night, and Goldie opened out and began to burn me right up. Nat'rally I retorts — I reckon things was said as ain't often heard between lovers — things as ain't often stated in the company of ladies, anyway. But then, 's I say, she set the tune and I had to face the music or — or take a back seat. Once take a back seat in matters of love —"

"— And you've just got to keep it for good," observed Mike Brannigan.

"— And you've got to keep it until *she's* found another man, who'll tramp on her," amended Mr. Dinkelspiel.

"She says you beat the stuffing out of her," drawled the wooden-visaged Mississip'.

"She's a liar. I appeal to any gentleman here what's made a study of female nature, ef that ain't just the kind of alligator a lady puts around —"

"He means 'allegation,'" explained the Colonel, in a very grave aside to the rest of the table.

"— ef that ain't just the kind of allegation," amended Dinkey, quite undisturbed by their laughter, "that a lady puts around the moment you happen to lay over her a bit in argument —"

At this point Big Frank, the bartender, appeared

with a tray of cocktails and mint juleps for the players; and pocketing his indignation for the moment, Dinkey, although taking no part in the game, paused to inquire "whether he didn't get a drink, too?" To which Jimmy Dillon suavely replied that "the management didn't undertake to set up the drinks for every long-stemmed, sun-dried, sponge-bellied dead-beat who chose to come in and talk up a drought, looking on at the game." Nor did he relent even when Dinkey offered to "play off at the table the very next $1000 that was sent him." So the loafer resumed his tale.

"Where was I?"

"You was about taking a back seat," rejoined "Cow" Comers.

"Not much, I wasn't. I was feeling real good, and I argued with her and reasoned with her in great shape —didn't allow no back talk either. Oh, you bet, I convinced her—convinced her so, that next morning I'd no sooner quit the house than Goldie packed her trunk and lit out for Big Alice's, leaving word as she didn't propose to live under my protection any longer. Wal, sir, I jest took my foot in my hand, and waltzed around there to fetch her back, right quick. But they seen me coming and shut the door on me. I knocked like thunder, though. 'Who's there?' says Big Alice. 'Me,' says I. 'The hell, you say! I thought it was that slab-sided, cross-eyed, lop-eared son-of-a-gun Dinkey. Why don't you walk right in?' 'Open the door then,' says I. 'Not much.' So then I come right out, and declared what I was there for. 'Wal, you can't have her,' says Alice. 'She says you don't treat her right, and she's come here now, and come to stay.' 'Empress of my soul,' says I, 'jest let me in once, and let's talk it over a time or two.' 'In a pig's valise!' says Alice. 'Ef you don't, I'll bust the —— house down,' says I. 'Sail in,' says she. And I was just lifting my foot to start the door—for I was as mad as a singed wildcat—when I took a notion to poke round to the side window and peek in first. Which is what I done. And there I seen Big Alice, standing right up alongside the door in her shirt tails, with a dog-gone long six-shooter in her hand ready cocked and waiting for me. Wal, sir, I studied a bit, and concluded I didn't want Goldie back so bad as all that. So I come around to the front door again — the side of it, that is, and says I, 'I'd allow 'em a spell to think it over, and be down again in the cool of the evening to set fire to the house, if Goldie didn't come home.' 'Cow,' you're winning a mint of money there — don't you want to stake me to five dollars and see me make a raise, too?"

"Give Dinkey a two-dollar stack of white chips," said "Cow" Comers, throwing four of his own half-dollar red "chips" across to Jimmy.

"And so you've done lost your girl, Dinkey?" remarked the Colonel, sympathetically. "Don't you know, there's many a man 'd mortgage his immortal prospects to suffer just such a horrible bereavement as that?"

"Yep," returned the abandoned lover, philosophically, "I guess that's so; ain't it, Jimmy?" and he winked with the most offensive familiarity at Jimmy, who reddened suspiciously, but said nothing. "Oh, I done lost her sure enough. Wal, now I can save money; she cost me a million a week, a'most."

"She says you never gave her anything but corn-cobs to eat," drawled Mississip', phlegmatically.

"Corn-cobs! *corn*-cobs! That's a nice charge to make against a gentleman! that's gratitude! when I wasted my whole revenue in supporting the durned little mule in amorous idleness and gilt-edged luxury! To hell with her corn-cobs! Ask John here—John, didn't I bring a lady into the restau*rant* one day last week, and blow her out to the most elegant meal you ever served, a'most?"

"One plork chlop, waffles, one clup cloffee, thir' five cent—you pay now?" inquired the Chinaman, literally.

Amidst the laughter of the others, Dinkey affected not to have heard this suggestion, and the entrance of Sol Poheim at that moment turned attention from him.

"Gembling, gembling! all de times gembling!" said Solomon, reprovingly, taking a seat at the table nevertheless.

"Take a whirl, Sol," suggested Mike.

"Give him some checks," said the Colonel to Jimmy.

"Eh! vat! me? I neffer play—you know dat. How dey coming, Cunnel?"

"Times they win, and times again they lose. Sit in and see how it is."

"Vell, gimme von stack—dem blues," and he threw down five twenty-dollar gold pieces and received a stack of blue counters, which, after carefully counting them, he began to distribute about the table in bets. "Say, Jimmy! vat vas de truth? dey say Dave Kellon sell out his share in dis house; is dat so?"

"Oh, I d' know; ain't nothin' settled yet, anyway. Guess he will, though, sooner or later. Dave don't have his health here, and he wants a change."

"You done let Billy Murray out, too; vat?"

"'Bliged to," replied Jimmy. "We'd warned him time and again, but he couldn't keep off drink, and — well, that wasn't all."

"Der reck'nings veren't alvays so stret vat dey might been, eh?" suggested Nix.

"There was disputes, anyway."

"Talking of Billy Murray, dog ef I didn't forget all about it! Did you hear what happened over to Billy's this morning?" asked a young miner. "'No?' you don't say! Wal, Phil Wade stayed in town last night, 'stead of going out to the camp, and way along about three o'clock this morning, as he was a-working home past Billy's house, he heard Mrs. Murray squealing to beat hell. So Phil steps in to see fair. Seemed as how Billy'd come home with a reg'lar three-masted jag[1] on him, and took the idee to kill Mrs. Murray with a carving knife. I ain't saying but what a little killing, maybe, 'd do Mrs. Murray a power o' good—"

"Me, either," coincided Mississip', pausing to expectorate with surprising accuracy and elegance. "Ef I had a wife like that, I'd swap her off for a yaller dog, and shoot the dog. If she'd been a good woman, Billy'd have been a different man."

"You're dead right. Wal, as I was a-saying, Phil dropped in, and there he seen Wild Rose and Billy fighting for the knife. I reckon, from what he told afterwards, that he wa'n't there none too early, either, for he'd no sooner chipped in than Rose let up. And she was that near pegged out she couldn't speak for ten minutes."

"What'd Phil do?" asked "Cow" Comers.

"Why, took the knife away, of course; and then he

[1] A fit of drunkenness.

slapped Billy over once or twice, to soothe him, and packed him into the parlour, — locked him up there, and slep' on the sofy himself."

"There's a girl that's got some grit in her," observed the Colonel, admiringly.

"Wild Rose? I should re-mark! Mrs. Murray says she didn't stop to talk, she shoved right in between them, and went straight for Billy. She was like to have got killed for it, too, for Billy was jest raving."

"Py golly, she's a dandy, sure!" ejaculated Poheim. "De tings vat I known dat gal do! She ain't no more like she vas, do — not so vild, not de sem spirits, vat! Der grit, ya — dat vas shtill da; fear she don't know — but de fun, no — dat vas not de sem wie formerly. Dem days, back in Montana, ven she firs' kem der mit Bob Hannaford, I tell you she vas 'live! — de flies don't settle mitin a block of her! Ach! dem vas de good days! Laugh? You bet we laugh. Vild Rose whoop 'em up all de time. And she was slick, too! Gee! — de slickest gal vat ever *you* see!"

"D——n it, Sol, she couldn't have been any slicker-looking than she is now," objected the Colonel. "Where're you going to pick a match for her to-day?"

"True, but de spirits vas der den. She ain't no more so gay like she vas. Der're times now ven you feel like a schmall schild peside her."

A slight commotion was heard in the adjoining bar-room at this juncture, and on peeping through the swinging doors which concealed the cause of it, Dinkey observed that "it was Red-headed Mame, and Chewing-gum Cis, from Alice's, drinking milk punches at the bar." A shadow of anxiety settled on Jimmy Dillon's face at the news, and thenceforward he became slightly preoccupied, although not sufficiently so to prejudice his interests in the game.

"Boys," said the Colonel, "what's this talk amount to that's going around town about Ned Chase's mine? Is there anything in it?"

"Vy, Cunnel, dey ain't got no title. De mine always stood in Dick Dutton's name, and dey ain't fixed up de papers before he died," replied Nix.

"So the heirs claim the whole carcass, eh?"

"Dey say de partnership don't go."

"Are they going to make the claim stick?"

"Dey're going to see anyhow — de case will be tried down to Las Casas."

"Is that so, Sol?"

"Ya, der Goddam olt Dutch money-lender vas right," assented Polheim. "Ef der's anytings to know he schmell it out mit his nose."

"And his nose ain't so long as dat Sheeny's, nieder," retorted Nix, dryly.

"Ef your nose vas like mine, you bin a better-looking fellow," said Sol.

"I mide; but dem noses ain't no more so popular like dey vas pefore de crucifixion. I likes better my own."

"Vell, der ain't nobody goin' to quarrel mit you for it, dat's sure. Say, Nixey, hef you got your snake's head [1] on to-day?"

---

[1] "Snake's Head": An apparatus affixed to the arm inside the coat sleeve. By pressing the arm on the table, a spring shoots a clip out of the cuff, in which cards may be placed that it is desired to use afterwards. The arm is then lifted, and the released spring draws the cards up the sleeve. When required for use, the arm is pressed on the table again, the cards reappear, and are exchanged for such inferior ones as the player happens to hold.

"You bet," responded Dinkey for him. "Whenever you see Nix with his great coat on, you can know he's got his 'hold out' up his sleeve."

Nix's denials were drowned in the laughter of the others, and soon afterwards he took occasion to leave.

"Him and Hannaford's the two meanest men in this country," observed "Cow" Comers.

"That's what," was the universal rejoinder.

"They do say," remarked the Colonel, "that Hannaford's kind o' mixed up with Dutton's heirs in this mine business — finds the money to fight the case or something."

"Wal, sir, there'll be trouble over that mine, you'll see," said Mississip', "and bad trouble, too, if them boys come to be cinched. You bet your sweet temper Ned Chase ain't going to be run out of any mine as he's a right to, and sit down under it."

"Joe Johnstone, either," declared one of the miners. "He's quiet so long as you let him alone; but ef a man *wants* trouble, he can get it there as quick as anywhere."

"I reckon —" began the Colonel.

But at this point the hilarity which had arisen in the bar since the advent of Red-headed Mame and Chewing-gum Cis degenerated into riot.

"Take the deal, Mississip'," said Jimmie with a curse, turning the dealing box upon its side as he rose to leave the room.

His entrance into the bar-room was the signal for a volley of badinage, replete with imagery of Oriental richness, from the two ladies — robust females in loose white wrappers and curl papers. They were not in the least afraid of Jimmy, and it was by no means unusual for them, when their social engagements left them at liberty in the afternoon, to come down to the Mint and defy him to put them out. This he could just accomplish when one of them came alone, but only just. When they came together they were more than a match for him, and had sometimes beaten him unmercifully. Nevertheless, Jimmy, who, like many another little man, was courageous, strongly disliked to ask for assistance, and always advanced to the conflict without wavering.

Addressing the ladies now with an air, at any rate, of studied politeness, he intimated that "the Mint was no —— travelling circus, and that he would dump both of them on the sidewalk if they didn't shut their mouths and quit fooling."

The damsels immediately hurled defiance at him in language as profoundly contemptuous as it was surprisingly blasphemous. They also hurled two milk punches in large glasses at him.

Jimmy evaded the glasses, although he received a good deal of the beverage, which seriously marred the beauty of his language and clothes, and quite wrecked his temper. He promptly made a front attack on Redheaded Mame, with a view to carrying out his threat. Redhead met him with a round-arm swing on the nose, which drew blood copiously. At the same time Chewing-gum took him in flank, and, throwing her arm round his neck, began to scratch his face like a wildcat.

Not without difficulty Jimmy released himself, and dealt the latter siren a box on the ears which tumbled her over on the floor, where he at once measured his own length, persuaded thereto by another of Mame's deadly round-arm swings. Before he could move, the lady sat down upon him hard, and with more regard for expedition than modesty, began to pull off her shoe, with a view to erasing her enemy's features utterly. Cis came to her assistance, and a rough-and-tumble fight ensued upon the floor, in the course of which Jimmy received by far the greatest share of the punishment.

The loafers at the bar, the players from the faro table, and a small party that had been quietly playing "Pitch" in a corner of the room, drew near the scene of combat, and stood round encouraging the principals. But Jimmy never had a chance of victory, and finally, when his opponents had him entirely at their mercy, and were beginning to wreak a permanent vengeance on him, he called Big Frank to his aid.

Frank, who hitherto had leant over the bar laughing, now advanced, and taking Mame round the waist under one arm, and securing the gentle Chewing-gum in like manner under the other, carried them both, still kicking vigorously, towards the door. This was opened for him by Jimmy, and by him slammed and bolted when the ladies had been carefully deposited "on the sidewalk."

For a little while they bellowed and swore outside lustily, but finally departed; and, under the auspices of the imperturbable Mississip', play was resumed at the faro table, while Jimmy changed his torn clothes in a back room, and otherwise did what he might to remove the traces of battle from his person.

CHAPTER VIII.

THE criticisms passed at the faro table upon Mrs. Murray's character were not undeserved. She was a soulless, selfish, little animal, whose sole motives were vanity, greed, and self-indulgence. Heaven knows whether she had ever cared or thought she cared for her husband! Certain it is that the sentiment, if it had ever existed, had long since vanished, together with others of a similarly unstable character that she had professed for men not so legitimately connected with her as Mr. Murray. Mrs. Murray did not stand high in the estimation of her neighbours. Dogtown was scarcely straight-laced, but it demurred to being made the confidant of irregularities that did not bear, at least, the stamp of courage and open defiance. It disliked to *see* any one deceived except in the way of business. Now Mrs. Murray not only deceived her husband, she deceived her lovers; she even did not hesitate to discuss virtue, and make as though she would impose herself upon Dogtown generally as an honest woman, a course of conduct which, but for its sardonic humour, would have wounded her fellow-citizen inexpressibly. Still, as there was no one sufficiently pious to usurp divine authority and denounce her formally, she was allowed to remain in peace,

The truth about her was not likely to reach Rose's ears; for it belonged to a class of gossip that, despite her reckless character, she never permitted to be broached before her. She saw or suspected enough about her landlady, however, to make her hold herself aloof entirely from anything like intercourse of a friendly nature with her, and she never spoke to her unless on some matter connected with her lodgings.

One afternoon Mrs. Murray came into her bedroom to say that "a gentleman wished to see her." When questioned, she replied: "He didn't give any name — he said, just like that, 'say that a gentleman wishes to see Miss Carlin.'"

Rose looked at her sharply, and saw that she was prevaricating.

"Who is it, Mrs. Murray? — you know."

And having tried to deceive Rose, with Hannaford's $10 bribe still in her hand, she turned round now and betrayed him also.

"It's Mr. Hannaford, I think."

"You think! You mean you thought I wouldn't see him."

"What an idea, Miss Carlin! Why, I never thought any such a — "

"Let him go into the parlour — if he isn't there already," interrupted Rose, shortly.

Bob Hannaford stood six feet two in his socks, and was magnificently proportioned. With his fair hair, long, fair moustache, and regular features, he was as fine a specimen of manhood as the heart of schoolgirl could wish to worship. But a sinister expression about his mouth and cold, pale blue eyes would have warned any less enthusiastic creature against him. The death of two or three men lay at his door, none of whom had been killed in altogether the fairest fashion. Even among men of his own type, therefore, he was looked at rather askance. He was a bully, without respect for age, or pity for helplessness; when not brutally sullen, he was a great talker, and to further his own ends could assume a great deal of a certain kind of veneer.

He knew that it was useless to waste any of his arts upon Rose now, and when she entered, therefore, she found him seated astride a chair with an air of bravado not altogether free from nervousness. He rose and held out his hand.

She looked at it, and laughed derisively.

"I must sink some way yet before I get as low as that," said she.

"Oh, dry up, Rose!" returned he, jocularly. "Climb down! Where's the sense in all those frills? — what are you playing me for, anyhow?"

"The meanest cur on all the earth," and she looked him squarely in the eyes.

He laughed. "You're getting childish."

Rose had brought in with her a handful of photographs, which she had hitherto omitted to arrange. Turning her back upon him contemptuously, she began to distribute them now about the room. "Say what you have to say, and go," said she curtly.

Hannaford moved his chair round and sat down. "Why, look at here, Rose, — quit fooling now — I've got a proposition to make to you, I'm here on biz. Rose," he said, leaning forward confidentially, "I'm a well-off man to-day — yes, I'm in red clover, knee-high. There's over $20,000 of my money lying in the banks at El Paso, and I own half of five thousand head of good graded cattle on the Gila! How's that strike you?"

"If it's true, — which I doubt, — it strikes me that

some poor creature has been robbed, that's all — some good friend of yours who trusted you, most likely."

Hannaford chuckled. "Go it, Rosey! You could always sling compliments when you wanted to. But hold on! that ain't all. Over and above that, I've secured a third interest in this 'Fresh Start' mine, that your friend Chase and his partner claim to own shares in."

"And they do own them, too."

"They don't own a —— cent in it. And they're going to learn it, too — learn it so d——d quick it'll make their heads swim."

"When their heads swim, we shan't be able to see your heels for the dust," she retorted sarcastically.

"Never mind. We've got those boys where we want them, Dutton and me. They haven't a leg to stand on —"

"You'd never go near them while they had."

"It's only a question of putting up a little money down to Las Casas, and the court will see that we get justice," he pursued, regardless of her remark. "They're cinched, I tell you. They've got no money to fight a case, — nor has Dutton, so far as that goes, — but I have, and I'll put it up, too. Before we're through with it, half that mine'll stand in my name, if not more. And I tell you it's a dandy, sure! it's out of sight! there ain't anything in the camp 't's a marker to it. Well, now, see here! You've got a score against me — I allow it. I didn't treat you right, there's no getting away from it. But, by gosh, you're the only woman I give a curse for, or ever did — ever *did*, mark you! and I'm willing to do the square thing by you. Come back to me and you shall have everything you're a mind to — you shall be handled like a gilt-edged princess. That mine'll stand it. And when the old woman dies, I'll marry you off-hand — it won't be long, either; for she's drinking herself to death at a lope, and I'm giving her all the money she needs for the job. Come! I can't speak fairer than that. It's your say now;" and Hannaford leant back in his chair, and looked at Rose with an air of considerable self-satisfaction.

Why did she listen to him at all? why permit him to pollute her ears with his proposals? For one thing, no mere request for him to go, or be silent, would have availed her. For another, she experienced a perverse delight, as she listened to him, in remembering that *this* was the nature of the man who had betrayed her — that she had once actually endued this brute, in her imagination, with qualities that had made him seem to her a hero. The error appeared so gratuitous now, so hideous, that, in submitting to the exquisite torture the contemplation of it inflicted, she found something of the solace afforded by the patient endurance of a voluntary penance. Only, what could one trust after being once so deceived by one's own faculties — wherein lay the joke of this ghastly irony of imagination?

Placing the photographs here and there, Rose had moved about the room, listening to her visitor without interrupting him; sometimes even pausing for a moment to make sure of his meaning. She turned now with her back to a little cabinet. Her face was very pale. It would have taken very little for her eyes to fill with tears.

For a moment she was motionless; then, lifting her hand quietly, she pointed to the door.

"You can go."

"I'll go fast enough; but I want your answer first. Come! it's your say."

"My say!" she repeated harshly, and a peal of mocking laughter burst from her lips. "What can I say? You yourself could hardly describe the foul thing I think you! Fetch me a coyote to talk to; I should like it better."

"Quit that!" thundered Hannaford, savagely, springing to his feet and towering above her. "Quit that, or, by the blue sky of God Almighty, it'll be the worse for you!"

He was stung at last.

She smiled.

"You terrify me."

"By God, I'll do worse than that! You may laugh, but come back to me you shall! — do you hear? — you shall, you shall!"

"Not in our times," she answered coolly.

"Let me see any other man monkeying round you!"

"Will you clean out the whole saloon?"

"You'll see!"

"Pshaw! I know *you*. You can bluff a tenderfoot, but you daren't face a man. Jim Tritton scared you like a child."

"Blast you!" he shouted, grasping her wrist in his rage. "Blast you! I'll bring you on your knees — on your d——d white knees to me yet! You were mine once — like any other woman I chose to buy — you shall be again, by God!"

With a cry she had wrenched herself free, and faced him, breathing heavily through her nostrils. She was quite still, only slowly her white fingers began to creep towards the pocket of her dress.

"You'd better go," she said hoarsely.

"Don't fool with any one while I'm a—"

"Go!—before worse comes of it!" she panted, and as she spoke she began to move inch by inch nearer to him. "Do you want to drive me to kill you? Go, I say! Go!"

Nearer and nearer she drew to him, her right hand stealing steadily towards her pocket, the fingers nervously feeling the texture of her dress as they moved. And Hannaford watched the movement, saw her clenched teeth, her rigid, white face gleaming before him, and realised the ungovernable passion that possessed her. Yet he did not move. Something about her fairly fascinated him. For the moment he could no more leave her than, now that she had fallen in his pathway again, he could abstain from hovering about her.

With an effort he roused himself, and a second later was gone.

Rose stood alone in the little room; she was trembling like a leaf.

Suddenly she became conscious that her hand grasped the revolver in her pocket, and with a shudder she let go of it.

"Ah, is it just—for one fault, one folly when I was such a child to have to suffer so much? It's horrible!"

* * * * * * * *

It occurred sometimes that old friends of Rose's drifted into Dogtown—friends that she had made during her earlier experience of mining camps. It spoke well for her that one and all were always more than delighted to see her again, and it generally happened upon these occasions that when her evening's work was over, there was an adjournment to one of the poker rooms at the back of the saloon, to enjoy a talk over old times. Here with champagne flowing, and laughter and many a good story, for the time being she would be the gayest of them all again, and many a pleasant hour would be stolen thus from the earlier watches of morning.

> "Fill the goblet fair,
> Every drop we sprinkle
> On the brow of care
> Smooths away a wrinkle,"

might very well have been their motto on these occasions, though it is doubtful whether, as a permanent cure for wrinkles, such late seances are effective.

One evening Toby Reed and Jim Van Ness, friends of Sol Poheim's and of Rose's — men who had come down from the North to look at a property in the camp that Poheim wanted to sell — were seated in a poker room with Rose and Sol. They had known the girl in her brightest days, and were themselves as light-hearted a couple of miners as were to be found in any camp.

"Well, 'God is good — but de debble isn't bad,' as the nigger kept on repeating when he was scared to death walking home in the dark. It's a good thing to have a string on both sides, if you can manage it," commented Van Ness on some story that had just been told.

"You bet!" said Reed, refilling the glasses. "It reminds me, that tale of Sol's does, of the fellow who was talking about early days in California. 'We made lots of money there — lo--ts of money, me and father,' he said, — 'should have made more if we hadn't been watched.'"

"Pretty dog-gone cool, eh?"

"You bet!"

"Say! talk about cool," cried Toby, "d' you hear of that cowboy the other day up in Montana 't came in town on a bend, an' shot the first man he met — shot him dead, right there, 'thout any words or anything? Well, when they came to have him up, there didn't seem to have been the least reason for it; the dead man was one of the quietest and most respectable citizens in the burg. They asked the fellow what he did it for — did they have any quarrel? No, didn't have any quarrel. Any trouble? No, no trouble. What were his reasons then? Well, he said, he was a man who always avoided trouble, and he *might* have had trouble with him if he hadn't killed him."

"Toby! Toby! And it happened 'the other day'!" remonstrated Rose, amid their laughter. "He has absolutely no respect for age, or he couldn't disturb a poor old story like that."

"Bad as body-snatching," declared Jim Van Ness. "The man'd tell that tale'd rob a grave."

"Rats! I invented it myself right now!"

"Oh! Drinks on Toby for that! Ring the bell."

"Say, poys! I vant to tell you a goot ting vat happent here —"

"Well, go ahead, Sol — Sol's 'goot tings' are generally expensive, but we'll risk it."

"Vell, ve got a blackschmidt here dot's sometings of a card sharp (Nix vas de name) and der come a fellow long here — Black Pat — maybe you known him — mit som' of dem snake's heads for sale — you know, dem hold outs.[1] Pat vas de first vat pring dem dam tings

---

[1] See note, chap. vii.

in dis camp. Vell, he solt von to Nix for $275, and den he clear out von here. Pretty soon 'long come a fellow after him, name' Weaver, vat Black Pat told to dot Nix got one of dem tings. So Weaver he lay round a bit, and get to know Nix, and play all de while like he was a sucker, and he ain't bin here long 'fore he gets in a poker game mit Nixey— who vas joost looking for a soft snap like dat. Vell, Nix he pegin to work de olt snake's head, and collect up de four kings up his sleeve. But he don't bin watching dot while he vas busy gedding out all de kings, Weaver he vas grabbing holt von de aces. Vell, de end vas dot Nix he run up a hand von four knaves and deal him to Weaver, and den he pull out his olt four kings, and dey geds to betting. First ting you know, dey both got 'bout $1100 apiece of der own money in de pot, and der vas a call. And Weaver he trow down his four aces, and sweep in de money, and says he, 'Oh, pshaw! I gif you $100 for you' olt trashing machine. Ef you can't work it no better 'n dat, it don't bin no use to you.'"

"Less noise, gentlemen! less noise!" said old Colonel Dodge, gravely, putting his head in at the door in the midst of their merriment.

"Come in, Colonel! come in!" they cried. "Where have you been all the evening?"

"Just setting a fellow's leg."

"You!"

"Well, looking on, and advising, and holding things, while the doctor did the mere technical part of the job."

"Whose leg was it?" asked Rose.

"Dinkey's. He was driving a bunch of steers up with 'Cow' Comers, and his horse fell on some loose stones as he was riding after a two-year old 't got away from them."

"Is he in much pain?"

"Well, he don't say much, but I reckon he ain't feeling altogether absent-minded about it — it ain't a very nice break."

"Who's looking after him?"

"Oh, some of the boys go in from time to time and see he don't want for anything."

"But there's no one with him now?"

"Why, just at present, I guess not. Chick's going soon 's he gets off duty."

The conversation changed, and shortly afterwards Wild Rose took her leave.

"Good-bye, Toby — Van, please look after him, and don't let Sol get the best of him over that mine," she said smiling.

"Sol? Sol can't beat me. He'll try, but — there! I've got lots of confidence in myself."

"You've got all there is, I guess," she replied demurely, amidst a burst of laughter, as she made for the door.

"Never mind; I forgive you," cried Toby above the banter of the others.

"Not yet, Toby — you really mustn't waste any charity on me until you're recovered from that deal with Sol. Good-bye."

"Good-bye! good-bye! See you to-morrow."

"Not if I see you first," was her parting shot as she closed the door.

As she left the house she called one of the "tin-horns" who were loafing about to show her where Dinkey lived. She found him alone and suffering considerably. Though she had little pity for herself, the pain of others always excited her sympathy; and for the rest of the night she remained there, doing what she could to make things easier for him. Nor did her good nature end there. In the days that ensued she was the most constant visitor at the poor little shanty; many a good meal went from the restaurant to the broken-down loafer at her expense; books, tobacco, and various other things had he from time to time to thank her for, and many an hour, that would otherwise have been as tedious as the rest, did her visits help him to while away pleasantly.

CHAPTER IX.

Dutton's intentions were now declared. A writ of ejectment had been served upon Ned and Joe, and the case was to be tried in due course at Las Casas. In the meanwhile, operations at the "Fresh Start" had been suspended, and Joe (whose disposition would not have allowed him to be idle, even had his means permitted it) occupied himself in working for wages in the adjoining mine, the Dutch Oven.

Despite the anxiety he naturally felt with regard to the dispute in which he was involved, those days were still the happiest that he had ever spent. His love for Kitty and her love for him made his material ill-luck appear comparatively trivial, and kept him from dwelling on it. It was so much more pleasant to think of Kitty — to picture her, neat and shapely, fresh and enchanting as a flower at daybreak, standing at their cabin door with a sunny smile to welcome him when he returned to supper. And when he had once reached her presence, he was not allowed to mention the mine at all; for she checked him directly with: "Oh! that wretched old mine! But why think about it, Joe? If we win our case, so much the better; if not — Shoo! I don't care! We'll find another;" meaning presumably another mine, not case. And thereupon Kitty would lean over Joe's shoulder, or tiptoe up and give him one of her fresh little kisses — kisses that seemed to fall and vanish like snowflakes upon the warm earth. Small wonder if others succeeded them before, sweet-eyed and flushed with colour, her pearly teeth glistening betwixt lips that were parted breathlessly, Kitty could escape from Joe's strong arms to reprove him demurely from a distance.

The time for the trial was drawing near when, one evening, Ned entered the Mint. It chanced to be a night when the rooms were rather deserted, a glove-fight up at the mining camp having attracted most of the habitués. Those few who were gathered about Rose made way for Ned as he approached her, and she inquired what news he had concerning the date when the action against him would be begun. He told her that the case would be tried in the following week, and that, in order to attend to it, he had just given up his post as stage driver for the time being, and was going to Las Casas to stay until the matter was settled. Joe, he said, would not join him until the fight in court actually began; for as Joe was married, money was a serious object with him — indeed, if the action went against them, he would be very nearly "broke." Besides, until Joe's evidence was required, he (Ned) could do all that was necessary himself, and in the event of his needing assistance could get all he required from other miners from Dogtown who would be in Las Casas on their own business.

"But, as Mrs. Joe always says," he concluded, "'bother the old mine!' don't let's talk about it. Have you anything to do to-morrow, Miss Carlin?"

"Nothing at all."

"How'd it be then if we rode over to Fallen-star Lake to picnic, and catch some trout, and fool around in that scenery there? It'll be my last day here for some time."

Rose assented to the proposal with pleasure, and their plans were soon agreed upon.

"By the way, who's that playing faro against Clint Morris?" she asked, as Ned was leaving.

"The fair kid at the other end of the table, in a light coat?"

"Yes — his face is familiar."

"It's some young Britisher who's ranching over on the Gila. He's up here to see those 'Scottish Chief' owners — least, so I heard the boys saying. Guess they want to rope him into that outfit to pay for their new steam pump — the mine's in a bad way, anyhow; it's about time some English company bought it."

"You didn't hear his name?"

"No; I wasn't paying much attention to what they said — I'll ask."

But it was not worth while doing this, she said, and, nodding good-bye to him, she began to sing again, whilst Chase went on into one of the poker rooms.

Her song finished, Rose's glance wandered again to the young Englishman. She was trying to make out wherein lay the resemblance between his face and another that she remembered. Presently she beckoned to a tin-horn gambler named Flynn, who frequented the room, and at that moment happened to be idle.

"What is Clint Morris about, Mr. Flynn?" she asked.

"The Englishman is the only one *really* playing at that table, for the others are only 'boosters.'"

"That's so; them two's only playing so's he shouldn't feel lonely. Clint's at his old games — just 'working' the tenderfoot a little. It gets away with me how a man can be such a nat'ral-born fool ez to play off his money at a game he don't know — he don't *begin* to know the first principles of."

"How is Morris beating him?"

"Oh, the Britisher's easy — he's making favourites — betting on the ace, king, queen, nine, and seven, and trying to *make* 'em win," replied the tin-horn, with a significant look. "Like all Britishers, I reckon he thinks *his* cards ought to win, anyhow."

"I see — and Morris is fixing them to lose."

"Clint's picking the dead-wood over all the time, and fixing them pertickler cards — the Britisher's — so's to lose next deal. Then he false shuffles and passes the cut. I know how I'd fool him, though."

"How's that?"

"I'd pike along, and wait till he'd got the deck good and readied for me, and *had it set in the box* so's he couldn't change nothing. Then I'd start in betting the limit on all those cards — the ace, king, queen, nine, and seven — and *copper all my bets.* The Britisher's backing 'em to win, and Clint he's fixed 'em to lose. Well, I'd just back 'em to lose — see?"

"I see," replied Rose, with a gracious smile. "Aren't you smart?"

"Oh, I've worked that racket on 'em, and fooled 'em to the queen's taste," remarked the tin-horn with honest pride. "I've gone in where they've been dealing a brace game, and played sucker on purpose — making favourites and betting in small amounts until I seen they was all ready for me. Right there's where I'd start in betting the limit, and switch around and *copper all my bets,* and just scoop hell out of 'em."

"Ah!" ejaculated Rose, dryly. "You're very clever, Mr. Flynn. How much has the Englishman lost?"

"'Bout a couple of hundred dollars; he ain't bettin' high."

Rose played and sang a little longer, and then, strolling down from the piano to the faro table at which Morris presided, dropped on a vacant stool near the Englishman, and began toying with the loose "coppers"[1] which lay about the table, while she watched the game.

Morris, a dandified gambler, well known for his skill in "influencing chance," greeted her with his best smile. Cold as her manner had always been to him, his confidence in his own personal attractions was such that he had not relinquished the hope of making a conquest of her. Vanity has more lives than a cat.

As the deal proceeded, Rose saw that the description she had received of what had been taking place was correct. In the intervals between turning the cards, and while the Englishman was occupied in placing his bets, she saw Morris occasionally shift a card casually from one of the two piles of dead cards to the other. She also saw that the Englishman lost all the bets he placed on the cards that he had made favourites.

"You're English, aren't you?" she asked finally.

"Yes," replied the boy, looking with mingled curiosity and interest at the beautiful face turned towards him.

"What is your name?" asked Rose.

"My name?"—and he laughed good-humouredly at the frankness of the question—"my name's Carden."

---

[1] Disks placed on the bets when it is desired to indicate that the card selected is backed to lose instead of win.

She shook her head unconsciously. The name did not throw any light upon the resemblance that had puzzled her.

"Well, Mr. Carden, you're out of luck, it seems."

"Dead out, ain't I?"

"Suppose you let me play your checks for you this deal?"

"Why not! You can't do worse than I've been doing, anyhow," and with a laugh he pushed his remaining counters across to her.

"Indeed, I hope to do a great deal better," she answered.

Though it might amuse him to sit down casually like this, and lose a little money, Carden was no fool. It was an experience, an adventure, a folly, the folly of which he appreciated, and to the extent of which he consciously indulged himself. Such a spirit is not understood on the frontier, where gambling is not a pastime but a business practised seriously for "the money there is in it." Prophets are often mistaken therefore, when, because they see a young Englishman losing a little money foolishly, they at once set him down as doomed to destruction. To their surprise the "pigeon" gets up from the table minus only a few tail feathers, and with a head clear of any illusions on the subject writes off the money left behind him as "money lost." When a young American gambles, it is far more often with the idea of making money, and generally with the utmost confidence in his own ability to do so. Regarding what he loses, therefore, as merely "money lent," he returns with all speed to recover it — a proceeding the results of which are inevitably fatal.

Thus, to Carden, who was simply playing for amusement, the turning of his money over to a strange girl to handle as she pleased only added piquancy to the adventure. Besides, there was a look in Rose's face which made it impossible for any one to connect her for one second with the idea of false play.

The cards had been already placed in the dealing box before she had spoken to Carden, hence it was impossible for Morris to alter the disposition of them. Rose began, therefore, by setting her whole capital on the inside corner of the king, to cover ace, king, and queen, and placed markers on the nine and seven for the same bet. Then she "coppered" both bet and markers. Thus she had a bet of her whole capital upon each of the cards that Carden had been backing; but whereas he had backed them to win, she was now backing them to lose.

"Why do you put these things on the top of your bets?" asked Carden, with curiosity.

"These are 'coppers,' and indicate that we back these cards *to lose* for a change," replied Rose, dryly.

A look of disgust was visible in Morris's face.

"I should think you'd let the gentleman play his own checks," said he, crossly. "He understands the game."

"Go right along, Mr. Morris, and attend to the dealing," replied Rose, crisply, and with evident reserve of power should argument be forced upon her.

"Yes, you needn't fret. It's *my* money," added Carden, who resented the interference.

The king lost at the second round out of the box. Rose won a bet, therefore, which enabled her immediately to double her stakes all round.

The two "boosters" were smiling covertly, and (unobserved by Carden) there was some suppressed mirth amongst two or three of the bystanders who were initiates. It had amused them to watch the "tenderfoot" being plucked, but their enjoyment was equally generous when they saw Morris caught in his own toils; for Rose scrutinised the dealing carefully, and the first time that he attempted to slide out two cards instead of one, politely corrected his "mistake," and proved it by reference to the "cases."

To make a long story short, at the end of the deal she had won over $400.

Thrusting the checks back to the boy, she said: "There! you won't beat that deal this evening. Leave off now, and come and talk to me about the old country."

Carden wished her to keep their winnings, but this she utterly refused to do, although, to terminate the discussion, she ultimately consented to divide them with him.

"Do you know," she said, when, seated together at the piano, they had talked for a little, "you remind me very much of some one. The resemblance doesn't seem to be one of feature; it must be in some trick you have, some way of looking, some —"

"You needn't say any more. I know who it is. Everybody says the same thing who knows us both. But I don't see how you could have met him; he never was out here before."

"We do go to England from here *sometimes*," she answered, smiling. "But who is it that you think you resemble?"

"My brother."

She shook her head.

"I never met any one of your name before."

"Oh, we're only half-brothers, the names are different.

His name's Drake. I knew who it was the moment you began. I've heard it all so often before," he rattled on, not noticing her look almost of consternation. "You're right; there is no resemblance in feature, only a strong sort of family likeness which you can't define. So you know Dick, eh! What a lark! Where did you meet him?"

"*I* didn't say that I ever had met him; *you* said that."

"Oh! — oh, I thought I'd struck an old friend of his. It would have been such fun, too! — he's out here now — come out to see me."

"Out here! — he's here now!"

"Ah, you do know him! Yes, he's here — round town somewhere with those 'Scottish Chief' fellows; they want him to — See! there he is! I thought he'd turn up directly. Dick, come here!"

A well-bred-looking Englishman, with square shoulders and a rather plain though pleasant face, had just entered the room with a couple of other men.

At the sound of Carden's voice he turned towards the piano.

Suddenly he recognised Rose, and a look of astonishment so complete as to be almost pitiable, transfigured his face. For a second he paused; then, recovering himself, he came forward rapidly.

"Mrs. Carlin! — is it really you?"

"Yes — really me," she echoed.

Rose had grown quite pale, but nevertheless she met his glance without flinching.

"But how — why — what does it matter, though? Here you are — at last! I am so glad to see you — so awfully glad! It seemed as though we never should meet again."

I

She was still looking at him, and she nodded slowly now, a little like one in a dream.

"Well, and — well — since we have met, tell me, how are the old Pytchley and North Warwick? We had some great runs, eh, — in those days?"

She spoke with evident effort, as though merely for the sake of saying something, and to obviate an awkward pause.

"Yes, they were great days. I have never ceased to think of them — although you did go off without saying good-bye to any of us, or leaving word where you were to be found. But we cannot talk here," he continued, unwilling to prolong a situation which he knew could only be painful to her. "May I see you to-morrow?"

"Yes. Come here, and ask —"

She stopped abruptly; for at that moment the circumstance that Ned came out of the poker room, and glanced at the group as he passed, reminded her of her engagement with him.

"No, I can't see you to-morrow; I will the day after. Come here, and ask them to show you where I live. They'll tell you. This is where — that is, I come here every evening."

Drake bowed. Not the least trace of surprise was discernible now in his manner, though he alone knew what it cost him to preserve this impassive demeanour. "Till then, good-bye," he said, shaking hands with her.

"Good-bye," and she bent over her music, while he left the saloon with Carden.

"Dick, who on earth is she? — she's the most beautiful creature I ever saw!" exclaimed the latter, when they were fairly outside. "It isn't — it can't be that same Mrs. Carlin who —"

Drake stopped short in the pathway and faced him. "Fred, old chap, it's the same Mrs. Carlin who had Hawthorn Lodge."

"And hunted with the Pytchley and North Warwick — the one they wrote me about, who used to ride such ripping horses and go so dead straight?"

"The same."

"But I thought you — they said you —"

"Yes, I wanted to marry her. She wouldn't have me."

"And what, in the name of Fortune, is she doing in that place?"

"For God's sake, don't ask me!" groaned Dick Drake. "But this I'll stake my life on," and his voice steadied as he spoke, "it's through no fault *of her's* that she's there."

It was nearly time for Rose to leave, when, seizing a moment in which she happened to be alone, Morris approached her.

"That was rather a rough trick you got in on us this evening, Miss Carlin," he said, leaning back on his cane, and eying her rather impertinently.

"First of all, here's my share of what we won, Mr. Morris," she replied sharply, pointing to the notes that still lay on the piano. "I don't take money that's won unfairly, even if you do. As to what I did, it was mere justice. The rough trick and the dirty trick was for you to steal a few miserable dollars from a tenderfoot."

"Business is business, Miss Carlin," rejoined Morris, getting red, "and if you —"

"Business isn't necessarily petty stealing. If it is, don't count on me to stand by quietly while it's going on. You don't cheat with Mr. Kellon's sanction or knowledge."

"I do what I like —"

"Well, I don't like what you do."

"That don't cut no figure with me," stammered Morris, angrily.

He was beginning to express himself in somewhat unmeasured language, but Rose checked him.

"Stop! I don't want to discuss the matter. Those are my opinions, and I'll act up to them."

"Not in this house."

Rose shrugged her shoulders in silence.

"Let me tell you, if you're counting on Kellon to back you, that he's sold out of this concern."

"To you?"

"Yes, ma'am, to me."

"And when does the sale take effect?"

"At the end of this month."

"Then he's master here until then, so have the goodness not to speak to me meanwhile — do you hear! — not at all."

"Oh, I don't want to speak to you. But just take a note of it: after the thirtieth you can get — see? You won't be wanted here."

"You divine my wishes intelligibly enough, Mr. Morris, although you express them in your own language. Good-evening."

Her encounter with Drake had vividly recalled all the happiest scenes of her life in England, and the contrast between them and those by which she was now surrounded was too cruel not to hurt her. It was the contrast between English country life at its best, with — while they had lasted — ample funds at command' to gratify every wish she had, and the life of a piano girl in a frontier gambling-den.

Rose had met Drake at Cowes, and it was what she had heard from him of the sport that had led her to take Hawthorn Lodge, on the borders of Warwickshire, for a season's hunting. Undoubtedly, this had been the happiest period of her life since girlhood. Drake had been extremely kind to her, helping her in the thousand and one ways in which a man of tact and nice feeling could help a woman who was a stranger in a foreign land. It was, in fact, owing to his good offices in her behalf that her life that season had been so pleasant. A strong friendship had sprung up between them. On Drake's side it had ripened into love, and he had asked her to marry him. This, as he had owned to his brother, she had refused to do. Nevertheless, the genuine feeling that she had for him, together with her gratitude for his kindly attentions, had made her anxious to do the best she could to cure him of his unlucky passion. The simplest way of effecting this had seemed to her to leave him. The season was already drawing to a close. Selling, or rather sacrificing, her hunters, therefore, for what any one chose to give for them, she gave up her house and betook herself to London. There she left three hundred pounds with her bankers, and with the remainder of her capital went abroad again to Monte Carlo, where a sequence of ill luck finally exhausted her funds. Returning to London, she fell in by chance with Drake once more, and her last evening in town had been spent with him and a cousin of his, whom she had met already in the hunting-field. Together they dined at the Bristol and went to a play.

Next day when Drake called at her hotel, he found that she had started early that morning for Queenstown, to catch a White Star boat for New York, leaving no address behind her.

CHAPTER X.

"HAPPINESS was born a twin," but trouble must be endured alone. Yet it rarely comes unattended, and this was as true in Rose Carlin's case as in most others. Drake's reappearance not only troubled her for his sake, since, with a woman's instinct in such matters, she had seen at once that his feelings towards her were unchanged and that he would propose to her again, but it worried her on her own account, for she shrank from the effort that it would be to her to refuse him. To tell the truth, for the moment she felt weary and weak in spirit, in no mood to resist without a struggle any temptation to a life of rest and peace. She was about to lose her present situation and means of livelihood; she knew that somewhere in the background she would presently discover the hand of Hannaford working against her; her best friend, Ned, was going away and in trouble himself; and, to crown all, a sequence of bad luck had beset her lately at the gambling-tables, and her funds were almost exhausted. When, therefore, Ned came for her with the horses next morning, he found her pale and distrait; but she was attired for riding, and was waiting for him.

Probably with no other person in the world would she have kept the appointment under the circumstances. With Ned, however, she felt at ease; with him she was not obliged to make conversation or to conceal any mood that possessed her. She had the feeling that, had it been necessary, she could have confessed every action in her career to him fearlessly. She believed that he would have judged her, not by the harsh letter of the law, but rather according to its spirit, weighing the good with the bad, the act with the circumstances which led to it; understanding and sympathising with her rather than condemning and despising her. She had full confidence in him. Nothing had ever threatened the security of their friendship. Once the same feeling had governed her relations with Drake, but unfortunately he had fallen in love with her; thus changing the whole aspect and basis of their connection. From love she felt secure with Chase. Here was one man at least whom she liked, and who liked her without his ever having breathed a word that could be taken as evidence of any such sentiment. When she had told him that she would sooner die than love again, she had uttered no more than the truth. Her disastrous experience in earlier life had given her a morbid dread, an absolute horror of love. Love! The very word made her shudder when she thought of what it often meant.

By degrees she emerged from her silence. They were nearing the summit of the pass, the country beyond which, during the first walk she and Ned had ever taken together, she had named "Never-Never Land." It had been a favourite direction of hers since then for their drives and excursions.

"I feel as though I were going into the Never-Never Land for the last time," she said, breaking a silence between them.

Ned laughed cheerily.

"Last time! Wait until this trouble about the mine is fixed and we've begun shipping ore again, and things will look rosy once more! Won't we have some record times!"

"You mustn't wait till things look 'Wild Rosy,' then, or the record 'll be poor enough."

"What's the matter? — blues?"

"Blues! Ouf! I feel as if I were at the bottom of some great blue sea — and all alone there."

"Hush! Listen to that mermaid's music, then — that old Texas nightingale! Did you hear that last trill? He's a dandy, isn't he?" and he laughed infectiously.

A mule, turned loose in the hills to graze, had caught sight of their horses, and was braying to them a long and doubtless interesting piece of gossip, of which, however, beyond marking their surprise and incredulity with some very expressive gestures of the ears, the latter took no notice.

"What do you suppose the old son-of-a-gun was saying?" pursued Ned, mockingly.

"I don't know — your horse looked rather disgusted, though. I believe the old mule was guying[1] him." And she smiled, too, at length.

"What d' you think he said? What was he giving you, Saucy?" and he bent down to his pony's ear. "If I thought he'd insulted you, I'd let you go back and kick him once."

"Don't you go, Saucy! That may be somebody's 'pet kickin' mule, Vilet,'" laughed Rose.

They had reached the summit of the pass, and she pulled up for a moment to enjoy the picture which the Never-Never Land presented.

[1] Chaffing.

"Doesn't it seem prettier each time you see it?—doesn't it!" she exclaimed, enthusiastically.

Right below them lay, like a mirror,—like a jewel in the head of the valley,—the little star-shaped lake they had come to visit. Away from it stretched the long furrow of the valley itself, intersecting the hilly country wherein it was embosomed. The sun was bright, yet not too warm, for there were clouds in the heavens that cast great fields of shadow on the mountains. A certain freshness was in the air, suggestive of rain; the atmosphere had that liquid clearness which renders near outlines more distinct, and enriches the colouring both near and far away. It was a scene made to be painted. Bluff behind spur, and spur beyond bluff, dotted with fir and juniper trees, dipped down from the lofty solitudes of the higher hills into the quiet cloisters of the valley. As the glance followed them into the distance, the contrast they afforded of deep-green foliage with dark-red soil became less and less marked. Gradually both greens and reds were lost in hues of lapis-lazuli, and these in turn grew paler,—paler and more pale still,—till in the faint peaks and ridges upon the far-off horizon, "Forget-me-not" was written most exquisitely across the view.

"Ah! Do you know that beautiful scenery—scenery like this, that is so rich in colouring—absolutely intoxicates me!" exclaimed Rose. "I feel—simply just as if wine had gone to my head. Isn't it beautiful—say? isn't it *lovely?*"

She turned and looked at the dark, reserved face beside her; there was a flush of enthusiasm even there. Not often did Chase betray his real feelings, but in her company he would admit a fondness for many things, never suspected in him by others who still knew him well. Most people thought his nature unromantic and practical, void entirely of all weaknesses for the things which really make life and the world beautiful. But this mask was lifted when he was with Rose, and she knew that beneath it were instincts and feelings which, had they been developed, might have made a very different man of him.

Ned was silent.

"Tell me, do you ever feel as I do about scenery? — say?"

"Yes, when there's colour in it, and — and feeling. A stretch of scenery like this, all wrecked hills and flashing rocks and broken splashes of colour, seems to me like shattered music, — music that was once unearthly beautiful and now, — oh, I can't explain, but *you* know what I mean."

"'Shattered music,'" she echoed, in a tone of pleasure; "music of the spheres. Yes, that describes it. And the plains, — tell me what they remind you of?"

"The great, hopeless, soulless plains?" he echoed thoughtfully. "Ugh! Give me the hills, with their effort and failure, their unrest and hope and strife, and moments of gloom or joy! They make one feel. The plains? — it's my belief that level countries and even climates breed liars and slaves. We need the strife of change."

Fallen-star Lake was a small, star-shaped sheet of beautifully clear water in the hills, between four and five miles from Dogtown. People often came there from the village and the mining camp to picnic, as Rose and Ned were doing. One energetic pleasure party had cut some fir logs and constructed a raft on which to pole about the lake while fishing, and it now lay grounded on the lake's lee shore. Ned had brought lines and bait with him, and knew where two long sticks, that would serve for rods, were hidden in the brush. So having tethered their horses, they were soon afloat, and intent on catching the little trout that haunted the crystal waters below them, in order to make a play of cooking them for lunch.

— "Oh, goldner zeit der Reise!
* * * * * * * * *
Da rann kein sand, und keine Glocke schlug."

Oh, golden hour! Tiny sprites of air — children of the winds it might be — came flitting up the valley, now hastening forward and now loitering, now halting altogether, until reaching the lake of many strange reflections, they paused in silence to wonder at its beauty. Suddenly they espied the laughing fisher-couple upon the raft, and swept towards them over the calm surface, whispering: "We come from the Great Beyond; we are the breath of One who Knows, and we are sorry for you — ah, sorry — sorry!"

Other sprites followed and lay, too, hushed by the lake-side. But soon in a fleet of myriad ripples, they also rushed across the waters, murmuring: "You are strong, oh man, and woman, you are beautiful; but fate can conquer strength and beauty both — fate — fate," and fled away.

And yet another troop drew near on silken wings, hovering like butterflies now here, now there, till they reached and stayed for a moment by the raft to give their message also: "The path you follow now seems bright as ours; but grief is born of happiness, the deepest sorrows spring from sweetest joys — grief! — grief!"

Beside the water's edge the fir trees rustled their sombre plumes and sighed: "Love not — for love is death to those who cannot read its message."

Above, the hills looked down from where they waited in infinite patience things that no man has knowledge of, and said among themselves: "Would they be happy if they knew? Poor Mortals think they know, and yet not one of them can see one day into Beyond. We see, we know, and so have ceased from strife."

But the mortals on the raft cared not, nor knew that aught was heeding them. The little fish were sharp and quick. They had often seen the shadow of the raft move slowly over the lake before, and knew that thereafter some of their companions were always missing. They had even beheld certain of them taken bodily up into the outer world on those occasions, nor had it escaped their notice that these ascensions had been performed by the chosen in anything but a spirit of resignation. Therefore they were shy, and bit charily, making it a trial of some skill to catch them, which led to keen rivalry between Ned and Rose, and lively merriment when one or other of them lost a fish that had been hooked.

They forgot the world, their cares and troubles, everything. For the time being they only knew that they were happy — happy as children are happy together, not wondering why nor questioning. Had it occurred to them to ask the reason, they must have paused full long before resolving on the answer. And when they had done so, laughter would probably have fled their lips and they would have grown serious.

With a take of three brace and a half of trout, weighing altogether not greatly over two pounds, they were content, and put ashore again. Then there was the fire to be built, the provisions in Ned's saddle-bags to be unpacked, the feed of corn in those on Rose's saddle to be given to their nags on an outspread saddle blanket, coffee to be made in a coffee-pot that had been packed in the corn, the little fish themselves to be roasted in a wrapping of wet paper over wood embers — in fact, quite a mass of labour to be accomplished. But Rose helped in everything, and both were in the best of spirits, so that rarely time went lighter-footed than it did for the present for these two.

The clouds had cleared away. All show of rain — it had never been more than a playful threat — had disappeared, and the sun shone now in earnest. But in the little bay beneath the cotton-wood trees, chosen by them for their camp, there was cool shade. And whilst they eat their lunch the million-voiced hum of tiny surf breaking upon the sand was heard in measured cadence, singing a song writ æons before the advent of man, but whether betokening prophecy or strange record, an eternal requiem or only a passing overture, was equally unintelligible now. In the crests of the cottonwoods the wind was stirring with a touch so light that its music seemed like the clashing of leafy cymbals; but above this, softened exquisitely, enriched divinely by distance, its long, low chords were heard upon the mountain's side, like the hushed breathing of a great sound that sleeps.

Now that her eyes were lit with gaiety and that mirth had brought a tinge of colour into her cheeks, Rose's pallor, and the blue splashes that a sleepless night had left below her lids, only enhanced her beauty. In her tweed riding skirt and little cover coat (relics of her life in England) she looked marvellously neat. Her figure was faultless — straight as an arrow, yet gracefully supple — as slim yet rounded as a Greek girl's is sometimes. From her oval hands to her slender feet, the stamp of race marked every line of her. As the Greeks said of Phryne, "She was beautiful all over."

Still not a little of her beauty's power was due to the unusual character of her face. Ancestors of hers, upon one side, had come from Andalusia to California, long before that state had fallen into American hands, and it was to this Spanish blood that she owed her type. Nay, it might have been traced further still; for, but for some difference in feature, it was a distinct reversion to the characteristics of the Moorish conquerors of Spain, whose last strongholds there had been in that province whence her forefathers had come.

Her glorious eyes, black as black skies at night when no stars shine, and beneath their curving lashes almost as mysterious, her full-lipped and imperious mouth, with its sensuous yet perfect curves, her snowy teeth, her creamy complexion, so clear, so exquisitely soft, even the mingled chivalry and passion, the recklessness yet melancholy in her nature was Moorish, not Spanish, least of all American.

CHAPTER XI.

Lunch was long since over; the afternoon was nearing on. But in idle enjoyment of the scenery and weather, they had remained where they were. A cotton tree uprooted by the wind harboured them. Seated on a cushion of fir-tops which Ned had gathered for her, Rose leant her back against it; a little way down the trunk sat Ned on the tree itself, his cow-boy hat tipped back and his elbows on his knees, as he leant forward rolling a cigarette.

"You found some friends the other night?" he said presently.

"Friends?" Her thoughts had been far away off when he spoke; his question brought them back. She sighed. "Yes — that is, I knew one of them — I knew him in England where he was very kind to me." For a moment she was silent. "What a queer thing fate is! How it drifts us about — brings us together — separates us — sometimes on a chance meeting builds the history of a whole life! — just as an architect might rear a beautiful building on a little ordinary plot of ground. Only fate doesn't build beautifully, as a rule."

Her thoughts had drifted from Drake again, and she was thinking of the day when she had encountered Hannaford, and the accident that had brought about their acquaintance.

"Yes, one seems to be the sport of chance — like

driftwood. Like driftwood, though, I reckon we're only the sport of certain settled currents. If we understood them we'd know about where we should land. All we do know is that we can't swim against them. And yet people believe in free will!"

"Don't you believe in it?"

He laughed derisively.

"No — if I believe in anything it's in fate, you bet!"

"Ah, no! — that's such a sterile, hopeless, soulless faith. It isn't a 'faith'; it destroys all faith. *You* can't believe that — you who said just now that you loved the hills for their effort and hope and strife and moments of joy;" and she looked at him with true concern in her beautiful eyes.

"You spoke of 'fate' yourself awhile ago."

"But not in that sense — not seriously. We build our own lives. Fatalism is only a cowardly excuse for shifting the responsibility of them from ourselves."

"Yes, it's a mean sort of belief, I allow. But one don't believe what one likes so much as what one sees."

"That's true nineteenth century materialism!" she said, scornfully.

"But if you *are* of the nineteenth century, what are you going to do about it?" he asked, laughingly. "I didn't choose my era, or it wouldn't have been this one."

"True courage makes no excuses; it only strives and strives to the end. When would you have lived if you could have chosen?"

"If I could have chosen?" and he smoked for a moment or two in silence. "Well, say in the time of old Queen Elizabeth — when there was still some romance and chivalry in men — when they still had some power to believe, and could believe in what they *felt* as well as in what they *saw*. How can you expect a man in whose bones there's the inbred scepticism of generations to pay any sort of attention to his fancies. The more we learn, the more we realise how systematically everything is ordered in this world. Where is there anything left to chance? You think you can choose for yourself. But what influences and decides you in your choice? You can't look forward and foresee the direct results of it — on others as well as yourself. You're not fit to choose. It would be the child choosing for the family, man for mankind."

She was silent for a little.

"I can't argue with you; what you say may be true enough in one sense, yet I *feel* that you're wrong, and so must you. After all, the final appeal for right or wrong is to one's *sense of it*."

"One's final appeal is to one's passing fancies and feelings, then? That's a tall order."

"To one's *convictions* — certainly — when they are good. You say everything is ordered, then even one's feelings are inspired. *We* don't consciously create them; all that we have power to do is to distinguish the good from the bad, the noble from the ignoble. Why not trust them, then?"

"But you can't ask one to believe seriously what, after all, is merely imagination."

"And why not? What is nobler than a beautiful creation of the imagination — an inspiration, in other words. What else but the fruit of these, takes us out of the mud of the world — what other road is there to that which is spiritual? If we don't cling to the thoughts which are unworldly and pure and beautiful, where shall we arrive in the end? Is materialism elevating?"

"It's a poor world if we have to look for all that is true and beautiful in it in imagination."

"Yes, if you persist in looking at imagination as idle fancy; but not if you believe that in imagination *is* the true and beautiful, the spiritual side of life. We cannot *see* our souls; why would you try to save them, then, only by what you can see and touch? The food for the unseen spirit is the invisible thought."

Ned laughed at her earnestness.

"Well, let's cultivate our imaginations then in future, and see where it will lead us to."

She smiled, too, and let the mood in which she had been speaking pass.

"But fancy having no imagination, and dealing with plain, hard, practical facts all the time! Ouf! And yet I guess there're any quantity of people like that."

"Rafts of 'em. *We* shall have to deal with a plain, hard fact, presently;" and he looked at his watch. "It's almost time to pull stakes."

"Ah, I don't want to go," she pleaded, enchantingly, nestling closer to the old trunk.

"Nor I, Heaven knows!"

"When do you go to Las Casas — to-morrow, you say?"

He nodded.

"I wish you weren't going at all."

"Why?"

"I've got a queer feeling about it — a feeling as though there were trouble ahead."

Ned laughed. "*That* isn't obliged to mean anything. I've been fooled like that too often. Every one who has nerves has those sort of fancies now and then."

"But *you* have no nerves."

He laughed ironically. "Haven't I?"

"How odd!" she murmured, looking at him curiously. "I might have known it, though. After all, what a little we know of one another. But still I have my queer feeling about Las Casas."

"Don't think about it, then — it's only fooling you. Anyway, I've *got* to go, so it doesn't matter. I've got to go and saddle up now; have you any 'queer feeling' about that?" he asked, laughingly.

"Yes — a hideous presentiment that I shall have to move directly."

"And what do you prophesy for me?"

"Oh, you shall stay behind."

"Not much!" and he threw away the end of his cigarette, and moved off towards their horses, a long ribbon of smoke curling behind him.

From her divan of fir-tops Rose glanced lazily from the lake to Ned, and from Ned to the lake again. With every minute that the sun declined the magical reflections there were growing stronger and more vivid. And lying down, as she was, almost on a level with the surface of the water, the ripples that floated towards her made all this maze of flashing lights, and colours, and inverted objects dazzle and dance in mad confusion. "Life at it's best," she murmured, smiling.

Ned came back presently, rolling another cigarette, and stooped down to brush aside the white ashes where they had had their fire, in search of a hot ember to light it with.

"Well!" said he, glancing aside at her quizzically,

"are you ready, or have you had another presentiment?"

She rose with something like a sigh, and clasping her hands behind her head stood for a moment gazing at the lake as though reluctant to move. The lithe figure of the girl, outlined against the dark boughs of a juniper, was a beautiful picture thus.

"Where's my hat?" she said, and he gave it to her. "Do you know I *have* enjoyed my day so. I don't want to go home a bit."

"I'm glad of that—that's just how I feel," he answered, simply.

What was it made her pursue the subject? Was it the innate feminine love of playing with fire?—a desire just *to see* whether beneath his friendship for her there did not lurk something a little stronger and deeper still. Did the day, the beauty of the scenery, their solitude disarm her for a moment? Or was it merely absence of mind and inadvertence? Who knows?—who knows a woman?

"What a lot I have to thank you for!"

"A lot of good-will perhaps, but mighty little else."

"Ah, yes—lots else. You don't realise what a day like this means to me—a day which takes me out of myself, away from all the—" she shrank as she spoke—"all the brutality and coarseness of Dogtown, and gives me fresh air and wholesome amusement. You can't imagine what your flowers, your books have been to me—the feeling that I could always come to you for help in any trouble. And then you—you have always talked to me like a gentleman. And"—her voice for the fraction of a moment quivered here—"you don't know, perhaps, what that means to any one situated as I am. Why have you done all this for me?"

As she had spoken Ned had stopped smoking. Unconsciously he had thrown away his cigarette. His cheeks had grown rather pale, and a light flashed in his eyes that should have warned her. But lulled in the security of complete ignorance as to his real feelings, she was blind.

"Why?" he echoed, scarcely above a whisper. "Why? Ah, don't you know? — don't you know, Rose? Because you're the only woman in the world for me! — because you seem to have awakened me from one long sleep! — because, thanks to you, for the first time I seem to be alive! — to feel! — to know the happiness that life can really give! Ah, the joy of living when one loves as I do. Hitherto I have slept in the cold and the dark — benumbed, almost blind, I think. *Now!* — you have touched all my feelings into life, and life is one long summer day!"

The words fell from his lips in a burning torrent. The whole man was changed. His reserve and imperturbable demeanour were fled. A warm flush was in his cheeks, and his grey eyes flashed with fire. She had lighted a train that had been laid for weeks, and there was no undoing her work.

At the sound of his voice, trembling as it was with love, her features lit up with wonder, and softened inexpressibly with happiness. A look of exquisite tenderness shone beneath her heavy lashes. Her lips were parted eagerly. But suddenly she seemed to remember — to awaken. And the light went out of her face and left it ghastly pale — stern, almost cruel in expression. She watched him coldly enough now.

"You forget my past, and all that I have told you," she said when he had paused.

"I? — what do I know of your past, or care? You were not — you never could have been to blame, whatever happened. Besides, what is your past to me! A love like mine sweeps away all the past and haloes all the future. Listen! I am poor, but give me a little time. How I will strive, and work, and scheme to gather wealth for you! Give me a little time. You shall have all —"

"This is madness!"

"No, no! listen —"

"I command you —"

"Ah, 'commands'! what are they to me now! Hear me out! — you shall have all that love can think of, or that wealth can buy. I have strength, and I *will* do this for you. For *you?* What is there that I couldn't do *for you!* Only love me, Rose, — love me as I love you. Ah, to be loved by you! It seems too good, too glorious, ever to be true; it seems impossible that joy like that can ever be mine. And you ask me why I have done the few poor little things that I have done for you? Why, I would lay down my life for you! — and love to do it!"

She still looked at him steadily.

"It was for this, then, that you were good to me," she said at length. But her voice trembled, and her lips were white with passion. A second later her anger burst forth. "For this, only for this! Because, like any common fool, you loved me! Ah, fool! Never speak to me again! never come near me again! I hate you!"

Ned Chase uttered a short, sharp exclamation, and recoiled as though a knife had struck him.

She did not see or hear him. With a few quick steps she reached her pony's side, and a second later was galloping rapidly away.

She never looked back. Through clenched teeth her breath came in sobs; she was deathly pale. Once she swayed in the saddle, and almost fell.

CHAPTER XII.

"Miss Carlin, you look like you'd lost your pet lap-dog and found his skin in a fur mat. You're looking worse than that,—you're looking real sick," said Kellon, kindly, that evening. "Hadn't you better take to-night off?"

She shook her head. "It's very good of you, but—I'd sooner sit here than sit at home alone. You've sold out to Mr. Morris, I hear."

"Why, yes,—I've been wanting to sell out quite a while. It's a good enough little camp, this, but somehow I don't have my health here; and then,—well, we gamblers are superstitious, as you know, Miss Carlin, and I've been out of luck ever since I opened bank here. There've been some ter'ble runs against me. You brought me about the only real streak of luck I've had here. There'd been a bad run against me for over a week when you come. First night you was here the luck switched right around, and for a fortnight I didn't hardly lose a bet, 'cept what you won yourself."

"Is that so? Well, if I'm a good Mascot, Mr. Kellon, perhaps you'll remember it when you're located elsewhere. I should like to come to you again."

"You don't reckon to stay on here, then?"

"I leave when you do."

"You don't say!"

"Yes; I 'got my time' last night"; and she smiled.

"The h—holy smoke! Did Clint tell you that?"

She nodded, and proceeded to explain to Kellon what had taken place betwixt herself and Morris.

Dave breathed some big words in his big moustache.

"Who is behind him with the money?" asked Rose.

"Why — I don't know as I'm altogether entitled —"

"I only wanted to know whether it was Hannaford."

Kellon brushed the ash very carefully from the end of his cigar, and took two deep pulls at it while he was thinking.

"Well," he began again slowly, "I certainly ain't authorised to say as it *isn't* Hannaford. Look here, Miss Carlin, I oughtn't to tell you this, and you don't want to let it get any further; but I do tell you, because some time or other it may be useful to you to know who's behind this show. Hannaford's buying me out, right enough, and he particularly don't want *any one* to know it. So his name won't appear, and no one'll know he's in it. I don't pretend to know what he's up to, but something mean, you can tie to that. I reckon he'll take the hair off'n Morris for quor'ling with you, and likely he'll have him ask you to stay on 'fore you quit. But I'll give you a pointer, right now; if you do stay on, don't gamble against the house any more. You won't get a fair deal. They'll run you in debt, sure, if you do; and you don't want to be in debt to either of those men. They're 'bout as mean men as there is for any lady to have to deal with."

"Oh, I shan't stay here."

"Well, you'll see Morris 'll ask you to, anyway. See here, Miss Carlin, I'm going away down to El Paso, to prospect around a bit, — now that that line's going through from there to the city of Mexico there ought to be a good show for a game there, — and just as soon as I open I'll send for you. You lay around here where I can hear from you, and if you'll undertake to wait for me 'twixt now and then, why, your salary shall run on same as ever."

Rose refused his good-natured offer as to the salary, but promised to keep him acquainted with her address.

Neither Drake nor Carden appeared in the rooms that evening, — a forbearance for which she was extremely grateful, although under the circumstances she had never for a moment expected to see them.

Drake called on her next morning.

He was a man of four or five and thirty, well off, and of good family. At one time he had been in the army. But having no particular ambition, and being, moreover, an exceedingly keen sportsman, — with his absorption in which pursuit his military duties often clashed, — he had left the service upon succeeding to his father's property in Leicestershire.

Until he had met Rose Carlin he had led the life of a confirmed bachelor, his time wholly occupied in sport. Excepting for an occasional week's shooting, he had hunted six days a week throughout the season. What this had left him to employ of spring and autumn, he had devoted to salmon-fishing and yachting. During summer he had fished and played cricket, until the grouse-shooting called him northward. Very little of his time had been spent in London, therefore; still less of it in the society of ladies, unless by chance he had met them at dinner. Not that he disliked, or affected in the least to despise them. On the contrary, he had an old-fashioned respect for them. They simply did not occur much in the life he led.

Chance had brought him into contact with Rose, and her love of sport being almost as keen as his own, they had drifted into companionship, with the unfortunate result that Drake had fallen desperately in love with her.

Drake was "good-looking enough for a man," as the saying is. And he looked a man, every inch of him, and a gentleman at that. If his face was not handsome, at least it was strong and pleasant; his smile was singularly winning, and he had those honest, lion-like eyes that alone will eclipse the most striking beauty in power of attraction.

It was characteristic of both Rose and Drake that neither made any reference to, or affectation of excuse for, the difference between the common little parlour in which they now met, and Rose's surroundings when they had known each other previously. She greeted him kindly, and asked a few questions with regard to mutual acquaintances and associations they had had. But Drake soon interrupted the drift of the conversation.

"Let's leave all that for the present, Mrs. Carlin," he said; and rising from his seat he leant his arm high up against the window casement, and looking down at her where she sat in a rocking-chair, paused for a little before he spoke,— even then his voice was not quite steady. "I — I don't suppose that you ever dreamed what it was to me to lose sight of you so suddenly — so completely. But, at least, I had the satisfaction of thinking that you were amongst friends, — that you were well cared for and happy, — otherwise I don't know what I should have done. Of course — of course your present position is your own affair, — I mean it would be impertinent in me to refer to it; but if you don't care for yourself, won't you try to think what your happiness means to me, and let me help you to get away from here? Mrs. Carlin, I asked you once to marry me,—I love you just as dearly now as then,—better I couldn't love you—I don't think any one could love you more truly than I do. Will you marry me?—will you trust your future in my hands and let me try to make you happy?"

"And this is your first question, Dick?" returned Rose, with a wistful smile; and her eyes were humid as she looked at him.

At home all Drake's friends called him "Dick." He was one of those men whose Christian names are always mentioned with their surnames, as thus, "Dick Drake"; and Rose had fallen into the habit of calling him "Dick" also.

"This is your first question, Dick?" she asked.

"Why not?"

"You've no curiosity, no doubts at finding me as — as you found me the other night?"

"Nothing that concerns you can be of indifference to me. But if I didn't trust you entirely, I should never have asked you to marry me at all. And do you think I'd doubt you just because I found you under circumstances that — that I couldn't explain?"

"This is Quixotic — absurd!"

"No, it's simply that I'd stake my life upon my faith in you. I know you. How could I ever doubt you?"

"It is good to have the power to believe as you do. But how many men have thought like you, and lived — to believe in nothing!"

"They may have been like me, but the women they loved were not like you."

She looked at him for a moment in silence, and his staunch faith in her brought the tears into her eyes. She wanted to thank him, to — she wanted a thousand things, but —

"Ah, what's the use!" she exclaimed nervously, dismissing all those futilities.

There was a pause. Her brows were knit closely, and her cheeks had grown pale; she looked away from him.

"Answer me," said Drake, "— or — or would you sooner wait, and —"

"No, no. There is no need to hesitate. As well speak now as speak to-morrow — ten years hence, for that matter. My answer must always be the same. You ask what is impossible. Dick, much as I like you, there isn't the least feeling of such love as you want in that liking."

Drake winced.

"Yes, it's cruel to tell you this, I know, but the cruellest thing that a woman can do in a matter like this, is to flinch one hair's breadth from the truth. Hope will catch at such a tiny straw. Even if I did care for you, I should never marry you."

"Aren't you free?" he asked, in a low voice.

"Oh, free enough, God knows! — free of every bond but the bondage of bitter memory. That makes no difference, though. Nothing could ever alter my decision. Face it, Dick — face it as you used to face those big doubles in Leicestershire, when the hounds were running — oh, those dear days! Dick, if I'd ever been going to love you, I should have loved you then — when I was almost happy. But it wasn't to be, and never will be. I don't love you, and even if I did I should never marry you. I shall never marry any one."

"But how can you tell? how do you know? Time changes everything — time changes all the world; why should *you* be so dead, dead sure? Take —"

She held up her hand.

"Let's close the subject, Dick," said she, gently. "You say you know me. If you do, you know how useless it is to pursue it after what I have said. Please say no more. Tell me anything else you like — anything, anything, only no more of that — for your sake, as well as mine — it's so useless, and *so* painful."

"At least let me help you, then," he said, in desperation, — "let me take you out of this life, and make you independent."

"By becoming dependent on you?" and she shook her head with a faint smile. "No, I am better as I am. Besides, you don't know what you ask. If I had half a million dollars to-morrow, I should spend it all in a year or two. You know how I gambled and spent money in Europe. Don't you see? — life's not a pleasure to me, it's a penance. It's only in moments of excitement that I forget the pain of it. And I *want* so to forget — ah, heavens! I should like to forget every hour as it goes. So I must have excitement, uncertainty — the feeling that I am on thin ice, and playing my last stake, all the time. I can get that better as I am. No wealth would last me long, for security and safety would drive me mad in a little while. Half the charm of that season's hunting in England was in the knowledge that there would only be that one for me — that there were just so many days of it, and that every day spent made a fatal inroad into the rest of them. To have known that I could hunt year after year would have spoilt it all. No, no! leave me as I am — and the best thing you can do is to leave me at once. If you stay here it will only distress me, and do no one any good."

Dick's eyes had grown moist as he listened to her.

"This is horrible," he murmured.

She sighed.

"Oh, no! the world is full of *us*." Then she laughed wearily. "If only I weren't so well — and *so* strong. Nothing ever hurts me — except that I get horribly nervous. Think if I should live a long while, Dick! — this life, eh?" and for the first time her lips quivered.

Something like a sob of pain broke from Drake.

"Poor old Dick! Go away — you'll forget in time — at least I hope you will."

"You ask too much. Rose, I can't leave you," he said, in a husky voice. "You must come away with me — if not as my wife, then as we were before — just friends — until you get back to some civilized place where — "

"This is absurd," she exclaimed, rising in her agitation, and moving away from him.

"But how *can* I leave you? — think — in this life? — among these men? Rose, I love you with all my soul, but I'll never breathe a word of it to you again, if you'll only trust me and let me help you. Have some mercy on yourself and me."

"Mercy! don't talk to me of mercy! There's none in this life! Will you go?"

"Not leaving you like this."

"What can I do then!" she exclaimed in distress, and she hid her face in her hands, pressing them tightly over it while she strove to think. "Listen, Dick," she said, and with her great eyes wet with tears, her lips quite pale, she extended both her hands towards him supplicatingly, "listen — Ah, why do you make me tell you things that I loathe to breathe — things that make me ashamed, and will make you despise me. No!" and she checked his protest. "You must hear me out. I'll tell you all now. When I was sixteen I ran away from school with a gambler — such a man as you see here. Afterwards I found that he was already married, and that my marriage with him was a mockery. Since then I have led the sort of life in which you found me the other night. I am known as 'Wild Rose' all over the West. I came to England only with the money that an old miner left me when he died. My family cast me off long ago —"

"But you were unfortunate — you were not to blame! You —"

"What has fortune or misfortune to do with blame! Punishment isn't measured by intentions, but by hard facts. Let me finish! To the man I ran away with I *was* married, at least I thought so. Since then —" and the crimson that had dyed her cheeks, since her confession began, burnt deeper and deeper still — "since then I have been more to blame."

"It's a lie! a base, base, damnable lie!" cried Dick involuntarily, and his face grew white as death.

She lifted her hand simply, like one who took an oath.

"Should *I* tell you this if it weren't true?"

"My God! my God!" he murmured brokenly.

"Will you go now?" she asked.

For a moment he was silent.

"Will you go?" she repeated harshly.

"No!" he exclaimed almost fiercely. "The more you tell me, the more you show your need of help."

A passionate gesture escaped her. Self-control was

becoming torture to her now, and she feared lest she should break down, and undo all that she had done.

"Fool! Do you want me to tell you everything?" she exclaimed hoarsely. "I said that I was free. I lied. I have reasons for staying here. I do not want to go. Now are you satisfied!"

It was a cruel blow. Drake quivered under it, but he took it without a word. He turned away in silence. As he went blindly from the room, he struck his face against the edge of the door, and stood for a second dazed with the blow. He was leaving without his hat. Rose put it into his hand. Their glances met for a moment, and in the brave eyes of the man there was a look of such unutterable suffering — the sort of hopeless suffering which exists for something dead — that she wavered, almost recalled her self-accusation, almost told him that her last statements had been untrue. But whilst she hesitated he passed on and left the house.

She stood there alone. The big, bright tears welled forth and stole down her cheeks unnoticed.

"If anything is forgiven, that lie will be," she murmured. "Poor Dick! It was bitterly cruel, but love like his dies hard."

* * * * * * * *

Drake went away without making further effort to see her. A week later, however, she received a notice from an El Paso bank saying that $5000 had been placed to her credit there by a client of theirs, and that the sum would be renewed as soon as exhausted. An intimation followed this to the effect that, should she ever find herself in any situation requiring assistance or advice, the writers of the letters were entirely at her service.

Needless to say, the money was never drawn upon by Wild Rose.

CHAPTER XIII.

As Kellon had foretold, long before the date arrived on which Rose was to leave the Mint, Morris came to her and did his utmost to induce her to stay. His manner towards her appeared to have undergone a surprising change. But Rose, since she knew who was providing the money to buy Kellon out, was able to account for this, and no argument that Morris could advance availed.

It was the day before Kellon had arranged to leave for El Paso, whither he was going by way of Las Casas. Both he and Rose had already severed their connection with the Mint, and they met by chance in the street.

"Say!" said he, after a little mutual banter concerning their out-of-work condition, "that's an understood thing, then, that when I open bank again, you're coming along to help with the music?"

"Yes — and the sooner the better. How long are you likely to be about it?"

"Well, that ain't so easy to figure on, 'cause you see it might be a week and it might be two months — might drop on to a good lay-out right away, and I might have to go further 'n El Paso and hunt awhile before I found one. But see here, Miss Carlin, ef you lay off and wait for me, it ain't but fair 't I should pay running expenses. Honest to God, I'd willingly pay you full salary to wait for me; you're worth it. Why, you're apt to make me more money in quarter of an hour 'n I give you in a month. Your singing and your playing just puts the devil into the boys. 'Fore they know where they are they're playing a big game, instead of fooling round and sampling."

She smiled. It was but a weary smile, however, and made Dave say: —

"Yes, it's a pretty poor kind of business, I allow. But when you're in it, there's certain fair tricks of the trade as you've got to make use of, — they help out the bank's percentage. You've got to set up the drinks for the boys, — all they want; and you've got to gin 'em up, and encourage 'em to bet all you can. And anyway, when they do buck against me they get a fair layout; monkey business don't go."

"I understand it all," she answered with a sigh.

"Then you'll wait till I'm ready for you? And meanwhile your salary —"

"Meanwhile, if you like to give me half pay, I'll take it."

"That settles it. Here's one hundred and fifty dollars for the first thirty days. If I ain't located by that time, I'll send you the money for next month. A rest 'll do you good, anyhow. You're looking kind o' played out."

"Oh, there's nothing the matter with me," said she, carelessly, and a few minutes later they parted.

Rose went on up the street alone. At every few yards some one or other of her numerous acquaintances would greet her. Sol Poheim and Colonel Dodge were standing in the road, and had her manner given them the least encouragement would have engaged her in conversation. But she did not care to talk to any one, and only nodded as she passed them.

"Sol," said the Colonel, looking after the enchanting figure, that with a certain languorous grace of motion was slowly receding from them up the hilly street, — "Sol, there's a dog-gone curious girl!"

"You bet yer!"

"Didn't she ever have any other lover than that whelp, Hannaford?"

"No, sir, — none dot effer *I* heard von, — and she vouldn't hef hed him, on'y she t'ought she vas married to de son-of-a-gon."

"There's an unlucky life, Sol; there's a girl that got started on the wrong track, and 's been paying sort o' blackmail for it ever since; there's a girl that might have been — well, just anything she'd a mind to — a queen, by God!"

"Dot's so — sure. Vild Rose is de true blod. She hes prains, und she hes plock, and feelings, too; und, py Gott, efry time vat you looks at her she sim more peautiful — don't it? Vat a lofty face! — eh, Cunnel? — so soft, so strong und proud! Ach, Himmel! I tell you der bin lots of men vou'd gif der souls to marry Vild Rose."

"And many that's done a d—d sight worse, Sol, you may gamble your fruitless existence on that," added the Colonel, shaking his head with an air of solemn conviction.

Solomon entered a mild protest against the term "fruitless," as applied to his existence. But the Colonel took high grounds, and maintained that mere symbols of personal prosperity could not be regarded as justifying the existence of any man, and that Solomon

were better dead than increasing his liability on the
Day of Judgment for time wasted in the present. He
agreed, however, to reconsider the verdict, if Sol would
immediately "set up the drinks"; and Sol consenting,
they repaired to an adjoining saloon.

Rose walked up the street slowly, and on until she
reached the hillside above the town, where she sat down
and gazed absently at the broad scene before her. By
and by she started home again listlessly. She was tired
— out of spirits, out of sorts, weary of the constant
battle that life was to her. Hers was indeed

> "The Vagrant soul returning to itself
> Wearily wise—"

for her very soul was weary — weary of its worldly
wisdom.

She had reached the main street of Dogtown, and was
about to pass a low-class "dive" or saloon, when the
door burst open and her late patient, Dinkey, backed
out in front of her, as hastily as his crutch and game
leg would permit, expostulating violently with a drunken
Irishman who was threatening him.

Another second and Dinkey was knocked backwards
across the boarded walk, falling under Rose's very feet.

His assailant was following him up with the avowed
intention of "Kicking the thon'ring loife out av him,"
when Rose threw herself between them.

"You coward, to strike a cripple!"

"Stand aside!" shouted the hulking ruffian.

"I won't," she answered fearlessly.

"Stand aside, I tell yez!"

"I won't. Run, Dinkey! run, you fool!"

The Irishman tried to pass her, but she clung to him.
The next instant he swept her aside, throwing her under

the feet of a cow-pony that stood waiting for its owner outside the saloon.

There was a snort, a little scuffle, the pony half reared, lashed out vigorously and dashed down the road. But he had done his work, and Rose lay senseless in the dust.

"Wild Rose, by God! Ye d—d fool, the boys 'll lynch ye for 't," cried a friend of the Hibernian, who stood now stupidly regarding his handiwork.

"What's that ye're saying?"

"They'll lynch ye, begorrah!—and serve ye d—d well right! This camp's no camp for you now, Moike; ye'll hang in an hour if ye stay in it."

The man accepted the hint, he was partly sobered already, and from the speed with which he took horse and "skipped the town," he was evidently much of the same opinion as a well-known western jury broker, who, when significantly invited once by a committee of citizens to leave their town within half an hour, said: "Gentlemen, ef my——old mule has half the respect for you that I have, we shall be ten miles away from here in less time than that."

A crowd collected. Rose was picked up and carried home. But it was night before she had recovered consciousness, and then only to learn that she had sustained slight concussion of the brain, and was doomed to many days if not some weeks of enforced idleness. She was so weak, however, that she could barely lift her hand, and so drowsy that for the next few days she dozed and slept almost continuously.

It was well for the man who had struck her that he had levanted, for the anger of Dogtown was such that a baptism of tar and feathers would have been a lucky escape for him.

For the next few days the cottage in which Rose lived was besieged by visitors. But she was soon out of danger. Dogtown was a busy community, and before long the inquiries after her progress dwindled in number.

Kellon and Dinkey, however, remained constant. From the first the latter had brought his blankets, and slept like a watch-dog in the verandah outside her window. He could not go indoors to nurse her, but he could hear her voice and hobble messages for her, or hunt up Mrs. Murray or some other woman in the neighbourhood, to send to her when she required waiting upon.

With the kindly feeling which always distinguished him, Kellon had deferred his departure in order to see that Rose had due attention from the doctor, and the best food and nourishment that money could procure in Dogtown. Nor did he leave until she was in a fair way to recover. He had not to delay very long, for her constitution and physique were excellent.

It was about midday when Kellon eventually arrived at Las Casas. Having (after — for the frontier — his somewhat fastidious fashion) changed his clothes and arrayed himself with spotless neatness, he lunched, bought the best cigar that the town afforded, and strolled up to the Court House where the trial *in re* the "Fresh Start" mine was proceeding.

As he approached the building, it became evident that some case had just been concluded. A crowd of men were streaming through the doors and down the steps of the house. Even whilst Kellon looked, a knot of them stopped, betwixt two men in which an altercation seemed to be taking place. Suddenly both drew, shots were fired, and with exception of three figures the crowd scattered and fled to cover in all directions.

Of the three left, one stood motionless. Close to him the other two were firing at one another.

At the second exchange one of them fell to the ground. The others then walked rapidly away down the path which led them to where Kellon stood.

"By —, it's Ned and Joe!" exclaimed Dave, as they neared him. "Why, boys, what's up?"

"Fair fight!" said Joe, hoarsely. "Both drew together. Ned's killed him, I guess."

"Killed who?"

"Dutton. He couldn't keep his mouth shut. He *had* to open on Ned and sneer at him, even after we'd lost the case."

Ned had not said a word, or taken the slightest notice of Kellon; he was walking on alone a little ahead of them.

"And what is he going to do?" asked Dave. "Joe, he'd best give himself up, if it's as you say; he'll get off easy."

Joe shook his head regretfully. "Dave, you know Ned 'll never give himself up — nor they'll never take him alive neither."

"Worse luck," assented Kellon, tersely. "Ned! See here, Ned!" he called.

"Blast you! let me be!" exclaimed Chase, savagely.

But with a glance at Joe, Kellon let the words pass unnoticed. "How are you fixed for money, Ned?" he asked.

"I've got plenty. Are you just in from Dogtown?" he inquired abruptly.

"Yes, just in."

"What's Miss Carlin doing? I heard she'd had an accident."

Kellon gave him a brief history of it, and the blood coursed back into Ned's haggard face as he listened.

"Come on!" he said, hurrying forward when it was finished. "There's no time to lose."

"What's wrong with him, anyhow?" asked Kellon, in an undertone, of Joe; for his quick eye had detected in Ned's face signs of trouble deeper than could be attributed to the trial, of longer standing than could be laid to the recent shooting scrape. He looked years older than he had when Kellon had last seen him.

"I'll be darned if I know, Dave," replied Joe, hopelessly. "He was like that when I came down here. He hasn't been himself in looks or temper all the time I've been here."

"Come on, boys!" cried Ned, now turning to them. "They'll be after me in short order. I must skin out of this. Dave, tell me anything else you know about Miss Carlin."

Kellon hurriedly gave such further news as he was able to, while the best horse in Las Casas was being saddled and bridled for him. A few minutes later he sprang into the saddle, shouting a curt "Adios" to those who stood near, and sailed away out into the country at a pace that defied pursuit.

And many a glass was drained to his escape, for Ned was a favourite with all who knew him; it was believed that the verdict in the trial had been bought, not fairly won, and the little known of Dutton was all against him.

CHAPTER XIV.

"Dinkey!"

"Who's there? ——! it's Ned Chase."

"How is she, Dinkey?"

"Fine — keeps mending right along. When 'd you come in?"

"Right now."

"How 'd you know it was me?"

"Dave told me I'd find you here."

It was still dark — the dark hour that precedes the first vague adumbration of dawn. Ned stood in the verandah of Rose's cottage, over Dinkey, an indistinguishable mass of blankets on the floor. Just outside the railings a tired horse might be heard breathing hard after its rapid journey.

Ned went out and took the saddle and bridle off the animal; then turned it loose and returned to Dinkey.

"Send a Mexican out after that horse to-morrow," said Ned — "it's Kirby's bay from Las Casas. See he gets it back. Here's the money;" and he gave Dinkey a five-dollar bill. "Now tell me about *her;*" and he sat down near the heap of blankets with his back to the cottage wall.

"Wall, the Doc, he was here last night, and said as she was picking up to beat hell. She still sleeps a lot, but he allows that's all right — the best she can do, in fact."

"And the man who struck her?"

"Mike Kearney? Wal, you'd better believe he ain't been heard of since, nor won't either, ef he knows what's good for him."

Ned sat on in silence.

"Why don't you go off home, and come around in the morning?"

"I'll wait."

"Likely as not she won't wake afore late."

"I'll wait."

And through the sombre pregnancy of false dawn; through the grey twilight of dawn itself, more suggestive still of mystery; through those fleet waking moments of young Day in all its glory, rich in chaplets of pearls and diamond drops, rich in soft tissues of silver mist and faint rosy hues, rich in gleaming gold and deepening waves of ruddy tone, Ned sat quite motionless, with his arms upon his knees, and his head bowed over them.

Out of the chaos of memory and present thought, useless regret for the past and visions of the future, what hell was the busy brain weaving within his mind in that time? God knows! But the drawn brows and contracted lips, bore testimony to the merciless mood of the man. A ray of golden sunlight fell mockingly upon the broad *sombrero* that hid his face when Dinkey rose from his blankets. The loafer looked at him once or twice curiously, but instinctively forbore to speak, and was shambling off into the village when, without lifting his head, Ned called after him:—

"Don't tell the boys I'm here."

A little later Mrs. Murray appeared, and after their mutual greetings, she asked Ned indoors to breakfast, casting a few sneers at the absent Dinkey, between whom and herself there was undisguised warfare.

Her lodger's accident had brought Mrs. Murray the best harvest she had reaped for many a long day. Not only did she regale herself liberally on the delicacies which one or another sent for the invalid, but by judiciously representing her as totally without funds, she so wrought on the better feelings of those who called to inquire for Rose, that she drew from them many a ten and twenty dollar piece which never came to her patient's knowledge.

In Ned she recognised at once a possible subscriber; during the meal, therefore — which he himself scarcely touched, she painted Rose's destitution in the darkest colours. She also mentioned having heard her husband say that a man who owed Ned $300 had left it for him at the Mint.

Rose still slept, however, and Chase refused to allow her to be awakened. But time was moving on. He had made such a fast journey to Dogtown that he did not expect any one to arrive there from Las Casas in pursuit of him until about noon. Still long before that time he knew that he ought to be off into the hills. It was now past eight. Whilst waiting for Rose, he determined to go into the village and secure a fresh horse, as well as collect the sum deposited for him at the Mint.

At the latter place he had to wait while a messenger was sent to request Boger to come and deliver the money, which was locked up in a safe. The bar-keeper came, the money was paid over, and the drinks which followed the transaction had just been finished when the door opened, and Nate Frost, the sheriff, entered.

Ned's whereabouts was unknown in Las Casas, for, short though his start had been, he had made the most of it. Men were scouring the country in all directions for him, however, and Frost had come in quest of him to Dogtown. Arrived there, he naturally repaired to the Mint first of all to prosecute his inquiries. But he was unprepared to encounter his man in this fashion.

Ned saw him first, and knew his errand. In a second his six-shooter was out. "Don't come any nearer, Nate," he said warningly.

Beneath his Boniface-like exterior Boger had nerves of iron, and confident that neither of these men was likely to shoot wildly or waste a shot, he continued to lean over the bar and watch the proceedings. Every one else in the saloon fled to cover, most of them crouching behind the sand bags with which the bar was lined to afford this protection.

There was a moment's dead silence whilst the two men, with the floor to themselves now, eyed one another keenly.

"Ned, I've got to take you."

"You won't do it alive."

"Put up your gun, and come quietly." The sheriff had made no attempt to draw his own weapon, for he knew that the moment in which he did so would probably be his last. Ned "had the drop" on him. "Put up your gun, and come quietly," he said. "The whole country is sure with you, and if you stand your trial you'll get off lightly."

He made a motion forward as he spoke.

"Nate, if you come a step nearer you're a dead man." Ned had grown very pale. "I'd hate to kill you in cold blood, but, by God, if you drive me to it I'll do it."

"It's no use talking, I've got to take you."

"You can't do it."

"Well, you've got the drop on me, but I've got to try all the same."

There was a dogged look in Ned's face, the import of which was unmistakable. The sheriff looked just as determined; but in his case the firmness was that of a man who steps out bravely to his execution.

He moved a step forward.

"Stop!" cried Ned. "Stand back to that door, and I'll stand up against this wall. I'll put my gun to my hip, and then you can draw your own. Boger shall give the word to fire."

"I'll go you," said the sheriff, coolly. "Thank you, Ned."

They took their places, the breadth of the room separating them.

Ned nodded to Boger.

"Gentlemen, if it's your will, I'll give the word," said Boger. "Are you ready?"

Silence.

"Fire!"

The shots were simultaneous.

For the fraction of a second neither man seemed to move. Then the sheriff threw out his arms and crashed forward upon the floor, with a black spot in his temples, from which the blood was oozing just above one eye.

Ned had already covered him again, but, dropping the point of his revolver, walked rapidly past the dead body towards the door, without a word. He was unhurt. But there was blood in his eye, and he still held his smoking pistol in readiness. All the wild-beast passion that slumbers within a man was roused in him. For the moment he was mad — drunk with the horrible drunkenness of bloodshed. This, too — this second crime had been forced upon him. He was a Pariah for all time, and he knew it. Well, let no man cross his path then! Human lives were no more to him than the lives of rats now. The more he took, the better.

As he flung the door open and stepped out, he came full upon Hannaford, in the act of dismounting. At the terrible spectacle Ned's wild face presented, the gambler was panic-stricken. He had heard the shots; he saw the revolver in Ned's hand; he knew the part that he himself had played, and he trembled for his life.

"Are you heeled?" asked Ned, hoarsely.

"No," faltered Hannaford.

"You lie! you lie! you lie, you cowardly dog!" yelled the other. "You're afraid to fight; you're only good to steal;" and as he spoke he crossed the path, and pulled a six-shooter from its sheath by Hannaford's side.

"Take it and fight," exclaimed Ned, handing the weapon to Hannaford.

"I've got no quarrel with you, Ned," whined Hannaford.

"You thief! you bastard! No quarrel with me? Take that, then," and grasping both the weapons in one hand, he struck Hannaford full on the mouth with the other. "Now turn to, and hunt me down," he said, and he swung round and left him, casting his six-shooter into the road.

"By God, I will!" muttered Hannaford, under his breath; "and better than that — better than that, Ned Chase. The woman you love shall suffer for this."

A few minutes later Ned galloped up to Mrs. Murray's, and, leaving his horse for Dinkey to hold, entered the cottage. Mrs. Murray met him in the passage.

"I must leave at once — can I see her?"

"She woke just after you'd gone out, and she's up now and wants to see you."

Seeing that Chase was pressed for time, and solicitous that he should not leave without making the contribution she expected, Mrs. Murray had awakened the invalid herself. She ushered Ned in to see her.

Rose was seated on a little sofa in the parlour. She still looked very pale, and seemed terribly weak.

Ned closed the door behind him and then — stood still.

She glanced up with a faint smile. But the expression of hopeless agony in his face chased her smile away. Instinctively she read that something awful had happened to him.

"Why don't you come and speak to me?" she faltered.

"I daren't," he answered hoarsely; and he spread his open hands before him mechanically, and looked at them with a shudder.

"You daren't!" For a moment a look of horror almost equal to his own lived in her features. Then, softly, "Come! no matter. Whatever has happened, I am your friend."

Half-way he came across the room, then stopped again.

"No, no — you haven't heard. They'll tell you — don't ask *me*. I shall never see you again. I only came for this: you have had bad luck lately; you must want money — Hush! I *know!* Please use this — this money's clean, and I have plenty. The only favour you can do me now is to take it."

He placed a roll of notes upon the table as he spoke.

There was a thousand dollars in it; he himself had less than a hundred left.

"Good-bye."

In vain had she striven to speak. The broken words she uttered were not heeded. And he was going! Where? — for how long? — under what ban? She knew nothing.

She had risen weakly to her feet, and her eyes were full of tears.

"Ned!"

From the door he looked back — one second hesitated. Then he rushed on and out of the house.

The muffled beat of his horse's hoofs died away down the dusty road, and Ned was off to the mountains.

CHAPTER XV.

The coach brought Joe into Dogtown in the evening. He had been arrested as accessory to the killing of Dutton. But there had been ample evidence forthcoming to prove that Dutton alone had been responsible for the quarrel; that neither Ned nor Joe had forced it upon him; that the latter had even been unarmed at the time, and beyond being present while the shooting occurred, had been guiltless of any participation whatever in the fray. He had been released immediately, therefore, upon giving bonds for his reappearance when called.

It was not until he reached Dogtown that he heard of his partner's encounter with the sheriff. Feeling sure, however, that Ned would never submit to arrest, he had been anxious from the outset lest further bloodshed should occur, and his fears were no more than justified when, from the verandah of the Mountain Pride Hotel, a dozen voices cried the news to him:—

"Ned's killed the sheriff!"

"Ned's killed Nate Frost!"

A few inquiries placed Joe in possession of such facts as were to be learnt concerning the event, together with the knowledge that nothing could be done at present to aid the fugitive. Breaking away from the throng that surrounded him, therefore, he hastened to join Kitty.

During Joe's visit to Las Casas Kitty had lived in town with the wife of one of his fellow-miners, by whom the news of the shootings had been mercifully kept from her. She had heard, however, that the trial had gone against the partners, and also a rumour that Ned had been in town that morning, but had left again suddenly. This alone would have been sufficient to alarm her. Unfortunately it was not all. From the first she had had a strong presentiment that trouble would grow out of this dispute, her predisposition was therefore to apprehend the worst.

Convinced that Joe would come to her as soon as possible, and expecting him to arrive by the coach that evening, she waited for him at the cottage gate. Darkness had fallen, it was already night — but a night so clear, so beautifully still that it was but daylight dreaming. The stars were not dim lamps in dimmer skies, but brilliant, palpitating jewels of every hue, some of which seemed even to change continually in colour, as they shed their soft rays through illimitable fields of blue that seemed to live and breathe.

A score of times the fancied sound of Joe's step set Kitty's pulses beating rapidly; a score of times imagination mocked her with his cheery voice. She was terribly nervous. Instinct told her that something had gone wrong. That Ned should have left without seeing her strengthened the conviction.

At length her husband's stalwart figure actually did loom up in the clear obscurity. With a cry of joy she rushed to meet him; her arms were locked about his neck, and for a moment neither spoke. Nobody saw them in the deserted road. Not that Kitty would have cared had all the world been watching her. Joe was back! Joe was safe! For the moment her fears were all allayed in that great joy. The rest seemed insignificant. Love makes us rather selfish.

It was almost in a tone of indifference, even of gaiety, that she said: " Well, Joe, so we've lost the old mine?"

"Worse than that, my girl," came the answer, in words that fell heavily from the lips that uttered them.

"Oh, pshaw! You're back, and I reckon Ned don't care, and— We'll find another, Joe, sure! I'll find one myself. Do you think I couldn't find a mine? Shoo! Didn't I find you,—and aren't you all mine?"

Joe was silent. They still stood where they had met, and he swept the star-lit heavens slowly with a glance before he looked down again at the pretty face upturned to his, its chin resting caressingly on his broad chest. Kitty looked so brave now, so lovable and innocent and full of confidence. He would have given worlds to have been able to keep from her the horrible news that he was forced to tell. It seemed like sacrilege to shock as sweet a nature as hers with such a tale of crime,— crime, too, that came so near them as did this. But it had to be done.

"Kitty, it ain't the loss of the mine that's — that's the trouble; that don't cut no figure in what I've got to tell you. There's —"

"There's been trouble down to Las Casas?" she asked in an awe-struck whisper.

"Bad trouble."

"Ah, Joe, not you? — not you?" she gasped, and for a second she shrank back, and then clung all the closer to him, with an agony of fear in her eyes.

"No, but Ned —"

"Don't tell me — Joe, I won't — I *won't* hear."

"Be brave, Kitty. Best hear it now, dear, and hear it from me, than have to learn it by and by from other folks."

He drew her trembling figure close to him, whilst in a few brief words he related what had happened. As Joe told his tale to Kitty, all the glamour and false romance that frontier custom hangs about murder fell away from it. For the first time, perhaps, the act of taking the life of a fellow-creature appeared to him in its true significance; for the first time he realised the full horror of Ned's position.

He ceased, and only the sound of Kitty's weeping broke the silence, as with his arm round her he moved slowly towards the cottage. Once within doors, the rough but kindly soul with whom she was staying aided Joe in his efforts to comfort her. But their words had little effect on her. Scarcely heeding them, she reiterated her entreaties to be taken away — right away — far from Dogtown and the mines, and everything that could remind her of them.

"Promise me! — promise me, Joe!" she sobbed. "This horrible bloodshed will drive me mad! What is a mine — a hundred mines — at such a price? All the world, with blood on it, would be a curse. Joe, take me away, — take me away from here. I love you so dearly, ah, so dearly, Joe, so dearly! If anything did happen to you, what should I do? Take me away; every breath I draw here now will seem to choke me."

And Joe, his handsome face full of the gravest distress and pity and patience, soothed her with promises to do all that she wished. At times she would grow calmer, — only for a little, though. Then her deadly fear lest something should befall him, together with her grief for Ned, would return in full force, and she would burst into tears again. Had Ned been closely related to her, she could not have felt any more acutely what had happened to him; for her brother he had been, in all but name, ever since Joe's courtship had begun, and standing as alone as she had stood, Ned's kindness to her had had a double value.

Brought up though she had been in a country where the wild-beast thirst for blood, and the sympathy with blood-shed that still lurks in human nature, lies very much nearer to the surface than is the case with other civilised races, Kitty still proved her kinship with Englishwomen by her horror of violent life-taking. And whenever she thought of the possibility of further bloodshed she was almost beside herself.

But she wore herself out at length, — sobbed herself into a species of coma; excess of emotion had finally deadened her sensibilities for the time being, and, able now to leave her alone for a little while, Joe went out to learn what he could of Ned's movements, the probable course of his flight if possible, and what steps had been taken to pursue him.

Almost the first place he visited was the Mint. Throughout the day and evening the rooms had been full. From the mines and adjoining ranches hundreds of men had crowded into them, to see the blood-stains on the floor, the bullet hole in the opposite wall; and hear from the lips of Boger, or some other who had been present, the story of the encounter. By the time that Joe arrived the crowds had already thinned out. Most of those who remained were in the inner room gambling. Hannaford, however, half drunk and, feeling that he had to do something to recover the reputation for courage which he had lost in the morning, very quarrelsome now, was hammering noisily on the bar counter with the butt-end of a six-shooter, calling up to drink all about him. When Joe entered, he addressed him at once. "Come up here, —— you! Come up and drink — drink that your ———— of a partner 'll be taken soon!" and he flourished his weapon recklessly.

At the sight of the man whom he regarded as the indirect cause of all the mischief that had occurred, the softness of sympathy and sorrow fled Joe's face; it became lined with rugged furrows, and grew almost black with hate. Well was it that Kitty had bound him fast by tears and entreaties, or twice within the twenty-four hours would the Mint have been the scene of a "shooting scrape."

"—— you! come up now — get a move on you! jump! or by — you'll never jump again," cried Hannaford, savagely; for Joe stood still.

"I'm coming," he said deliberately.

"You bet you are," sneered the other, as Joe walked towards him; and hitting the bar counter again with his revolver, he shouted to the bar-keeper to hasten with the drinks.

Taking his stand next to him, Joe backed a little. He seemed to be measuring the distance between them carefully with his eye. Hannaford, however, was not noticing what he did.

"Name your drink, you claim-jumping thief," he said, turning on Joe.

As Hannaford did so with his full force Johnstone struck him on the point of the jaw. The blow was terrific. There was not a man in the camp so powerful as Joe Johnstone, and rage now lent him exceptional strength.

"God! he's dead, Joe!" exclaimed a spectator, stooping over him where he lay many feet away from the man who had felled him.

For all intents and purposes Hannaford was dead for the time being. It was over four hours before he showed any signs of returning consciousness, and fully forty before he could be said to have properly recovered his senses. As for his jaw, that had sustained compound fracture.

Dogtown was not to be cozened out of its genuine dislikes by the intervention of any misfortune that left the objects of them still alive. No sympathy, therefore, was expressed for Hannaford, nor, the doctor excepted, did any one go near him until some days later. Even then, the little deputation of miners who waited upon him came not with any idea of paying him a visit of condolence.

Hannaford had recovered his wits, although his jaw was still bandaged, and he himself was still in bed, forbidden to talk. He motioned to his visitors to be seated.

With a vast deal of deliberation they complied with the invitation. A pause ensued. Then Bill Clanton, the elected spokesman of the party, — an old "hard-shell," with light blue eyes, a cedar-bark complexion, and a grizzly beard, — tucked his quid in his cheek, spat slowly upon the floor, and said gravely: —

"The boys hev been a-considerin' of yer conduc' lately, Hannaford, in regards to certain matters, and we disapproves of it." The speaker paused to give weight to what he had said, and to impress it upon his hearer with an uncompromisingly glassy stare. "The camp hez come pooty nigh takin' action — pooty dog-gone nigh," he repeated very slowly and significantly.

"I reckon you'd best lay low for a while — d——d low! you're hell-fired onpopular."

He ceased. The various members of the deputation conferred silently together by means of an interchange of looks. Apparently there was no more to be said on the subject. As if by common consent, therefore, and as a sort of intimation that the interview was at an end, each spat deliberately upon the floor, and rising heavily they filed slowly out of the room without uttering another word.

Such an intimation of public sentiment was not likely to be cast away upon Hannaford. He realised that any further movement on his part which tended to increase the unpopularity aforesaid would be hazardous. No one had a greater respect for his personal safety than he. For the present, therefore, he abandoned, among other schemes, certain projects of revenge against Joe which he had already begun to elaborate.

At the Mint Joe himself learnt but little about Ned. Boger, it appeared, had followed him to Mrs. Murray's, where he had given him a couple of pots of Liebig's extract and a flask of whiskey, and had been commissioned by him to tell Joe that, even if he escaped, he should not write, whilst if he were taken he would be very unlikely to be taken alive; he — Joe — therefore was not to trouble about him. The bartender knew nothing of the line of retreat that Ned had chosen, but since the latter at one time or another had prospected all over the surrounding country, and was probably far better acquainted with it than any of the men who were following him, his escape seemed not unlikely.

Under these circumstances Joe was left to his own devices. Personally it went sadly against his nature to abandon the struggle for the mine. He might still have appealed the case to the Superior Court, or, in the present state of public feeling in the camp, have rendered it impossible for Hannaford or his agents to take possession of the property — possibly have even forced them to compromise. But submitting to Kitty's wishes in the matter, he relinquished all such ideas, and decided to strike out for some altogether fresh location.

CHAPTER XVI.

PAYING prospects had been discovered recently in the foot hills of the Sierra Madre, near Floretas, a little Mexican town some forty or fifty miles over the border. Fine fruit and farm lands were also to be bought there cheaply. The consequence was that a number of settlers, among whom were a good many Mormons, had begun to emigrate thither from the United States. From what Joe had been able to learn, it seemed probable that a small farm there would make a comfortable home for Kitty. Moreover, once established there, he would be able to "grub-stake"[1] Mexicans to prospect for him, whilst he himself remained at home and improved his farm, in order to prepare for the "boom" in land which was expected to take place in the neighbourhood.

Kitty's youth had been spent on a farm; she was not only accustomed to, but liked the life. Under present circumstances the idea of returning to it was greeted by her with particular delight, for Ned's situation and the trouble they had gone through had so shaken her nerves that she longed to get away from Dogtown and all its associations. For the time being, at any rate, the dream of rapidly acquiring a fortune in order to buy a home in the "old country" was overshadowed by her fears for her husband's safety. Love had made a coward of her, and all her influence went to encourage Joe in this project of emigrating to Old Mexico.

[1] "Grub-stake": to furnish the expenses of a prospecting expedition.

Needless to say, perhaps, the question was soon decided as she wished, and once decided, but a little time sufficed to make the few preparations that the journey required. Joe's fellow-miners, when they heard of it, held an informal meeting in one of the bunk houses in camp, at which it was unanimously resolved not only to present him with a good Studebaker wagon, and a pair of strong mules and harness, but among them, also, to relieve him at good prices of all such household effects as he would have to leave behind him. They were thus able to make a good purse for him when his auction took place. Beside the mules, he had the mare that had been used to hoist ore from the mine, a good draught-animal that upon occasion could serve him very well as a saddle-horse, no slight recommendation when his weight was taken into consideration. The emigrants, therefore, were by no means ill-equipped when they set forth.

Easy stages brought them in three days to Wilbur, the nearest town on the American side of the line to their destination in Mexico. Here they remained for a few days purchasing farm implements, together with such stores as were necessary for the journey, and gathering information with regard to the country they were about to enter. Finally, their preparations being complete, they drove five or six miles out of town one afternoon and camped, in order to ensure an early start next morning. Sunrise saw them under way, Kitty in a big sunbonnet, on the box-seat of the wagon beside Joe, and already engaged in building magnificent castles in the air in connection with their new departure.

The country before them was almost level. In the

clear air, beneath the sea-blue skies of the Mexican frontier, however, even such scenery as this had its charm. Grease bush, *mesquite, gatunias,* sage bush, several kinds of cacti (among them "Spanish bayonet," "hen and chickens," and *Amolia* or "soapweed,") with many another bush and plant, covered the wide plains; mingled here and there were patches of *Can' agrio,* the use of which makes tanning an almost rapid process, or *Yerba vigora* ("snakeweed"), the chewed leaves of which, applied to the bite of a rattlesnake, effects a certain cure.

Crows and hawks sailed in the pure atmosphere. A few varieties of small birds flitted among the bushes. Lizards flashed from cover to cover over the sand and stones. "Cotton-tails" scuttled about among the *mesquite* roots, while "Jack rabbits," their larger brethren, were visible in all directions. Now and then a solitary coyote might be detected slouching off in the distance with the cringing gait of the professional tramp; once a small band of antelope appeared moving south; for, deserted though the broad expanse of country might seem, it had its own wild population.

In the course of the morning they met a "prairie schooner" from Mexico, bearing a family that was evidently moving like themselves in quest of a fresh location. It was the first sign of any traffic that they had seen, and the piles of tattered quilts, bundles of old clothes, blackened pots and pans, festoons of dried beef, garland of red chillies, and Winchester rifle, conspicuous among the baggage; the dark-eyed women and black-headed urchins that peeped from under the patched and torn wagon cover, were all objects of interest to Kitty. As for the wagon itself, no joint or square foot of which there was but was mended with nails, or spliced with wire or rawhide, she followed it for a long way with her eyes, expecting every moment to see it collapse. But that which chiefly moved her to compassion was the sight of the hurdle-thin little horses that drew it, the consumptive-looking loose stock and colts that scuffled along ahead of it, the tail of half-starved dogs in its wake.

On they went, now and then passing a "bunch" of horses, or a band of cattle grazing towards one or other of the windmills that dotted the country, marking the wells at which their mid-day water awaited them. To any but very close observers the scene would have been monotonous; but Joe and Kitty were full of hope and health, great wealth of love and reasonable contentment, so all the world seemed fresh and bright to them except when the thought of Ned, a fugitive from justice, checked the flow of their spirits.

One of the hints they had received at Wilbur was that some knowledge of Spanish would be indispensable to success in their new life. With characteristic energy, therefore, Kitty was already desperately busy with a Spanish phrase-book, learning herself and making Joe repeat after her the names of all such things as they were likely to want.

"I reckon," observed Joe, reflectively, while this was going on, "it won't be wuth while for you t' learn the name of anything as we've got already. When they want to borrow anything, it'll be just as well not to understand them. They do say as they've got that borrowing business down to a fine point in Mexico, and I'd like awful well to keep even with 'em somehow."

Shortly after ten o'clock they reached the last well

windmill[1] they would pass before arriving at the river on which they were to camp that night. The remainder of their day's journey was a long stretch of dry country. They decided to rest where they were, therefore, until afternoon, in order to allow the mules and mare to roll, and graze for a little, while they themselves took their mid-day meal. It was while they were thus engaged that they made their first acquaintance with one of the race they were to live amongst. A solitary Mexican overtook them on foot, and sat down by the well-side. He was a strongly built man, of medium height, clad in old blue canvas overalls and a flannel shirt, which, though ragged, was tolerably clean. From beneath his well-worn *sombrero* — the silver braid on which was frayed and tarnished — straggled long grizzled locks, and these, with a small grey beard and moustache, framed a face as brown as tanned leather, in which deep lines and wrinkles not only marked the angles of the features, but were deep-cut in cheek and chin and forehead. His blue eyes had a pleasant expression; if his face was grave, it looked both honest and kindly; his speech was slow, but a frank and sympathetic ring in his voice inspired confidence. The only baggage that he appeared to possess was a blanket, or *zarape*, carried, together with his coat, across one shoulder, and a beer bottle in one hand containing, or rather no longer containing, water.

There was natural grace in his simple greeting which won Joe's good-will, when he approached the well to fill their kettle. Seeing that the man was travelling like themselves, only without being so well provided with

---

[1] Used to provide the horses and cattle that range these plains with water.

food, he asked Kitty — who was now frying bacon at their camp-fire — whether she knew enough Spanish to offer him something to eat. Kitty's vocabulary already included the word for "hungry," and with that and signs they would doubtless have been able to convey an invitation. But the stranger, who was returning from working in a lead mine in the States, — the owners of which had failed, owing him, among others, some sixty dollars of wages, — had far more English than they Spanish, and a conversation was soon established in the former language.

They gave him some food, he in return giving them some useful information concerning the road. After a while he thanked them courteously, filled his beer bottle at the well, and, shouldering his jacket and *zarape*, resumed his journey. An hour later, reharnessing their "spike team," they themselves set forth again.

They were jolting along at a jog-trot in silence, for the heat of the day had quieted them both, when a long way ahead of them Kitty espied a speck in the road, which, after some speculation, she decided must be the old Mexican. They had not asked him whither he was bound, nor had he told them; but, remembering how familiar he had seemed to be with Floretas, she determined now in her own mind that he must be going there as well as themselves, and the fact that he should be trudging thither under a hot sun, while they were seated in the shade of a wagon-tilt, was quite enough to make her decide that they must offer him a ride. Joe was somewhat averse — and wisely, too — from picking up casual strangers on the road, but yielded to please Kitty, and when they overtook their new acquaintance, pulled up to offer him a lift.

He proved quite an acquisition. Like many another *old* Mexican, he had natural tact and good manners. Whether these be peculiar to age or not in Mexico, it would be difficult to say. Young Mexico, however, is by no means as remarkable for them as his parents.

The present man knew the country they were passing through well, having prospected all over it for mines; he was able, therefore, as they went along, to tell Joe a great deal concerning its mineral, as well as agricultural, resources. He was not in the least degree greedy or selfish, either; he was very grateful, and when the spot was reached where they were to camp for the night, made himself exceedingly useful in watering and picketing the mules and mare, collecting firewood, carrying water, doing, in short, all those little tasks which enter into the economy of camp life, and doing them, too, in such a natural and unostentatious way that Joe was finally won to admit his concurrence in the good opinion that Kitty had formed of him from the beginning, and was induced to invite him to complete the journey with them.

Their next day's drive was quite a short one, along a pretty river-bottom full of great *alamos*, *palos-blanco*, and willows. The full distance to Floretas might have been covered by them had they so chosen, but Joe was unwilling to risk overtiring Kitty; most of the day, therefore, was spent lounging in the shade, learning Spanish from their new friend. Long before they had reached their destination the travellers had acquired quite a friendship for him, and had asked him whether, if they eventually settled at Floretas, he would care to come and work for them.

But to this Crispin Lucero — for that was his name — shook his head, declaring that he had been a miner all his life, and knew but little concerning farm work. He told them, however, that his brother, Justo Lucero, who was married and lived in Floretas, was a good farm hand, accustomed to work for the Mormon colony near there, and that he would be glad to come to them. They could assure themselves in the town as to his reputation for honesty and industry.

It was evening before Lucero piloted them to the Custom House in Floretas, where they had to report themselves immediately upon entering the town, and where, with many expressions of gratitude, he left them, upon finding that he could no longer be of any service to them.

The office was already closed; they were consequently unable to transact their business there until the following day. Since, however, it would have been unpleasant for them to camp in the roadway, and the law did not permit them to go any further until their papers had been made out, the *Administrador* of Custom (a young fellow named Julian Padilla) invited them to turn their wagon into the Custom House courtyard, and put their animals into the corral behind it.

The Custom House offices occupied the whole front of the building — a one-story barrack of *adobes*. On either side of the open courtyard behind extended the rooms in which the *Administrador's* own family and a few of the employees lived. In the rear of the courtyard was a second enclosure, the corral.

Joe's frank manner won over most people, and Padilla proved no exception to the rule. He invited him to bring Kitty into the house, introduced them both to his mother — a plump, motherly old lady, whose face beamed with good nature — and to a crowd of half-a-dozen equally good-natured-looking sisters, most of whom understood *some* English, and all of whom vied with one another in ministering to the wants of the pretty American.

It was their first experience of Mexican hospitality, and, proverbial though this is, it was carried by the Padillas to a pitch unusual even in Mexico. Nothing could have been more delightful than their tact, their total lack of ostentation or pretence. The girls themselves did the housework; for the old lady, a housewife of a school that is disappearing, had brought them up to follow in her own footsteps. She herself was as warm-hearted as she was industrious, and treated Kitty like one of her own children, so that, among them all, the young wife had a sense of relief and comfort such as she had not felt for many a long day.

Supper over, they sat out in the courtyard, where Padilla and some of his sisters sang pretty Mexican songs to the accompaniment of the guitar. It was late before Joe spread his blankets near the wagon. As for Kitty, her new friends would not part with her at all, but insisted that she should occupy the best bed in the house.

Next morning, Joe received an insight into the intricacies of Mexican customs laws — a lesson which not only occupied him for several hours, but made a large hole in the sum of his slender resources. Fortunately, the officers he had to deal with followed their superior's example in forbearing to use the considerable discretion allowed them, to the unjust disadvantage of the stranger; so the matter proceeded as satisfactorily as, all things considered, was possible.

In the course of the morning, their travelling acquaintance, Crispin Lucero, returned to look them up, bringing with him his brother Justo, a small, desiccated edition of himself, whom, at first sight, Joe was inclined to think too old to be of any service. Padilla, however, vouched so strongly for his honesty and industry, that he was induced to promise him a trial later on when there was work to be done. It was a promise that he never regretted; for the little old fellow proved to be as active as a monkey, as willing as a stanch horse, and as faithful as a good dog.

During the morning, also, Joe was introduced at the Custom House to a brace of worthies named José Vasquez and Luis Duran. Both spoke English, but the latter, proprietor of a small store in Floretas, having lived some years in the States, spoke it fluently. He was an undersized, rat-featured creature, with black whiskers and beard, a pinched-up, cunning, and perpetual smile, a small but prominent paunch, and spindle legs in very tight trousers, which, with the enormous *sombrero* that he wore, gave him the appearance of a mushroom, or rather toadstool.

Vasquez, on the contrary, was strikingly handsome. His eyes were magnificent — the volcanic eyes of an Indian; it was said that there was Indian blood in him. Be this as it might, he was a man of fine presence, and when he pleased, of extremely agreeable manner. Better educated and far shrewder than the majority of his neighbours, he would have been comparatively well off but for his passion for gambling, and other reckless propensities. Evil report had a good deal to say about him, and half the scoundrels in Floretas were at his beck and call. He had the reputation of being a great smuggler. Both Julian Padilla, with his *celadores* or guards, and the military officer who was quartered at Floretas with a handful of soldiers, would have given a good deal to have caught him in flagrante delicto. But Vasquez was too clever for either of them. It was said that he brought in the goods he smuggled in from the States by way of the Chinacate Mountains. As this range was the stronghold of the Apaches who were fugitives from the reservation, no ordinary person dare enter it. It was supposed, therefore, that Vasquez bought immunity from interference on their part by furnishing them with whiskey and ammunition.

While Joe was extending his acquaintance and passing his household goods through the Custom House, Kitty, in company with a couple of her friends, went house-hunting.

The houses in Floretas were all one-story buildings composed of *adobes*. A few of the best of them were plastered and whitewashed within and without. But bars and shutters in the absence of glass windows rendered their interiors gloomy, an objection accentuated by the total lack of decoration or taste that prevailed. In rare instances the broad expanse of bare walls would be broken by a crucifix upon a small bracket, a fifty-cent oval mirror in a gilt frame, or a lithograph of similar value. As a rule, however, the room, if a living room, contained nothing but the best bed in one corner of it, with chairs and a table arranged against the walls with painful formality. If there was any fireplace at all, it looked like the entrance to a dog kennel, excavated in the thickness of the wall. The redeeming feature in such rooms was their cleanliness, any taste or prettiness about the houses at all being found in the *patios*, where birds and flowers helped to relieve the natural ugliness of the buildings.

For a dollar a week Kitty found that she could have the temporary use of a small, three-roomed house that was empty, — empty even of furniture, — together with a small corral attached to it which would serve for their animals.

"But, Joe dear, it's got no floors, only beaten clay, and just whitewashed walls, and no glass windows, only shutters," said Kitty, when she had otherwise described it. "All the houses here seem to be like that, though; there's hardly a pane of glass in town. Will you mind very much?"

"It'll be rough on me at first, that's a fact — y' see, it ain't like I was a big stout woman like you. But I'll make a bluff at it, and see if I can't tough it through," laughed Joe, and he stooped to kiss the fair face of the little woman. "Why, Kitty, the wagon's a palace to me when you're there!"

CHAPTER XVII.

A WEEK had elapsed, during which time Joe and Kitty had cemented their friendship with the family at the Custom House. Kitty and the Padilla girls had become inseparable, an intimacy extremely useful to the former inasmuch as their assistance, combined with her own natural aptitude, soon enabled her to acquire what she described as "a regular rag-bag of Spanish," besides obtaining considerable insight into the mysteries of Mexican housekeeping. Doña Paz, the mother of the family, was an artiste in Mexican cookery, and although she omitted to tell Kitty nothing that could be of service to her, it was in matters pertaining to her own particular hobby that she took the greatest delight in instructing her.

A sorry little place was Floretas. But for all its toothless, wrinkled, sunburnt, and tattered appearance it had something of the charm which seems inseparable from Mexico; something of that original individuality, too, which always attends slow development and natural growth. No irksome straight lines or ostentatious angles challenged the eye there, none of the offensive smugness and soulless monotony of a "well-laid-out" town oppressed the stranger within the limits of Floretas. Untidy the streets were certainly, but the glimpses occasionally to be caught from them of *patios* with quaint well-heads, piazzas, flower beds, and bird cages were very attractive, and here and there there was a note of pleasant contrast to be marked where the emerald foliage of some young cottonwood tree, or a cluster of great fig leaves rose like the crest of a curling wave above the corner of a crumbling wall.

The inhabitants were so many typical studies. They took life in a philosophically idle, fatalistically hand-to-mouth style, the only sustained effort in which they seemed to indulge being that of prolonged conversations held at a few chosen street corners, or favourite haunts beneath walls bestowing shade. Here the broad-sombreroed loafers, blanketed in their coloured *zarapes*, collected in picturesque groups, smoking the eternal cigarette, while they stroked their black beards, and discussed village gossip or national politics. Occasionally a point of difference would be reached, and their smouldering talk interrupted by an explosion of argument, when the oaths in which the language is rich would fly freely for a while. Like summer storms, however, these disturbances would soon die away again in harmless growls, and the wanton wind of gossip resume its desultory meanderings.

It must be admitted that the wants of the gossipers were few; moreover, that in bearing their deliberately chosen poverty they displayed illimitable patience. After all, why struggle for the doubtful independence of wealth when, as in their case, a *zarape*, a handful of beans, and a little tobacco ensured contentment?

Here and there in Floretas a man was to be found who, unlike his neighbours, possessed both energy and thrift. Unfortunately, these exceptions bore too strong an approximation to practitioners in usury, erring as greatly in one direction as their thriftless townsmen did in the other. Such cases are common enough in Mexico, and it is to be regretted in the interests of commercial prosperity in the country that this strong contrast should obtain. So few men illustrate the happy medium. They either lack business capacity altogether, or else are narrow-minded, hard, and usurious. Rich Mexicans rarely embark in legitimate business enterprises; they content themselves with lending money at exorbitant rates of interest. It may be said in extenuation, that the sense of security for business ventures is of comparatively recent growth, that these men grew up in revolutionary times, and are unable to change confirmed habits. Be this as it may, since the gambling spirit which permeates all classes encourages reckless borrowing, the results are disastrous. One of the reforms most essential in the country is the stringent enforcement of a law greatly reducing the rates of interest at present legal.

On the day succeeding their arrival in Floretas, Joe and Kitty moved into their new house. They soon unpacked or procured such things as were required to make these temporary quarters habitable; which done, Joe set himself to work to examine the surrounding land. There were plenty of men only too willing to aid him in the task. Indeed, no sooner did it become known that he wished to purchase, than his door was besieged by owners anxious to sell the little holdings and accompanying water rights which they themselves were too lazy to utilise.

To follow him through the experiences he gathered in the days which ensued would be tedious. Suffice it to say that, at the end of a week, although he had obtained some insight into the quality and value of neighbouring property, he had made no advance towards obtaining what he required.

Among others who, with a great show of disinterested kindness, had busied themselves in pointing out purchases to him, were Vasquez and Duran; it was under their auspices that he eventually secured what he needed.

The land along the river-bottom near Floretas was divided among the townspeople into *terrenos*, or holdings of about forty-four acres each. Three miles out of town was a prettily situated *terreno*, on which stood a house with some large trees scattered about it. The owner wished to sell. The quality of the land was excellent; half of it was cleared of *mesquite* and *gatunias*, and had been cultivated. The house itself, though small, was large enough for Joe and Kitty.

At either end of it was a large room, the one serving as a kitchen, the other as a bedroom. Between them was the *portal*, a space the size of another room, beneath the same roof, but by a broad archway left entirely open in front, whilst at the back it was walled up, a doorway giving access in this direction to the corral behind the house. During most of the year the climate was such that this open room could be used as a sitting-room, and it was here that the inhabitants of the house were accustomed to take their meals. Adjoining the kitchen, at the back, was another and a smaller room, occupying one corner of the corral, which could be used as a storeroom.

Before the house was the well, — there was another in the corral, — near it a little flower bed, bricked up until it was raised some eighteen inches above the ground. Beyond, crossed by a large log which did duty for a bridge, ran the *asequia*, or irrigating ditch; on either side of it grew a few vines and fruit trees, with patches of melons, vegetables, and garden stuff. A few large *alamos* about the house lent shade, and that air of support to it which trees in such cases afford. For nothing can exceed the loneliness, the orphaned look, of a house with no trees near it.

So far as an attractive home for Kitty was concerned, the place answered all that was sought. But there were further considerations to be taken into account. Forty odd acres of land was less than Joe required. At this point, however, Duran came to his assistance with the information that a man who owned one of the adjoining *terrenos* wished to sell for $200; and since Vasquez and Duran both declared this, as well as the earlier bargain, to be extremely cheap, since also Kitty was pleased with the house and its neighbourhood, the purchases were eventually concluded.

Not that this was done without the expression of some little foreboding on Kitty's part. Despite his extreme civility, she had imbibed a strong prejudice against Vasquez. The warm looks of admiration that he was accustomed to lavish on her were of a kind that she entirely disapproved, and although she had not mentioned the subject to Joe, fearing to create ill feeling between the two men, she was unable to dismiss it from her mind. Moreover, Justo evidently mistrusted both Vasquez and Duran, and between Kitty and the old man a strong feeling of mutual confidence had arisen. Already much of his time was spent about her cottage, and notwithstanding the fact that Joe had no settled work to give him as yet, he had regularly attached himself to the newcomers. Every morning he came to turn the mules and mare out to graze; every evening he drove them home again. Occasionally he brought wood or hay; he did

most of Kitty's marketing, and when unemployed was
generally to be found somewhere within hail, if she
wanted him to do anything for her. For Vasquez and
Duran he appeared to possess a strong aversion; on
more than one occasion when he had seen Joe go off
with them, he had shaken his head ominously, and once,
with a great show of secrecy, had said:

"*Mucho ojo, señora, con esos señores. No son hombres
de bien — son muy magñoso! muy templado!*"

Still both Joe and Kitty were anxious to settle; the
little farmhouse suited them, the land was undoubtedly
good, and, judged in the light of their knowledge of
values in the States, the prices seemed cheap. It was
not until some months afterwards — when they had
begun to speak a little Spanish — that they learnt how
Vasquez had secured the house and land for a debt of
sixty dollars, and how Duran had won the other *terreno*
against a stake of twenty dollars at *monte*. Neither
had appeared in the negotiations with Joe, everything
being ostensibly arranged by the original owners, who
probably received a few dollars each to stand forward
as the principals.

Padilla's time was fully occupied with his own business, besides which he had already gone a good deal out
of his way to serve Joe in various ways. The latter
did not like, therefore, to appeal to him for advice at
every step, and consequently consented to the terms
of the bargain without referring to him. He did, however, request him to glance over the transfers, before
accepting them. It was a fortunate precaution. Presuming upon Joe's ignorance, Vasquez and Duran had
had them drawn up so imperfectly that, had he accepted
them, he might have found himself called upon to give

up or practically buy the property over again at any time.

Owing to the lax methods of doing business encouraged by the character of the people, documents of this kind are frequently faulty in Mexico. It is no uncommon thing for property, not of the first importance, to pass through two or three hands without any transfer being given for it at all, in order to evade the heavy stamp tax otherwise incurred. In the present case, intending to sell as soon as they were able to do so, and confident in their power to enforce transfer whenever necessary, neither Vasquez nor Duran had secured titles to the *terrenos* mentioned. The man from whom Duran had won his piece of land had not himself any transfer to show for it from the original owner. Moreover, his wife's signature was omitted from the one he now offered Joe. The transfer to the Vasquez *terreno* was equally deficient, since the signatures of the proprietor's children — he being a widower and they of age — had not been affixed to it. Apart from the question of signatures, the irregularities in the terms of the transfers themselves were such as practically to nullify them, whilst the fact that they were not properly stamped would have made both purchaser and sellers liable to heavy fines had the defect ever come under official notice. To the vendors this was not of such importance as it was to Joe, who had something to lose, and was naturally anxious to comply with the requirements of the law.

Julian Padilla at once declared both documents to be useless, and being well acquainted with the form in which they should have been drawn, himself prepared fresh ones. He then saw that these were properly stamped; that the stamps were properly cancelled; that the signatures of all parties interested in the matter were duly affixed and witnessed. In short, he saw that Joe was secured in his title to that which he had fairly purchased. If the prices paid were more than double what they ought to have been, it was not his fault. On this point his advice had not been asked, and he did not feel called upon, in a place where he himself had to live and support a large family on a slender salary, to make two dangerous enemies of Vasquez and Duran by forcing them to forego whatever might be in excess of a fair market value for the land in question.

Joe and Kitty removed now to their new possession, engaging old Justo and his wife Juana to live there with them.

Taking advantage of one of the sand hillocks that lay scattered over the plain of the valley,—sand hillocks the origin of which is uncertain, but which are called by the natives "Montezumas," and when disturbed are often found to contain fragments of old Aztec pottery,—Justo, with Joe's assistance, constructed for himself, within hail of the house, a dug-out cabin with front and roof of wattling and mud. This done, he and Joe set to work in earnest to prepare the land for sowing corn (maize), a considerable crop of which it was the more urgent to ensure since the season was already far too late to plant wheat.

But even the season for sowing corn was advancing, and, dissatisfied with his progress, Joe bethought him one day that he would go over to the Mormon colony of Hidalgo, a few miles from where he lived, and try to hire some assistance. He had already met some of these colonists at the Custom House, among them two to whom he had taken rather a fancy. They were partners — the one an oldish man named Keck, with good Roman features and a patriarchal aspect; the other, a man in the prime of life named Bell, whose immense frame, for all his six feet in height, gave him when he stood alone the appearance of being short, and whose broad physiognomy was full of good-natured shrewdness.

Joe's intention was broken to Kitty as they sat at their mid-day meal in the *portal*.

"I guess I'll ride over to the Mormon colony this afternoon," he said casually.

"Guess again," laughed Kitty. "If you think I'm going to have you foolin' round that colony at odd times, and sparking those Mormon ladies, you're away off."

In the excitement of arranging her new home, — to assist in doing which Chata, one of the girls from the Custom House, had come to stay with her, — Kitty had begun to recover her gayety.

"Well, maybe I guessed wrong then," returned Joe, with a placidity that was perhaps not altogether guileless.

At any rate his submission caused Kitty to ask what he wanted at "Mormon town."

"Oh, nothing — nothing of any consequence, that is."

"Of course not. Still — what is it, anyway?"

"Wouldn't interest you a durned bit," replied Joe, unconcernedly.

"I'm the best judge of that, Joe — ah, Joe, tell me; I'm dying to know."

"I wouldn't die about a little matter like that," said Joe, calmly.

"Yes, I will, too, and you'll feel ter'bly about it forever afterwards if I do."

"Oh, I d' know," he chuckled. "There's some mighty nice-looking folks over to Mormon town."

"Then I'll never die as long as I live!" declared Kitty, and they all three laughed at her bull. "Joe, what is it you want there?"

"Just a little help."

"Help! what sort of help?"

"Well, kind o' looked to me's though you'd got rather more 'n you could tackle here," he rejoined with a twinkle in his eye; "and I was allowing that maybe another wife or so'd come in handy."

"Oh, ho! you—you *ree*—probate!" laughed Kitty, in delight. "Well, now, you may just go right along and bring them here. I'll undertake that *they* won't think I've got more 'n I can tackle. *How* many wives did you say?"

"I reckoned 'bout three more 'd do to begin with."

"Three! Chata! but listen to him! Joe, aren't you *ashamed* of yourself?"

"No," said Chata, gayly; "no have no shame, Mr. Johnstone—no can blush even."

"All right, get a move on you, Joe; go and bring 'em—quick. You bet you can't bring 'em as quick as they'll go back again. And while you're gone, me and Chata 'll fix things so's to have it nice for them when they do come."

"*Que si! que si!* Dey going be very *comfortablé*, your tree wives," cried Chata, merrily; "no you have no care for zat."

"*Muchas gracias*," replied Joe, with his best accent. "But I guess I'll have to give that plan up. I can see you wouldn't make the ladies welcome. What's the matter, though, with my hiring a little help with the ploughing? It's getting late now, and the sooner the corn's in the better. 'Sides," he added diplomatically, "I kind o' thought I'd look around over there and get a few chickens for you."

Now Kitty was longing for some fowls.

"Oh, Joe! do you think you could? — and bring them back with you? And *do* you think that you could try and borrow a cow? Chata says they'll lend you a cow if you promise to look after the calf. And it won't be any trouble, because if you keep the calf up in the corral, the cow can be turned out to graze all day and will always come back at night. Yes, you can go — only mind you're back to supper! And, Joe," she tiptoed up here, and kissed him prettily, "no trifling with those Mormon ladies! Mind! I won't have you look — not even *look* at any one but me."

For developing a new country there are probably no better colonists than Mormons. Within their ranks are men of every handicraft required in an agricultural community. Wherever they settle, they bring these with them. They are sober and industrious, expert farmers, stock-raisers, and fruit-growers, quick to see and to turn to advantage the capacity of any undeveloped neighbourhood. Moreover, since they are naturally very clannish, and obliged by their religion to help one another, they are less liable to be interfered with by outsiders than are ordinary settlers.

The little colony of Hidalgo, one of four or five that had been planted lately in the foot hills of the Sierra Madre, in the State of Chihuahua, contained about six hundred inhabitants, and, with its flourishing gardens, neat houses, and general air of prosperity, presented a very different aspect from that of Floretas.

Joe found Keck in his farmyard, engaged in putting a new block into the brake of a wagon, whilst a tribe of healthy youngsters, from children just beginning to walk alone up to lanky boys and girls that would soon begin to work, stood round and watched him. The old man left his task at once, and greeted Joe cordially. Before long, chatting as they went, they were walking round the farmyard.

"O' course this ain't the shape we used to have things in, back in Utah," said Keck, half apologetically, waving his hand towards some long, low *adobe* stables, on the roof of which were piles of fodder. "All the same, there ain't much amiss with the stock — yes, best give her leg room, I reckon," he observed, as Joe steered wide round the heels of a smart but wicked-looking Jenny mule tied to a snubbing-post near the stable doors. "The boys on'y got her up the other day, and are making a saddle mule out of her. She's a bit skeary yet, but she'll come to it — she'll come to it in time."

With some pride he showed Joe a good-looking stallion in the stable, some fine colts in the corral, and some exceedingly well-bred Berkshires in the pigsties, all of which were well and appeared to be well fed. Joe remarked upon their conditions, which drew from Keck a story.

"My father always had fat hogs, and a neighbour of ourn, name of Langell, his'n was always poor, stunted hogs as didn't hardly pay for the killing. Happened one day as Langell met the old man, and says he, 'Keck, I'd like awful well for to get a couple of your pigs; they matures early,' says he, 'and they're always fat. I reckon there's suthin' in the breed.' 'Wal,' says my father, 'send a boy along to-morrow to fetch 'em over. I've got a litter of young pigs right now, as I'm a-goin' to wean,' says he, 'and you can get a couple of 'em.'

To-morrow come the boy with the wagon, and my father give him the pigs. And then he takes a sack, and throws a handful of corn in it, and says he, 'Sonny, there's the pigs, and (giving him the sack with the corn in it) tell your father *there's the breed!*' There's a durned sight in it, too — yes, sir, if you wants good-looking stock around you've got to feed 'em — 'specially hogs. Some folks thinks hogs can pick around like chickens till you wants to fatten 'em. But there ain't nothing saved by it. Ef the hogs ain't stunted for good, it takes twice the time and twice the corn to get the flesh on 'em afterwards."

It so happened that at the time Keck was fairly at liberty, for his own corn was all planted. He readily agreed, therefore, to come over to Joe's farm for a couple of days, with his partner, Bell, and do what was required. The following day they arrived, and stayed three days, in which time, with the sulky-ploughs they brought with them, they quite allayed their host's anxiety as to the amount of land he would be able to sow that season. Moreover, they brought with them some fowls for Kitty, and in response to her apologies for being unable to give them any milk or cream with their meals, offered to lend her a cow.

CHAPTER XVIII.

Rose's state of health was far from satisfactory. She had regained strength enough to move about in a tired, listless fashion, but the dash and spirit characteristic of her before her accident had not returned.

To be sure, her life was no longer very cheerful. Most of her time was spent alone, one reason for this being that, despite her devotion to children, she had entirely ceased to take an interest in Bee. The child's nature repelled her. Although still indulgent towards her, therefore, Rose no longer cared for her company.

Another cause which contributed to her isolation was the impossibility for a woman of her frank nature and stanch character, of feeling any other sentiment than that of disgust for Mrs. Murray, who would otherwise have been her natural support. Two days had sufficed Rose to measure her correctly; and once aware of its futility, the gambler's wife had thrown off all disguise, resorting to the simpler course of sponging openly upon her lodger, robbing her in all their mutual transactions without even the affectation of concealment, whilst hating her none the less bitterly for each fresh benefit received. To be brought into daily contact with one whom she saw bear and forbear so much, one who never asked a favour or claimed consideration, who did what she herself thought was honest and right, and cared not what others thought about it, could not but make Mrs. Murray feel how contemptible were her own shortcomings; and not unnaturally, being the kind of woman she was, she hated her lodger for it.

Notwithstanding the hypocrisy used to cover them, Rose was fully aware both of Mrs. Murray's sentiments and character. It was but natural, therefore, that she should limit their intercourse as far as possible. Indeed, charity alone induced her to remain in the house. The truth was, however, that almost ever since she had taken up her quarters there, the money furnished by her had constituted in effect the sole support of its inmates; indeed Murray himself had gone to El Paso in search of work, leaving his wife and child entirely dependent upon Rose.

In her present enfeebled condition, Rose had not the energy to enter into and assume the boisterous tone, the crude, careless, vivid spirit of the frontier. As people often do before death, or when suffering from the effects of a severe illness, she had reverted unconsciously to the habits and feelings of early life; for the time being she had become again the creature of mental refinement and well-bred physical expression she might always have remained, but for the fatal step that had blighted her career. The miners in Dogtown were not accustomed to people of this description. When they called upon Rose now, they felt abashed and ill at ease. The novelty of the feeling did not compensate for its unpleasantness, so one by one they dropped away, and for the time being the invalid was left almost alone.

Dinkey remained faithful to her. He hung about the house like an ownerless dog that had once been well fed there. Possibly Dinkey had not pride enough to permit of his feeling abashed under any circumstances.

He was not credited by Dogtown with any sentiments at all, — none, that is, of a loftier nature. Of course it was presumed that he had the capacity to be conscious of his own general inferiority. Possibly this was so. At any rate, he was undeniably one of those imperturbable, all-round failures, who accept insult and imposition, misfortune and discomfort, without any manifestation of impatience; who are regarded by others, and seem to regard themselves, as mere on-lookers in the game of life, the self-accepted inheritors of obscurity and injustice. Dinkey was one of those men whom every one knows when they see them, and no one remembers in their absence. To be sure, when Dinkey was pointed at as a failure, the fact was overlooked that he had never attempted anything, — a consideration that might have made not a few of his scoffers envious had they seriously pondered it. As Talleyrand observed, "*C'est un terrible avantage de n'avoir rien fait.*"

One morning, from her seat in the verandah, Rose saw Dinkey loafing about in the road which led from the cottage to the main street of the village, and beckoned permission to him to come to her.

"How d'y, miss?" said Dinkey, cheerfully.

She nodded her acknowledgment of the greeting gravely, the faintest possible smile, induced by his perky manner, quivering upon her lips as she did so. "Dinkey, did it never occur to you to ask any one to give you work?" she asked compassionately, though, unaware that he was any object for pity, it may have been doubtful whether Dinkey so construed her tone.

"Why, no, miss. Work! You bet yer ef I was to ask anybody for sump'n, it 'd be sump'n as I wanted wuss 'n that."

Looking out at the red hills beyond, Rose smiled her belief in that assertion. "It might be worth while to try it once,—for a change."

"Wal," rejoined Dinkey, judicially, "it *might*, of course."

But he seemed in no wise confident on that score.

He sat himself down on the edge of the verandah, and producing through some rent in his ragged coat a bag of "Durham" tobacco and a packet of yellow papers, proceeded, with all that nimble-fingered deftness which characterises the worthless, to manufacture himself a cigarette.

"It might. But then again — there's objections;" he resumed. "There's the pers'nal trouble, and — and the anxiety as ter th' result, and the duberous value of success — even ef it did come up thet way. 'Tain't no sure thing ez anybody 'd give me work — nor it ain't no ways certain if they did ez it's just what my nature requires. Then again, I seen a mint o' hustlers drop back into my financial condition, after trying all their lives ter get money out of their neighbours by the most honourable bizness methods, and they seems just as full of remorse as pious missionaries when they dies. And them as does make a ten-strike and hold on to it! — you don't never see one of 'em lay off a day and take his ease! — you don't never see one of 'em paintin' th' town with his friends, and heving a time! They're a-kicking right along, just blistering for more, hungry ez buck skeeters outside a skeeter bar. It's my b'lief, miss, as that there what they calls 'success in life' is a put-up job; it fools the slickest of 'em."

"Try it, Dinkey."

"Wal, thet's ez you say," returned he, with his usual

placid indifference. "I reckon there ain't no trick in becoming a millionaire ef a man sots right down to it, and gives up all self-respect and idee of pleasure in life — listens and looks into everything what don't concern him like, and shets his mouth 'bout everything 't does."

There was not much mirth in Rose's laughter, yet she laughed outright for a moment.

"Become a millionaire — do — to please me."

"Oh, I'll give it a trial — nex' chance as comes along," replied Dinkey, dispassionately. "But it's a dirty bizness, nips all your feelin's, dwarfs all your idees — 'tain't fit for no self-respectin' gentleman of course. How kin a man be a gentleman wot's got all his senses, an' intelligence, an' energy sot on gettin' money for himself out of other fellers, whether they kin afford it or not? A man gets so he don't hev no mor'l sense — so he don't see nothin' 'thout the dollar sign in front of it — so 't anything outside of gettin' dollars ez pure dreamin' 'n' idleness. There ain't no beauty in the world for such folks — no happiness — no good. They can't hear, they don't see, they don't feel — don't do nothin' on'y bite off an' chew, — and they bites off more 'n they can chew, most of 'em. I tell you, they gets narrowed so they don't even know they're narrow. Bizness is the blight of human nature, it pizens all the springs of thought and feelin'. Thievin' does less harm to a man, 'cause he don't fool himself that he's honest like them bizness men does. A thief may reform, but a bizness man's a goner."

Silence ensued for a little while, whilst Mr. Dinkelspiel blew cigarette smoke out of his ears and nose, and did some very artistic expectorating.

"'Sides," he ejaculated, evidently after further consideration, "there ain't nothin' in money-makin'—don't even pay— A man 'cumulates wants, 'n' obligations, 'n' duties for every cent there is in it."

Rose only sighed.

"There don't come no news in camp 'bout Ned Chase," observed her companion presently, changing the subject.

"No?"

"Not a word," and the speaker shook his head. "Ned Chase is a dandy, too; he'll give 'em all a job to take him. Like as not they never will take him." He paused to con the question in his own mind before he proceeded. "Thet's the most pro'ble in my 'pinion. Ned's a darling when he's set a-goin'."

Warming to his subject, he recounted a string of incidents illustrative of Chase's pluck and resource, his devil-may-care spirit and good nature.

Rose listened in silence — half absently it seemed.

"Oh, dear!" she yawned, wearily, when at length he ceased. "And where do you suppose he is?"

"Wal—wal—I kind o' suspicion 't he's way down in Texas—somewheres round there. Thet's where they're looking for him now. The sheriff of Las Casas went down that way two days back—I reckon they're on some kind of a clue."

"But they won't catch him, you say?" and with a glance at once critical and absent she watched Dinkey through half-closed eyes as he answered.

"Na-ar, not they!—not unlest he gets tangled up buckin' agin some faro bank, and goes broke. Ned's got some sagass to him. Tell you the man what 'lights out to trap him when he's in hidin' 's got to play slicker 'n a peeled lizard! Ef on'y he don't run out of checks!—that's the pint!"

"Does any one know how much money he had with him?" asked Rose, curtly.

"Why, some of the boys was a figgerin' on thet the other day, and I hearn 'em say as he couldn't have less 'n seven or eight hundred dollars along — as they *knowed* on. In course he might hev had more 'n that: but that 'll do ample ef he's kep' it."

Rose was silent.

"And if they catch him?" she inquired abruptly.

"If they ketch him? — alive? Why they'll bring him back to Wilbur fust of all and hold him there for trial."

"I don't know Wilbur: what sort of place is it?"

"A little one-horse hearse of a burg, with a two-room brick jail in it."

"It wouldn't be difficult for him to escape from there then?"

"I reckon not," returned Dinkey, cheerfully; "with the help of a little wad of money, in course. They'll watch him close enough — f' fear he shed get away without payin'."

The conversation lapsed, and after smoking on for a while in silence Dinkey rose and took his leave — a fact merely noticed by Rose with a little motion of the head.

For a long time after he had gone she sat there quite motionless. But finally she, too, rose. Mechanically she went indoors to her own room where, with a little tired sigh as though worn out alike in body and spirit, she cast herself down on the bed and buried her face in the pillows. Not a sound escaped her, but when at length she moved, her lashes were wet with tears.

Interviews like this between Rose and Dinkey came to be of daily occurrence. From her rocking-chair in the verandah she would see him leaning against a fence, seated upon some felled tree or stump, or loitering aimlessly about in the offing, and beckoning to him, either allow him to sit and talk to her, or send him on some trivial errand. He brought her the news in Dogtown, such as it was, especially such fragments of intelligence concerning the search for Ned as were current in the saloons and dives which he frequented. And since a fool hears more in a day than a man reputed to be wise is allowed to hear in a month, and Dinkey being regarded as a fool every one spoke freely before him, he garnered a good many odds and ends of gossip.

Meanwhile Rose's condition remained practically unchanged — if anything, she grew a little thinner and paler. She certainly became quieter and more sombre. Whole days would pass during which she sat in the verandah almost without intermission, doing nothing, scarcely interchanging a dozen words with any one. Even Dinkey's placid stream of small talk would hardly elicit a remark from her.

The dapper, good-natured little doctor of Dogtown shook his head. He was compassionate and really clever, and the case at once concerned and puzzled him. Rose's physical apathy contrasted so strangely with the feverish glow and mental restlessness betrayed in her great, dark eyes. Had the failure and misery of her life penetrated the armour of world-scorn and outward indifference with which she had clothed herself, and begun to conquer her at length? Were her pride and pluck giving way? She certainly was not gaining ground in health.

It was generally late before she retired to rest; for she slept so little now that it was her custom to postpone the night's penance as long as possible. One night she had just begun to undress when she heard the door of the cottage opened and closed again softly. Since she had seen Mrs. Murray go out earlier in the evening, and nocturnal excursions were by no means unusual with that lady, she merely supposed that she was now returning. But at the first footfall in the passage she stood still. She knew the step: it was not the step of Mrs. Murray.

A second later her door was opened and Hannaford entered.

She flew to her trunk, and threw up the lid.

"If it's your six-shooter you want, it ain't there," he remarked.

He was right: the weapon was gone.

"You miserable coward!" she exclaimed, anger overcoming her fears, as she faced him with flashing eyes. "You bribed that woman to take it."

"You bet! I knew your temper, Rosy, and I didn't allow to have anything as ugly as a six-shooter interrupting our little conversation."

He had evidently been drinking a good deal, and for the moment was inclined to be jocular.

She stood at bay; she was silent, though her breath came and went heavily.

"Sit down," he pursued banteringly. "How's your health?—sit down and make yourself at home;" and, seeing that she glanced swiftly round her, he laughed again. "No show, Rosy: you're cornered." She turned towards the door. But Hannaford was too close to it, and, interposing himself, he seized her by the bare shoulders and thrust her back.

"Not much, I tell you. I haven't come all this way for nothing."

For all his assumed coolness, he was evidently labouring under strong excitement. He advanced a step towards her, whilst she, her eyes never leaving him, retreated.

"It don't strike you what I came for?"

"I neither know nor care. If it concerns me, you came in vain."

"That's as may be — that's what we're going to see. Rosy, I love you still — do you hear? — I love you still. Strange — isn't it? By God, I'd hate you if I could — as well as I ever hated any one! But I can't; I love you — love you better than I ever loved you before — better than I ever loved any other human being in all my life. You can't get away; you've got to listen," he said, seeing that she was still covertly seeking some means of escape. "Come! the offer I made you awhile ago holds good: will you take it?"

"I'd die a thousand deaths first! — a thousand deaths!" she exclaimed, turning on him again with an outburst of ungovernable passion. "Listen to me! I am unarmed now, but I shan't be always. To-morrow — the next day — what matter when! if it's years — long, long years, only drive me to it and — " she lifted her face and hands to heaven and spoke with awful calmness — "and while I have eyes to see and strength to stand I'll follow you. Drive me to it, and I'll hunt you like a dog and kill you like a dog! If it must come to that, so be it, your life or mine."

"'Your life!'" he echoed, speaking almost softly in the rage that possessed him. "'Your life!' Yes, see that it doesn't come to that! You love Ned Chase."

She laughed scornfully. She disdained to deny anything that he might accuse her of, false though it might be

"You love him! Well, help him, then, if you can. The sheriffs have him safe."

"It's a lie."

"It's true, — true, true! — the God Almighty's burning truth!" and he laughed triumphantly. "They're bringing him back from Texas now! And Ned Chase shall swing, so help me Heaven, if it costs me every dollar I have to bribe his jury and buy his death."

She had grown quite white and quiet.

"Well — well, now you have said it, you can go."

"Can I? — not without you! Once for all, do you take my offer?"

"I have answered you."

"Then blame yourself, by ——."

"Stay there! Another step and I'll rouse the house."

"You fool! the house is empty."

"Think what you do!" she cried, still keeping him at arm's length. "Touch me, and as sure as there are men in Dogtown, they shall lynch you to-morrow."

"I shall be far enough off to-morrow. No one knows I'm here now. I've fixed a sure alibi; they'd never believe you. And — Hell! what do I care if they do! I can die to-morrow, but you shall be mine to-night. Quit —"

With a short, sharp cry, as he seized her, she struck him on the mouth. But his arm clasped her waist firmly. In vain her screams rent the air, — shrill and clear for a moment, then muffled and choked. What could she do, unarmed, against Hannaford's enormous strength?

But the struggle lasted only for a moment. A pistol-shot rang out outside, and a bullet crashed through the window. The brutal hands which held the girl released her. For a second their miscreant owner stood undecided; then, dashing her aside, he fled through the door and out from the back of the house. He knew that even if he escaped that pistol, lynching would surely follow if he were recognised.

A few moments passed, and two more shots were heard away down the road. Then there was silence for a while, until some one tapped at Rose's window, and a voice asked:

"Are you all right, miss?"

"Oh, Dinkey! was it you?" answered Rose, in broken accents, as she lifted the window.

"Why, yes. I — I seen yer shadders on the blind a-fightin'. What was up, anyhow? — some dog-gone sneak-thief?"

"Why — why, yes; a man broke into the house, Dinkey."

"He did, eh? I reckoned it was suthen like that. Lucky I allowed to take a *pasear* around here 'fore turnin' in. That's how I come to hear you shoutin', and then — wal, then I seen your figgers on the blind, and lets drive to scare him. Hearn him skootin' away down th' road afterwards, and took another drive at him. But I reckon he was goin' faster 'n bullets. Wal, you're all right? — sure? — on'y frit? That's good. So long; I'll be round in the morning."

"Come early, Dinkey! we must go down to Wilbur."

"Hev they got him?"

"I'm afraid so."

"The hell you say!"

"To-morrow, early. Good-night," repeated Rose, and she shut the window.

"The hell!" ejaculated Dinkey again, softly, as he

turned away. "They've got him, then! Wisht I'd got Hannaford just now; we'll hev him agin us, sure."

Morning came. Mrs. Murray, however, did not return. Bee was absent, too; but since she often went to spend the afternoon with the children of a neighbour, and invited herself to remain with them for the night, this did not surprise Rose. Neither did the prolonged absence of the child's mother; for she naturally supposed that the woman was unwilling to face her after having stolen her revolver at the instance of Hannaford. In the midst of preparing her frugal breakfast, something, however, seemed to flash across her mind. She quitted her occupation suddenly, and, hastening back to her room, began to search in the trunk from which Mrs. Murray had abstracted the revolver.

At first she only dived into it, and turned over its contents hurriedly; but soon, not finding what she sought, she began to throw the contents, one by one, upon the floor, turning and shaking them in eager anxiety. In vain. Her search was fruitless, and she finally abandoned it, with the conviction that Mrs. Murray had stolen not only her revolver, but her money also,—every dollar that she possessed including the $1000 left with her by Ned, which she had religiously preserved in order that she might return it to him.

Rising from her knees, she stood up amidst the disorder that she had created, with great tears in her eyes, and lips that quivered tremulously. She glanced slowly round her at the scattered articles upon the floor, and there was something pathetic in the simple survey,—it was so entirely mechanical, so entirely an instance of the body still following an impulse the mind had given it, though the mind itself was leagues away in thought.

But Mrs. Murray had evidently made good her escape, and the girl she had robbed was not one to waste in tears time that should be spent in action.

She dried her eyes and sat down to think. A moment later a cry of joy escaped her. Her glance had fallen upon two handsome rings she wore, the one of diamonds, the other of a ruby and diamonds, — relics of her brief spell of extravagance in Europe. She held them in the sunlight now, rejoicing in their beauty; for she saw in it a means of escape from her difficulty.

But her thoughts were interrupted by the appearance of Dinkey in the verandah.

"Dinkey, she's gone!" she said, as he came inside.

"Mrs. Murray? You don't say!"

"And she has stolen every dollar I had."

"The — the son-of-a-gun!" ejaculated Dinkey, fervently.

"Who is there in town who will buy these rings?" and she began to remove them.

"Why, dog ef I quite know," returned he, slowly. "Sol Poheim he's gone West, and Dave's away, and the Colonel, and — you couldn't afford time to raffle 'em?"

She shook her head. "I want the money at once."

"Wal, maybe Abey Einstein, or — or Clint Morris 'd take a notion to buy 'em."

"Try Einstein, or Ben Schuster, not Morris. Stay! there's this" — and she unfastened a pretty little jewelled watch from her dress; and then, from a small case on her dressing-table, took an emerald lizard brooch and some other trinkets — "and these. Take them all, and see what you can get. We must have five or six hundred dollars at once. The rings alone are worth three times that."

"They'll want to know how I come by 'em."

"If any one wants to buy, bring him to me, then."

Dinkey set off on his errand. In the course of half an hour he returned with 'Abey' Einstein, a little Jewish ore buyer, who offered Rose $300 for the articles she proposed to sell.

But although desperate she was firm.

"Six hundred or nothing, Mr. Einstein," she said. "You know their value better than I do, and I know that at that price they are given away. If I can't sell them here for that, I'll take them down to El Paso with me. Will you buy or not?"

Abey hesitated.

"Very well, I've no time to waste. Dinkey, take them up town again, and if you can't sell them, borrow enough money from Boger to carry me to El Paso — Boger will lend it to me."

"Sthop, mine dear lady, sthop!" cried Einstein, effusively. "Of course ef you vos so hart prest like dot, here vos de money. I di'n't know you vos vant money so badt;" and without more ado he paid her the $600, and disposed of the jewels in some concealed pocket.

A few hours later Rose set out for El Paso with Dinkey, leaving most of her baggage behind her in Boger's care.

CHAPTER XIX.

In the inner of the two brick-built rooms which composed Wilbur jail Ned Chase lay handcuffed and ironed.

A small window near the ceiling admitted light; the only communication with the outside lay through the adjoining room. This, day and night, was occupied either by Quandt the sheriff, who had charge of the prisoner, or by one of his deputies, the former himself always going on guard at night. For in Ned he knew that he had to deal with a desperate man who was likely to seize the first opportunity that suggested a chance of freedom.

And desperate indeed Chase looked. It was difficult to recognise in his fierce, haggard, and reckless visage the self-reliant, handsome face of the stage-driver who had driven Wild Rose up to Dogtown only a little while before. Ned Chase to-day looked fifteen years older than he had done on that afternoon.

He had almost made good his escape when captured, and, had it not been for his generosity to Rose, would have succeeded in leaving the country by way of Galveston. But lack of funds had checked him in his flight at Dallas. Obliged to go to work there in some livery stables, he had been recognised and watched, and one night, whilst endeavouring at a faro table to win with his day's wages enough money to pursue his journey, had been stunned and overpowered before he had been able to draw his revolver.

Since his arrival in Wilbur several of his old friends had sought access to him, but this request had been refused to all except his lawyer, to whom he paid but little attention.

It was past twelve o'clock; the west-bound train was punctual, and Dinkey stood on the platform of Wilbur station watching its engine head-light as it floated towards him through the darkness of the plains in the direction of El Paso.

"Said as she'd be in here to-night — to-night or to — to-morrow," he muttered, hiccoughing loudly.

Truth compels the admission that Mr. Dinkelspiel had had just one glass too many. Not that this had in anyway impaired his faculties, spoilt the charm of his manner, or even greatly affected his speech. Nevertheless an experienced person would have noted the influence of the extra glass. The engine bell rang out harshly in the breathless night, the train drew nearer rapidly; soon it pulled up before him. Only a few people descended, for the Pullman through passengers were all asleep in bed, and the local traffic was small. Dinkey, apparently, was doomed to disappointment; for among the arrivals there was not a single woman. He was on the point of leaving when a young Mexican wearing a broad *sombrero* and muffled in a *zarape* addressed him.

" Mr. Dinkelspiel ? "

" You've struck him, sirree," returned that worthy, eying the speaker curiously.

" You were waiting for me — not ? "

" Not much — not unless you've got a message for me."

" Why, Dinkey ! "

"———! " he exclaimed, and then in more cautious tones, " I didn't know you, miss — "

"José," corrected the young Mexican, quietly.

"Wal, I didn't know you, José, and that's a fac' — not until you spoke up in your own voice. Durned ef I'd got any idee who it was. But, say! what's the meaning of this rig, anyway?"

"Oh, well, if I had come in here in my own dress, they'd have suspected something — Hannaford would, anyhow, and he's sure to be down here directly."

Dinkey nodded, chewing a muttered curse savagely.

"And so, as I speak Spanish, — some of my people back in California were Mexicans, — I thought I'd work this disguise for a little."

"Guess your head was level; you done right."

"Where am I going to stay?"

"At Cow Comers' — it's safest. Cow's a good friend of Ned's — mine, too — an' he won't let on even ef he s'spects who y' are and what our game is. 'Sides," and he glanced again at his companion's costume as they walked along, "Cow has dealin's crosst the line — cattle — and 'casionally has Mexicans come up here an' stay with him, so you won't 'xcite no 'tention there 'n that rig!"

They crossed the station yard to Cow Comers' little board "gin mill" to deposit the bag Rose carried, and then walked up the town in quest of supper for her.

Late as it was, the "China restau*rant*" was open. Indeed, it never was closed day or night, often doing a better business in the small and disreputable hours of morning, among "faro fiends," "poker" players, and similar birds of the night, than amongst its more reputable customers who plied their callings by day. There was nothing unusual therefore in Rose and Dinkey entering the place after midnight and ordering a meal.

The "restau*rant*" consisted of a single room, one side of which was subdivided by board partitions into three private compartments, the entrances to which were hung with calico curtains. Along the line of the opposite wall, were ranged three dining-tables, and lastly, at the back of the room was the little counter or desk where "Pig-eyed Jim," the proprietor, presided, kept his accounts, received orders, and shouted them into the adjoining kitchen through the doorway at his elbow. Although not scrupulously clean, the room was by no means as dirty as it might have been. It was evident that the floor was swept, the table linen changed from time to time. And if the pungent odours of the kitchen were distinguishable, if everything, from the gaudy, blistered, and torn wall-paper through which the bare boards of the walls were visible to the Japanese fan which lay upon each table, was absolutely freckled with fly blows, it was only what the habitués of the restaurant were used to, and therefore was scarcely noticed by them.

When Rose and Dinkey entered and took seats in one of the private compartments, the public room was empty save for a gambler who was on the point of finishing half a grilled chicken and some coffee. A Chinaman soon came from the kitchen to take their orders.

"Whar's Pig-eye?" asked Dinkey, after having, with a decision that bespoke long practise, selected from the list of dishes detailed in a marvellous jargon by the Celestial.

"Him play li'le blit flalo — black allesem dlectly."

"Him play faro," repeated Dinkey, querulously, in the moral mood it pleased him to assume when, as in the present instance, he had indulged in just one glass too many. "Him play faro — all the same 'Melican gentleman, eh? Can't never keep off this gambling. Why ain't he here to 'tend to bizness? I tell yer right now he's going to lose my game if this goes on."

"Me fetchim supper allesem," laughed the Chinese boy, retreating.

"If they ain't the dog-gonedest race of gamblers as is, them Chinamen! And the sons-of-guns wins too, that's what gets me," complained Dinkey, enviously. "If ever *I* sets in to play a stack,[1] it's sure gone. *I* can't never pull out no fifties, nor hundreds, nor seventy-fives, like they do."

"What's the matter, Dinkey?" asked Rose, rousing herself at the sound of his injured tones.

Recognising his condition, she had forborne to discuss with him to-night the matter they had in hand, and had retired within her own thoughts. Not that he was drunk, or even approaching that condition. But his manner slightly betrayed the influence of liquor, and woman-like, for all her frontier experience, she instinctively shrank from going into the subject in greater detail than was necessary for the present.

"What's the matter?"

"Nuthen! — oh, nuthen!" rejoined he, resignedly. "On'y Pig-eye's gambling 'stead of being here to pass the time o' day with his customers."

"Time of *day!* why it's past midnight!"

"Bizness in my judgment shouldn't never relax. S' long as the doors is open, it's bizness hours," remarked Dinkey, with borrowed dignity proper to the sentiment. "Let a man be consistent and he'll b'come cel'brated. Ef bizness ez his pint, he don't want to take no stock

---

[1] A "stack" of checks, or counters.

in gambling. An' if he's a gambler, he don't want to go outside of his profession and 'sociate with no bizness sharps, for they'll call the turn on him every time."

Rose smiled.

"If those are your notions, Dinkey, how is it that you don't take something up, and persevere with it?"

"I hev done so," rejoined Dinkey, sententiously. "I hev took up the perfession of loafer, I done it deliberate. An' I tell you there ain't no occupation ez satisfactory ter look back on ez that of loafer — ef it's consciensushly adopted and systemac'ly carried out. A loafer don't have to look back on no wasted work; 'sides a loafer 'xcites pity, an' compassion, an' char'ty, an' f'bearance, an' rebukes pride, an' ez a warnin' to everbody. Theore — (hic) theorecccly work is useful an' noble, but prac'ly it's degradin' an' foolish. Contemplation's the boss. I become a loafer on princ'ple, and there can't no one say but what I been consistent in my bizness. And what's more, I hev the private satisfaction 'f knowin' 't if I wuz to choose to take my system into bizness, I could lay right over more 'n half of these Smart-Alicks ez is pilin' up money f' their children, an' trouble f' themselves — an' I could do it every time."

But the arrival of their food put an end to Dinkey's discourse, which was perhaps fortunate. For although commenced in his usually mild tones, with the conviction and sense of justice in his arguments, which grows with speech in those who have "partaken" even slightly, the strength of his voice was gradually rising. Given a little drink to start him, a man can easily talk himself into a very fair imitation of drunkenness. Before the meal was over Dinkey had subsided again into his wonted monotone, and they were yet at table when

Pig-eyed Jim, a plump, happy, well-to-do-looking Chinaman, in spotless white, with his pig-tail neatly coiled on the top of his head, returned. A desperate gambler according to his means and opportunities was Jim, and a shrewd one too, like most of his race. But for all that most of his earnings were converted sooner or later into losings by the invincible coolness and deadly percentage of the "bank."

"You gottim slupper allloightee?" he inquired, putting his head in past the calico curtain.

Dinkey nodded, too busy now to indulge in any lecture.

"No wantee nlothing?—nlother genlman no wantee?" and he looked across at Rose in her rough Mexican *vaquero's* costume.

Rose shook her head and Jim disappeared into the kitchen. They paid for their supper presently and left the house.

"Dinkey," said Rose as they strolled up the street, "point me out the jail, and I'll walk round and study the lie of the land there. You had better look through the saloons and see if you can hear anything."

They separated shortly afterwards, Dinkey moving in the direction of the Wigwam Saloon.

He was leaning on the edge of a "craps" table, following each "shot" of the dice with gratuitous observations, but without playing himself save when he could borrow a stake from some winner, when he was roughly grasped by the shoulder and turned round.

Hannaford stood before him.

"Come here. I want to talk to you."

"Wal," drawled Dinkey, "I kin listen to all ez you've got to say 't's of any importance to *me* 'thout takin' my coat off," and he resettled the collar of that ragged garment with an air of dignity.

"Quit fooling, and come here!— get a move on you!" exclaimed Hannaford, savagely, drawing aside as he spoke.

Mr. Dinkelspiel got the slowest "move on him" that was at his command, and sauntered after his interlocutor.

"Where's Rose?"

The loafer scratched his uncombed head under the edge of its dilapidated felt hat, and considered with provoking deliberation.

"What Rose?"

"Where's Wild Rose?"

"How shed I know?"

"She left Dogtown with you."

"Yep — I druv her far's the Santa Fē railway. Ef you'd a mind t' know whar she was heading for, why di'n't you ask her the night afore?"

"I never saw her."

"Why, now, thet's strange," retorted Dinkey, coolly; "I seen *you* tho' — talking along of Mrs. Murray where your buggy was drawed up by the *'royo*, east of town — me and 'nother gentleman happened t' be takin' a *pasear* round thar — Don't do nothin' foolish now!" he interrupted, seeing that Hannaford was on the point of assaulting him, "'cause it ain't such a hell of a ways from here to Dogtown but what you could be reached. And, you bet, some of them Dogtown boys wouldn't want no better 'xcuse for to lynch you 'n what you done last night you was up thar."

Hannaford turned ghastly pale. For a moment he eyed Dinkey irresolutely. Then with a muttered curse he moved rapidly away, for the loafer's usually mild features wore a very truculent expression as he looked his antagonist straight in the face.

It was afternoon on the following day; with his back against the wheels of an old buggy in Cow Comers' back yard, Dinkey lounged, whittling a stick perplexedly. Rose stood before him in her Mexican disguise.

"We couldn't get them from Cow Comers?" she asked.

Dinkey shook his head. "Cow'd help us if he could — Cow'd do 'most anything for Ned, but he ain't got no horses — nor money either. Times is pretty rocky — bed-rocky with Cow just now. 'Sides, miss —"

An angry gesture from Rose checked him.

"— José, I mean. Durn my lame tongue! Ye look a sure 'nough Mexican, too, in that rig; there ain't no cause to make mistakes! But what I was a-going to say was, what's th' use of getting horses till we see our way to fetch Ned out?"

"Leave that to me. Do you know where you can buy cheap a couple of horses — with saddles and bridles — good horses?"

"Will you want to know *where they come from?*"

Rose laughed recklessly; it was a laugh to conjure tears.

"No. I don't want *you* to steal them, but you needn't ask any questions except '*where they're good for.*'"

Dinkey pondered a little, whittling small shavings from his stick with the utmost care and delicacy. "Like ez not Jim Steinway's got suthen out to th' ranch ez he'd be glad to get shut of 'thout any questions asked. They do say ez Limber Jim's gettin' so's he ain't respected much by the ranchers round."

"Go out there this afternoon and see what you can do— Good horses, mind, and you'll have to get the whole outfit for $100."

"I'll go. Do you want 'em brought in town?"

"Not yet—besides, it might not be quite safe—"

"That's so."

There was a pause while both reflected a little.

"Ef you get him out, it'll have to be done at night, I reckon," observed Dinkey.

Rose nodded.

"By the way, who was that I saw on watch at the jail last night?"

"Thet? Why, thet's Quandt, the sheriff of Placer County. And he's a pretty slick old duck. There ain't much show to play Quandty, so I tell you right now. He's a hard game."

"And we couldn't buy him?"

"Oh, hell, yes! buy him easy 'nough ef we'd got the money. But he'd come high. He's got too smooth a job to risk it for a few hundreds. How'd you get to see him?"

"Through the open door when the Chinaman took his supper into him."

"Pig-eyed Jim?"

She nodded.

"Reckon Pig-eye feeds Ned, too—that wouldn't be no bad way to send him a letter."

But she negatived the notion with a gesture. "It would be taking risk for nothing. We shall find Ned ready whenever we are. Does Quandt always take the night watch?"

"Yep."

"And have supper brought into him?

"I guess so — Quandty's fond of good eatin'."

"What sort of a man is that Chinaman?"

"Pig-eye? Pig-eye's a peach!"

"Unscrupulous?"

"Unscrup'lousness is the strongest pint in his character."

"A gambler, you say?"

"Gamble his mother's soul away."

"Then he'll take risks?"

"Wal — yes — " rejoined Dinkey, reflectively, "I reckon Jim 'd take chances — purvided they was balanced with a show at profits — 'nough profits — an' 'nough show."

"He's fond of money?"

"Reach's far for a dollar's any millionaire in th' country."

Rose thought for a little, while Dinkey scratched his bent head pensively with the sharpened stick, and watched her obliquely from under his eyelids.

"Well — well, we'll see," she said finally. "You look out for some horses, Dinkey."

"Thet'll be all right. I'll get them. But see here, ef you're reckoning to rope Jim into any scheme, you can't handle him too cautious. He's slicker 'n an oiled eel, and he'll want all you've got to give him, and more too."

Rose sighed.

"Yes, I suppose he will, but it can't be helped," and she turned to go indoors.

"Oh, say!" exclaimed Dinkey. "Durned ef I didn't 'most forget to tell you — I seen Hannaford last night."

"I saw him myself — passed close to him in the street soon after I left you. Did he speak to you?"

"Yes — asked where you were."

The dark stained face of the young Mexican grew darker still.

"It's lucky for him, perhaps, that he doesn't know," and she turned shortly, and went indoors.

"I guess it is," coincided Dinkey, significantly, as he moved off on his errand in quest of horses.

Rose sought the poor little room she occupied,—it was but a boarded-off pen, the walls of which did not even reach the ceiling. Here she lay down on the rough stretcher which served her for a bed, whilst the passion that had stirred her at the mention of Hannaford's inquiry subsided, and her features waxed stern with hard thought and busy scheming. Finally, overcome by the heat and excitement and worry of the past few days, she fell asleep. But, even then, the disjointed murmurs that broke from her from time to time, the strained lips and anxious expression of the brows, proved that she could scarcely be said to be at rest.

Nothing but force of will kept her going now. She was literally living upon her nerves. For years she had led a life of excitement at high pressure, and her late accident at Dogtown had been a much more severe shock to her system than she had chosen to admit. Rest and complete immunity from all mental stress would alone have counteracted the ill effects of it. She best knew how far she had enjoyed such advantages. The strain was beginning to tell on her now. The fearful headaches and fits of horrible depression from which she had long suffered—and which, at times when she was alone, even led her to contemplate suicide as a relief—had become more serious, and more difficult to shake off. There were moments when she felt that the whole world was against her; when she felt utterly reckless as to what she did or what became of her; when she knew that she was incapable of judging coolly or rationally of anything, and had to exert the utmost self-restraint to keep from doing the most extravagant things; when she realised that the road she was travelling led to madness, and when she looked in despair for some escape. How would it end? Even in her calmer moments she had almost ceased to care. She only hoped and prayed that the end might not be long.

Dinkey returned before she awoke, — indeed it was his knocking at the door which roused her. She let him in, and then lay down again wearily with her cheek upon her hand, to listen to his report.

"I've done fixed it."

"Good horses?"

"Dandies."

"Did you know the brand on them?"

"No, but Jim give me a pinter; he says best not to take 'em up on the Gila."

"How about saddles and bridles?"

"He'll let you have 'em."

"How much?"

"All told? — hundred and ten. Twenty five dollars each for the horses, and thirty each for the saddles an' bridles."

She nodded approval. "What time is it?"

"Half after nine."

"Let's go up to the Chinaman's. I've had nothing to eat since morning. It's just between times, too, and there won't be anybody there. We may get a chance to speak to Jim."

They rose and went out into the street.

"Ain't you takin' big chances in lettin' Pig-eye into this?" asked Dinkey, as they walked along.

"Not as great as they look. I've thought it all over. We've got to give Quandt a sleeping powder. I might try to do this without Jim knowing it, but it would take longer to — to arrange, and there'd always be uncertainty up to the last minute."

"Thet's so. And Jim's pretty slick, he might catch on, an' make you pay as much for holdin' his mouth as he'd take to do what you wanted himself."

"Precisely. Now as he's only a Chinaman he'd get nothing for telling them what I proposed to do, even if they believed him. There's just the chance that they wouldn't — they'd think he was trying to work them for a reward, and beat him up well for his impudence."

Dinkey assented.

"He's smart enough to know all that, too."

"Just so. On the other hand, he has no scruples, he'll do anything for money, and as he's a born gambler it's in his nature to take risks; so the chances are all in our favour."

"Yep, you're right. Wal, let's hope ez he ain't around gamblin' somewheres now," said Dinkey as they entered the restaurant.

It happened that the Chinaman was at home, engaged in making up some accounts in strange hieroglyphics with a reed pen, behind the little desk at the back of the room.

Entering one of the private compartments, Rose and Dinkey ordered supper, and when they were served, bade Jim stay and talk with them.

"What's th' news in town, Pig-eye?" drawled Dinkey.

"Nlews? Why, me takim' out plapers to b'clome 'Melican clitzen."

"Gwine t' get naturalised and become a man 'n' a brother, eh? You don't say! Wal, hope you're going to get your language naturalised, too; for ef you go around talking that duck music when you're 'n Amer'can citzen, some feller 'll kill you sure for libel."

Pig-eye grinned expansively.

"Is that all you got to tell us?"

"Ye', me no lear no nlews; blizns vlely ploor."

"I hearn you got a prisoner here anyway."

"Nled Chlase? Mles. Mshleliff gotim dlown Tlexas, blingim here maybe tlee, maybe flor days 'go. Mlisser Quandty saym gloin' hang Nled Chlase."

"Is thet so? Wal, it 'd be pretty rough on Ned ef he was to hang while you went loose, Jim."

The Chinaman smiled sweetly. "You tinkee? Me no blad mans."

"I reckon you have the feeding of Ned, don't you — gets his meals from here?"

"Mles."

"Hanging's a quicker death 'n that, anyway," observed Mr. Dinkelspiel, sarcastically. "D'ye take Quandt in his supper, too?"

"Mles — evly nightee, me takim fline slupper."

"You want to make some money, Jim?" asked Rose.

"Mloney? You blettee! Me wantim mloney allatime — vlely poor."

'Twas a hard fight. The Chinaman was shrewd. A few hints sufficed to make clear to him what they required, and he had not the slightest moral objection to oppose to it; but he set a high value on his yellow skin, and saw every aspect of the danger likely to threaten it in the matter. "Mlisser Quandty's" summary methods were known to him, and had inspired him with considerable caution. However, he had also a very strong desire for the money offered to him, and the question soon resolved itself into one of price. In the end this was agreed upon, he consenting to take $400, and promising for this to mix such powders as Rose should give him in Quandt's jug of coffee and milk. At the same time he declared his intention of sending off one of his assistants by the night train, in order to divert from himself any suspicion which might arise concerning his complicity in the act.

With her own costume Rose had procured in El Paso a grey wig and false beard wherewith to disguise Ned. With considerable forethought she had also provided herself, in case of necessity, with some sleeping powders of sulphate of codeine. Some of these she now promised to bring to the Chinaman on the following evening.

"And, Jim," she said with a queer smile, tapping her six-shooter, "don't go back on us! No need for any threats; but don't try it."

"*Will* the cuss go back on us, d'y' think?" asked Dinkey, as they left the restaurant.

"Not much! he's too keen about the money."

"Still he might fool us a little mite after he'd gotten it."

Rose laughed harshly.

"I'll meet him on his way to the jail, and fix the coffee myself before I pay him. If he holds back after that — well, I'll frighten him worse than he's frightened of Quandt. I don't *mean* to fail."

To tell the truth, no one observing the decision in her voice as she spoke would have been troubled much with apprehensions of failure in so far as success depended upon herself.

"As to his telling any one beforehand," she pursued, "it isn't likely. He'd get nothing for doing so — unless it were a thrashing for daring to be tampered with. We're safe enough."

"It leaves you mighty little dough to get away with," remarked Dinkey, after a pause. She sighed.

"Yes — yes, we may get him out, but there won't be much to get him away with — unless we hold up a train — or raid a faro table," and she smiled wearily at the idea.

CHAPTER XX.

WITH the morning came Dinkey to Rose to conclude their arrangements. A long discussion ensued, as the result of which it was decided to adopt a bold suggestion made by Rose; viz. that she and Ned should leave Wilbur by the midnight train, joining Dinkey, who was to precede them with the horses, some way down the line, and thus stealing a good march on their pursuers, who would certainly not be long in setting out after them. Some ten miles from Wilbur the railway crossed the Whitewater, a stream always dry except in the rainy season. Here Dinkey promised to await them. Rose, on her side, undertook when they arrived there to stop the train by pulling the cord of the alarm bell. She and Ned would then be able to slip off and hide in the *mesquite* brush until the train had resumed its way, when a revolver shot would indicate their whereabouts to Dinkey. The point mentioned was the nearest on the line to the Mexican frontier. Starting thence, they could before morning be well across the border, where if not actually beyond reach, they would at any rate have left the sheriff's posse hampered with the burden of the international legal formalities to be discharged before it could enter Mexico. In the event of their being prevented by unforeseen circumstances from boarding the train at all, Dinkey was to come down the line towards Wilbur on the chance of meeting them on foot.

Towards evening Mr. Dinkelspiel slunk quietly out of town in the direction of the Steinway ranch. Rose spent the day in her room, where food was brought to her by Cow Comers, who, although aware of her identity and of the object that she had in view, professed to ignore these facts, and treated her merely as a Mexican friend of Dinkey's.

Not until nearly eleven o'clock did Rose move out, and then issuing by the back way, muffled in her Mexican *zarape*, she strolled in the direction of the jail. But here she was doomed to disappointment. The door of the front room occupied by Quandt was wide open, and as she passed slowly by, she saw by the light within a cheery party at the table playing cards.

She passed again, this time a little nearer — near enough to distinguish Hannaford among the players, and note the "stacks of checks" upon the table before them. It was evidently a poker party; and there was, therefore, every probability of its lasting until daylight.

To attempt Ned's rescue under the circumstances was out of the question. Tears of rage moistened the flashing eyes of the Mexican watcher, as the fact was reluctantly recognised by her. For a few moments she still lingered, the expression of hatred that had settled on her face even deepening when, with a derisive laugh, Hannaford threw down a hand and swept in a "pot." Conscious, however, that suspicion might be awakened if she were noticed loitering in the neighbourhood, she soon moved away in the direction of the Chinaman's restaurant, where she waited until Jim appeared carrying a large tray, which evidently contained supper for the whole party. "It's no use trying anything tonight, Jim; there are too many of them there."

"Mlot lyou gloin' do, eh?" inquired the Chinaman, unconcernedly.

"Wait till to-morrow — I'll meet you here at the same time."

"All loightee. Slay! blette' lyou come lestaulant t'mollow — flix um cloffee there allesame."

"Me to come to you there?"

"Mles — more safee."

"All right, I'll come — and mind you wait till I do come. How about your boy going off to-night?"

"Mle klepee here till t'mollow allesame," and Jim went on light-heartedly with his tray, whilst Rose, mad with disappointment, and excitement, and impotent impatience, set out to walk down the line to meet Dinkey.

Even had she ever doubted his capacity for true feeling, the relief he displayed when he learnt that nothing more serious had happened than the actual cause of delay, would have proved it to her. Weary as she was, she thanked him with all the charm of happier moments, and presently set out again to return to Cow Comers', where, worn out with fatigue and excitement, she cast herself down in her clothes as she was, and slept the deep, dreamless slumber of exhaustion until far into the morning.

Another day of intolerable suspense! There were moments during its long hours of torture when she felt that she must shriek aloud, rush out into the streets, and declare who she was and what her business there; do anything, no matter how wild, to vary the maddening bondage of waiting. But as the day waned and the time drew nearer for action, she became cooler.

As before, towards eleven o'clock she left the house, and strolled in the direction of the jail. The door was closed to-night. Turning the corner of the little building, she glanced warily round. No one was within sight, so, stealing softly up to the window, she peeped under the blind, which was not entirely drawn down.

Quandt, a square-built, iron-grey, weather-bronzed veteran, sat near the table in the bare little room, reading a newspaper by the light of a lamp at his elbow. His coat and shirt collar had been removed, his boots were off, and his feet, in socks once white, rested on a chair before him. From time to time his massive jaws worked as he chewed the black stump of a cigar that was in his mouth. He was alone. The door which led to the adjoining room was closed.

Rose crept silently away and gained the shadow of an unfinished house at a little distance from the jail, where she stood still to collect herself. How her heart beat! She half regretted now that she had decided to use the train in escaping. It complicated matters, involved a nice adjustment of time, left something to the element of luck. To be sure, before Dinkey had left town that evening, Cow Comers had ascertained for them that the train was expected to arrive punctually; still betwixt then and now something might have occurred to delay it. But even at the same time as these disturbing thoughts crowded upon her, she became conscious of a growing disregard for them, conscious of the sense of iron will and icy coolness that was taking possession of her.

Dead silence reigned over the little town, broken only by the occasional creaking of a well-windmill near at hand when a breath of wind turned or shifted the bearings of its sail wheel. Once the voices reached her of a broken dialogue between two men traversing the end of the road in which she was — "Done him up. . . . They'd got it in for him long . . . well, all as I know —" and the speakers passed beyond hearing. An opium-fuddled Chinaman toddled by in the middle of the road, muttering to himself. Stray dogs trotted to and fro — one diverged from his course to reconnoitre her. A lame, loose horse limped past. At some distance she could see the light streaming across the street from the open doors of a little Mexican eating-house, or "*tamale* joint"; once some men issued from it, indulging in rough, half-drunken horse-play. And ever and anon the rasping of the rusty windmill grated on her tense hearing.

Here she remained for several minutes, when she deemed that it was time to go to the Chinaman's. The restaurant was empty except for Jim himself, who was behind his little counter with his hands crossed idly upon it, evidently awaiting her. He motioned to her to enter one of the private boxes, and went himself into the kitchen, whence he reappeared with Quandt's tray in his hands. Setting it down before her, he lifted the napkin which covered it, and pointed to the jug of coffee and milk.

"Is it hot?"

"Allesame bloiling."

Rose tasted it with a spoon to see whether it was warm enough for her purpose. Then rapidly producing a couple of little packets of codeine powder, she emptied them into the jug and stirred the coffee until they had dissolved.

"Take that to him," said she, replacing the napkin.

"You glivim mloney nlow?" inquired Jim, politely.

In the preoccupation of the moment she had forgotten this point of the arrangement; but taking a roll of notes from her pocket, she handed them to him.

Pig-eye counted the notes methodically, then depositing them in a place of safety within the folds of his voluminous garments, he removed the tray to one of the tables outside, and calling a Chinaman from the out-house behind the kitchen, bade him convey it to the jail.

"Him glo away t'nlightee," he whispered with a look of significance, as the boy went out with his burden. "Tlouble clome, him dlone it, not Jim," and he smiled sweetly.

Nevertheless Rose deemed it advisable to follow the tray until it should become evident that the bearer of it had no intention of playing her false. Indeed, as Jim had hinted, it seemed likely that he was only an unconscious tool in the matter, whom his master was ready, if necessary, to sacrifice as a scape-goat. Near the door of the jail, therefore, Rose dropped behind, and from a little distance watched him enter and leave it again almost immediately.

A great calmness had come over her now. All her senses were preternaturally alert. She was strung to the highest pitch of excitement, yet possessed with a deadly coolness — strong in the consciousness that she could face certain death without the quiver of a nerve. She was no longer subject to the least feeling of irresolution or of impulsiveness, but was aware of doing everything by the direction of cold-blooded calculation. She could see, weigh, and decide with a clearness and unhesitating firmness that surprised even herself; for the whole mental process, although so swift, was yet so evident, so orderly and logical, so entirely devoid of any influence from instinct.

After waiting for some minutes, she stole up to the window, and peeped in. Quandt had laid aside his paper and, with the corner of his table napkin tucked inside his collar, was already demolishing his supper.

Rose watched the massive jaws at work, marked the ravenous gusto with which he eat, and noted how, with the testy haste which the dry, nervous atmosphere of the frontier begets even in Germans, he slashed savagely with his knife at a fly which was teasing him. Under other circumstances she might have smiled. But the look of strength and decision about the old ogre occupied her mind at present to the exclusion of all other considerations.

Presently Quandt took up his cup and, draining what was left in it, refilled it from the jug. With burning eyes, though her breath came softly and regularly, Rose watched him drink this also some moments later. Then she glided quietly away, and remained at a distance for fifteen minutes by the old watch which she had borrowed of Cow Comers. It was ten minutes to twelve now.

The action of codeine is very rapid. Moreover, it leaves behind it no nausea or other after effects by which its use may be detected. When Rose returned, Quandt was already dozing, with his cheek resting upon his hand.

She watched him for a few minutes. Once or twice he half lifted his head as though vainly endeavouring to shake off his slumber, but at length his arm slid from beneath him and fell forward upon his plate; simultaneously his head dropped and his face was buried in the angle of his elbow. The codeine had done its work.

Five minutes later Rose turned the handle and, entering the room, softly closed the door behind her. She glanced at her watch. It was on the point of twelve. The west-bound train was due at a quarter past, and would probably be a few minutes late. There was no time to lose.

Her first act was almost to extinguish the lamp, so that the room was left in obscurity. Then she approached the door that divided her from Ned, and tried it. It was locked, but a rapid search in Quandt's pockets provided her with the key, together also with the keys of Ned's irons which were attached to the sheriff's belt by a steel chain and clip.

She opened Ned's door.

"What in hell do you want at this time of night, Quandt? — — you! let a man sleep, anyhow!" exclaimed Ned, angrily.

"Hush! it's a friend. Quandt's asleep. Here are the keys of your irons."

Chase was alive to the situation in a moment. He sprang from his truckle bed and took the keys. Rose returned to the outer room to watch.

In a few moments Ned rejoined her, fully dressed. He had removed Quandt's belt and six-shooter, had buckled it on himself, and was in the act of looking round for the carbine, which he knew was at hand, when the sound of voices and laughter was heard approaching.

"Lock that door!" he whispered fiercely, at the same moment grasping the carbine which he had found in one corner of the room. "Lock that door! — they're coming to see Quandt;" and as he spoke he turned the light out entirely.

Rose, he had not recognised in her male attire; indeed, in the hurry of the moment he had scarcely looked at her. All that he knew was that a friend had come to help him.

There was a moment's breathless silence before the voices were heard again close to them — only on the other side of the door in fact. Ned was right; the men had come to see Quandt.

"Oh, Quandt!"

"Let us in, Quandt; we've got a bottle of whiskey."

A little way withdrawn from the door Rose and Ned stood close together. Rose was as motionless as a statue. Ned was breathing heavily. His release had been so sudden and so unexpected, that he had not as yet recovered his usual coolness. But a wild beast had been safer to handle at that moment than he.

"Quandty — oh, Quandty! let us in, the night's young yet!"

"Quandty, you old stiff! open the door; we're losing precious time."

"Quandt, don't you dare to let them in. If you do, I'll never speak to you again!" exclaimed a shrill woman's voice a little behind Ned.

He started. For the moment he thought that it was a woman. Then he realised that the ruse was due to the wit of his companion, and he muttered an exclamation of applause under his breath.

A burst of laughter had greeted Rose's words.

"Crimes! he's got a gal in there!"

"A great old Quandt! That's a good 'un on you, Quandty."

"We'll tell the boys."

"Who is it, Quandty?"

"Dat'll do no'!" exclaimed Ned, gruffly, imitating Quandt's voice and accent. "Enough vas enough! Joost quvit!"

And "quit" they did. The roysterers were not so intent upon fun as to forget that Quandt could be very "ugly" when angered.

For a minute or so Ned and Rose listened breathlessly to their laughter and voices as they went away up the street. These gradually became indistinct, at length were lost entirely. Then Ned relit the lamp, closed the door of his own room, and silently he and Rose left the jail, locking the door behind them.

Free!

"Where to now?"

"Follow me — there's not a minute to lose," said Rose, and, crossing the road, she slipped round the corner of some houses opposite, and led the way rapidly through the sand hillocks and *mesquite* brush at the back of them towards Cow Comers' place, which, as already noted, was close to the station.

In the shed at the back of the house she produced the grey wig and beard for Ned and saw by the light of a match that it was properly arranged, communicating to him meanwhile her plans for their future movements.

"Who are you, anyway? I don't know you, do I?" said Ned.

"No," she answered hurriedly; "friends of yours sent me — sent Dinkey, too."

"Wild Rose did it, I'll bet!" exclaimed Ned, under his breath.

"And look here," she pursued. "I've about got through the money they gave me, bribing the Chinaman to physic Quandt's coffee and buying horses."

"Horses! you ain't coming with me?"

"A little way. But it's fair to tell you that I've only a few dollars left."

"——! Then d——d if I don't hold the train up."

"Hark! there's the whistle! I'll get the tickets. Meet me on the train."

"Which car?"

"The next to the Pullman."

She was gone.

The prolonged, hoarse whistle of an engine was echoing across the level prairie, signalling the approach of the train. In the stillness of the night its rush and rattle could be heard distinctly, growing perceptibly nearer. A minute more and it was already in the station, the buildings of which were on the opposite side of the line to that on which Ned was. In a little while the engine bell sounded again, the train gathered way, and Ned swung himself on to the platform of the car indicated by Rose.

There stood the little Mexican muffled to the eyes in her big *zarape*, her *sombrero* drawn well down over her brows; and next to her, almost touching her, was Hannaford, bidding good-bye to some men on the platform of the station on the other side of the train.

The next moment Ned's ticket was thrust into his hand, and with a backward gesture of the head Rose motioned to him to enter the car. He did so, and took a seat close to the door, Rose taking the one next beyond him. The car was wretchedly lighted and sparsely tenanted, the few people who were in it being scattered about further up the aisle, and either asleep or endeavouring to sleep.

"Yes, right back to-morrow—tell Quandt—I'm only going up to Grainger," shouted Hannaford to his friends as he followed Rose and Ned into the car.

Meanwhile Ned had leant over to Rose and whispered:

"See here, I'm going to uncouple the Pullman coach and go through the passengers. Are you in it?"

"Ned, don't you know me?" it was on her lips to say. She never quite knew what restrained her afterwards — in a few hours more she knew that he must discover who she was.

"Quick! we *must* have money. Are you in it?" she heard him whisper again fiercely.

And mechanically she nodded. "I'll back you."

Is it destiny which sometimes makes a human being acquiesce in an act against which its whole being is crying, "No"? Is it destiny which unstrings all the powers of resistance and makes a human being, without reason or desire, act blindly entirely against the voice of judgment? In this case it might have been that Rose's consent was won by some false and exaggerated estimate of the necessity for money for Ned's safety. She was in no state to judge coolly of anything just then, and she often thought afterwards of that moment and of what followed it with wonder.

A drowsy guard came round and took their tickets; with the exception of themselves and Hannaford — who had taken a seat close to them on the opposite side of the car — every one else was either dozing or asleep.

They had ten miles to run to the White-water *arroyo*, which at the rate the train was moving would be reached in about twenty minutes after leaving Wilbur. Occasionally Ned looked out of the window to keep tale of the landmarks they had to pass; occasionally he glanced from beneath the shadow of his broad-brim hat at Hannaford, whose first sign of recognition would have been his last sign of life. Ten minutes had passed when Chase left the car to examine the couplings. In a few minutes he returned; instead, however, of resuming his seat, he dropped into the one occupied by Hannaford.

"Ain't you got enough room over there 't you want to crowd me?" asked the latter, irritably.

But even as he spoke he felt something hard, like the end of a stick, thrust sharply against his ribs.

"That's my pistol! Don't stir," whispered a voice he knew well, and beneath the grey wig and beard he recognised Ned Chase.

Involuntarily he shrank back.

"Another inch, and I'll kill you." In the grim white face that was bent towards him in the semi-obscurity, he read Ned's meaning more forcibly than it was conveyed even in the curt warning.

Hannaford was almost blue with fear.

"I want you to get up directly and go outside that door. I'm going through the Pullman coach, and I'm going through you, too. Don't utter a sound."

On laboured the train, rattling monotonously. One—two—three—four—five minutes must have passed. To Hannaford they seemed like a lifetime.

"Now!" said Ned, at length, rising and going out into the aisle to make room for Hannaford to pass before him.

The situation was absolutely grotesque. A word would have roused the half-dozen men who were sleeping further up the coach; but Hannaford dare not speak it, for he knew that if he did it would be his last.

Mechanically he rose and moved towards the door, and, beckoning to Rose, Ned followed him closely.

The next moment they all stood outside, in the darkness, and the rush of air, and smoke and cinders, on the platform of the Pullman car, with the door of the other closed behind them.

Ned's first act was to take Hannaford's pistol away from him, and thrust it in the belt of his own trousers. Then he tore his own false beard and wig off and tossed them aside on the track. Stooping down, he grasped the ring of the bolt which locked the couplings, and as a forward jerk of the train took the strain off, it pulled it partly out. Another jerk and he removed it entirely.

Meanwhile at his request Rose had cut and knotted the alarm-bell cord. Lifting the wedge of the crank, Ned next seized the handle and wrenched it back.

The Pullman car, the last car attached to the train, was separated from the others. In a moment more the latter began to go ahead of it. The distance between them widened rapidly. They were left behind.

"Get in there," said Ned, opening the car door, and pushing Hannaford before him with the muzzle of his pistol, he left him in the vestibule under cover of Rose's six-shooter, while he himself entered the smoking-room to rouse the black porter.

Having searched him for arms and keys, he returned and rapidly went through Hannaford's pockets. Then locking them both in the smoking-room, he proceeded with Rose to the body of the car to awaken the remainder of the sleepers. These consisted of three men, two women, and a boy. The women were not disturbed; the men and boy he made stand up in the aisle betwixt the berths.

"Boys, your lives are in your own hands. The first man that makes any break will be shot!" said Ned, tersely.

It was a short matter for him to search their berths

and clothes; for he took only money and from the boy's clothes not even that.

Meanwhile the car came to a standstill in the midst of the prairie, and all had become strangely quiet. Not a man spoke — one fat old gentleman was breathing heavily with fear and excitement, but otherwise only the convulsive sobbing of a woman behind one of the curtains broke the stillness.

The search completed, Ned turned his attention to the drawing-room. Hitherto its inmates, if there were any, had given no sign of being awake. Leaving the others under cover of Rose's pistol, Ned now entered it and found it occupied. The curtains of the lower berth he dropped as soon as he discovered that it was tenanted by a woman. Placing his foot upon the edge of it, he raised himself to a level with the upper berth, and shook the sleeper — a man whose face was turned from him.

"Climb down! — quick! I want your —"

Suddenly he stopped. The sleeper he had roused — considerably older than himself, although strangely like him in face — had turned, half-raising himself, and was looking at his intruder, aghast with wonder.

"Ned!" he gasped.

It was the first time they had met for six years, and thus they met, — the wronged and he who had wronged him.

But Chase recovered himself almost immediately. "Yes, Ned! D——n you, come out here! You're no more to me than the rest. I want your money."

Slowly, like one dazed, the man obeyed and slunk outside, where Rose, who stood there with drawn revolver, motioned to him to pass down into the body of the car and join the others whom she was guarding.

Ned took a pocket-book from under the pillow, and searched the clothes upon the sofa.

Whilst he was thus engaged the curtains of the lower berth were parted swiftly and a woman's face appeared — the face of a fair-haired woman, fresh as a child's is fresh, lovely as a flower is lovely, but startled and full of perplexity and fear.

Ned had finished his work before he noticed her. She was gazing at him, with open lips and eyes dilated, fascinated.

He turned and she breathed his name.

"Ned."

For a second he paused. A bitter smile was on his lips — bitter words hovered there too, perhaps. But, if so, he checked them, and with a glance of scorn, turned on his heel and left the room.

"Come along, that's all!" said he, curtly, and together he and Rose left the car, locking the door behind them.

"Who—oop! Horses!" shouted Ned in the dark.

From a little distance came an answering shout. The car had rolled on past where Dinkey was waiting them, but seeing that it was detached, he had suspected what had occurred and had followed it. In a few minutes more they were mounted.

Brief time had they to spare. Dinkey had to return his own horse to Steinway and show himself in the Wilbur saloons as soon as possible, and the less time Rose and Ned lost in starting the better.

Scarcely a word passed. Rose declined the whiskey flask Dinkey offered, but he and Ned took a pull at it, and then with a hurried grip of each other's hand they separated, and the fugitives struck out, steering by the stars due south for the Mexican frontier.

CHAPTER XXI.

In a hillside furrow, at a point where the *amolia* and *mesquite* bush were clustered a little more thickly than elsewhere in the vicinity, Ned sat watching while Rose slept. Near them their tethered horses, saddled in order to guard against surprise, were grazing — none too eagerly; for they had had a rapid journey the night before and were feeling the effects of it.

Dawn was just breaking, its first red pennant streaming in the east, and Ned, his eyes fixed on the ramparts of the Sierra Madre, of which the elevation he occupied was but a detached outwork, saw ridge behind ridge and peak above peak of that wild world emerge dimly outlined into view and then sink back behind their cloudy curtains for a few minutes more slumber. Gradually the folds of mist parted. There was a moment when one fanged summit alone was fringed with fire, and all the world beside was waiting. Then, with stately march, a burning segment of the sun's disk rose above the horizon, and the glittering earth awoke to greet the day. Soon the broad yellow plains and rugged hills were revealed, and the chain of emerald *alamos* and willows lining the stream which flowed at the foot of the isolated hill whereon the fugitives were concealed, became a striking feature in the landscape.

A coyote, returning from his night's foray, was trotting

diagonally across in front of the little bivouac, when he noticed the horses feeding and stopped to scrutinise them. Ned raised his rifle and covered him, but he did not fire. Cartridges might soon become worth their weight in gold, and besides he did not wish to wake his companion. Suddenly the marauder espied him and set off at a lumbering canter.

Lowering his rifle, the watcher began to roll himself a cigarette, stopping occasionally to follow some absent thought, or scan the plains in the direction whence pursuit might be expected. When he had lit the little, yellow twist of paper and tobacco, he thrust back his hat, baring his hot brows to the morning breeze, whilst he smoked — still in the same preoccupied manner.

Once he turned, and glanced casually at Rose. Half wrapped in her Mexican *zarape*, she lay on the ground, her head resting upon and partly crushing the crown of her *sombrero*. Her face was hidden from him.

It was curious that he should not have recognised her yet; but not the faintest suspicion of her identity had entered his mind. To be sure, hitherto, he had only seen her in the semi-obscurity of an ill-lit railway carriage; and since in the little attention he had bestowed upon the subject he had jumped to the conclusion that his companion was "just some Mexican half-breed sent by his friends to see him safely across the border," he had had no more curiosity about the matter. The sight of the slumbering figure reminded him how little he knew of his ally. Again he looked. "Who was he, anyhow? — and who had sent him?"

Rising quietly, he moved a step nearer to obtain a view of the sleeper's face. Then the blood rushed wildly into his own haggard visage, and he stopped dead.

"Good God, it's Rose!" he exclaimed.

Every line of her face was familiar, every line of it was dear to him. The false moustache which she had worn for the last few days was gone,—lost during the night, or cast away when disguise had ceased to be necessary,—and now her full lips were revealed, parted exquisitely. Beneath the dark fringe of her lashes he noted the deep blue splashes betokening mental as well as physical exhaustion. The morning wind from time to time was lifting the short-cropped tresses from her forehead, but not a movement, not a sound, escaped her. Utterly worn out with fatigue, she lay as one dead.

For one long minute Ned gazed without stirring. Suddenly all that Rose had risked, all that he had led her into, the full misery of her situation, flashed upon him. In one glance he saw and realised everything, and, turning aside, he struck his brows in despair.

He moved a few steps away blindly, for the paroxysm of his anguish wrung his whole frame, and some minutes elapsed before he regained his self-control.

Why had the girl done this? As his thoughts slowly gathered round this problem, the blank look of perplexity in his grey eyes deepened. Was it possible that after all she cared for him? Mad hope! The very suggestion sent the blood tingling through his veins like liquid fire. For one joyous moment he accepted the possibility, for one joyous moment he ruled the whole world of his desire. And then reason laid its cold hand on his heart and he was only a blood-stained outcast again, whom, even when his hands had been clean, she had driven from her with scorn. No; love had naught to do with her motives. They were engendered in the quixotic generosity of her nature—in some chivalrous sense of pity for one who had befriended her, who, in turn, had himself been unfortunate, and whom ruthless men were now hunting to slay. Such an act was but in keeping with Wild Rose's character. But, ah! the misery of it! That an impulse of generosity on her part should have made him of all men responsible for the danger and hardship to which she was now exposed, the charge under which she now lay! The irony of it was cruel. And as he thought again of the face that was lying there, completely unstrung and expressionless save for the faint cast of anxiety, which even in sleep was manifest, the hunted ferocity which had grown of late in his own face gave place to a less sombre expression that was better to look upon.

Rose was the one friend who had stood by him in his hour of need. With that service destiny had locked their fates. For better, for worse, they were thrown together indefinitely. Well, so be it. What a man could do in the circumstances to show gratitude, that he would do by her.

"Ned!"

Rose was awake and sitting up, and as he turned she held her hand out to him.

He took it silently, while she, looking up in his face, saw more there than he could have told her.

"I ought to have spoken — last night — before we boarded the train," she faltered. "But — oh, what's the use! I can't tell you why I didn't — I don't know myself. And then — I had no money — they stole all that you gave me," and rising as she spoke, she dashed aside a tear. "Come! let's be moving. What's done is done," she said coldly.

Ned laughed with a recklessness that he was far from feeling.

"Yes; what's done is done, no good to think about it." And then he looked her in the face and would have thanked her; but what words were there that could have uttered what he felt? "Thank you," he said simply, after a moment's hesitation. She raised her hand. "Oh, you needn't stop me! You've done too much for me to try to tell you what I think."

He brought the horses up to where she stood, and they rode away slowly.

"The sooner we get into the foot hills the better," said Ned. "I know a road there we can follow which runs due south."

By degrees they fell into conversation. None of the recent news of Dogtown had reached Ned; Rose, of course, knew it all. Particularly interested was he in what she had to tell him with regard to Joe and Kitty.

"Gone south! — into Mexico, to farm?" he echoed. "And where have they gone to — didn't you hear the place?"

"A place called 'Floretas' — "

"But Floretas is close here! — we crossed the Floretas road about an hour before we camped. The town lies away off there to the west, in the bend of those brown hills."

"Then that's where they are."

On they rode, forcing the pace whenever possible; but picking their way across country and avoiding roads as they were doing, their progress was necessarily slow. With increasing frequency Rose had recourse to the water canteen which Dinkey had attached to the pommel of her saddle. Ned watched her unobserved, and saw by her air of lassitude, her parched lips and burning eyes, that she was suffering. But the few questions he asked she answered in such a way as to discourage further inquiries; and apart from a wish not to worry her when he could do so little to help her, he durst not say much lest she should fancy herself an impediment to him.

Long before midday, however, he called a halt, pleading — what indeed was true enough, although in other circumstances he might have disregarded it a little longer — that the horses required time to graze. The fact was, he had made up his mind to change his route; for he could see that Rose was ill, and that with very little more hard work and exposure in her present state she would break down completely. Floretas was only about fifteen miles west from where they were, and, dangerous as the loss of time might prove, he determined to seek shelter for Rose with Joe and Kitty until she was sufficiently recovered to pursue her journey. Possibly, she could be safely left there altogether, if she chose to adopt the guise of a Mexican girl, which her intimacy with the language rendered easy; and thus she would be saved all the dangers and hardships she must inevitably incur if once the news of their flight got ahead of them.

The long hot hours of midday dragged slowly by. Most of the time Rose lay in a half-drowsy state, staring vacantly at the cloudless sky. Once or twice she asked Ned whether it would not be wiser for them to push on. But he quieted her with the plea that their horses must have time to feed.

Finally she roused herself and said: "Ned, don't linger here and risk recapture for my sake."

"No fear of that; I'm not doing so," he answered cheerily. "They can't follow us across the border until they have a permit, and that takes time. We're safe enough if the horses don't play out. But we've no corn to give them, so they must have plenty of grass."

"Well — you know best. Only if I find that you are running any risk to spare me, we must separate. There's no occasion for sparing me. My constitution has been my greatest curse; I live through everything."

"And you'll live through this, you bet! — live to forget it all and have a good time yet."

She smiled — a strange, "wearily wise" smile.

"Joe has a farm south of the town, you say?" he pursued.

"Yes — near some river — so Dinkey told me," she replied.

"We'll find it out and stay there to-night."

"I thought you were going to push on south," and she glanced at him keenly.

"So I was, but since Joe's so near I'll go and see him. It's like this: — as far as Floretas I know all the country well, south of that I'm a stranger. It'd be a good scheme to get a few 'pointers' before we strike out — besides, Joe can do a little reconnoitring for us if necessary."

"Well — you know best," she repeated after a pause; "you must know what I shall feel if you're retaken through having solicitude for me, so you'll spare me that if possible;" and with a little tired sigh that went to Ned's heart she lay back upon her *zarape* beneath the scanty shade of a *mesquite* bush.

The sun was already sinking when they set forth again, and it was evening before they reached the river below Floretas — dry now save in places where the water stood in the deeper holes. The question arose as they followed its course in the direction of the town: — which of the little ranch houses that they saw at intervals belonged to Joe? It would have been easy enough to inquire, but Ned was loath to attract attention or name their destination unless obliged to do so.

They had passed two or three places, which from their utterly uncared-for and slovenly appearance they knew could not belong to hard-working Joe, when they came in sight of a cottage which was smarter looking than the rest, and they pulled up in a clump of willow bushes to reconnoitre it. Two well-fed American mules grazing at a little distance from the house, encouraged the belief that they had found the place they sought. Suddenly Ned uttered an exclamation of pleasure. From behind a sand hillock, covered with *cacti* and *gatunias*, a horse had fed into view near the mules.

"We're right. There's old Cocktail — the mare we used to have at the mine. Let's get off here and lie low for a bit. There's a saddle-horse hitched to the snubbing-post in front of the house; it might belong to some one from the Mormon colony near here. We don't want to see any strangers, anyhow; they might prove old acquaintances."

They dismounted in the screen of the willow thicket and watched the house for a while, while their horses nipped the tender tops of the willow shoots. It was getting dark before a Mexican came out of the house, and rode away in the direction of town. Joe saw him off, and then began to give Cocktail and the mules their evening feed of corn.

"I guess we're safe now," said Ned; "but you stay

here with the horses while I go up to the house and make—" He stopped, for glancing at Rose he saw that she was leaning upon her saddle with her face buried in her arms and was paying no attention to him.

"Worn out, I reckon," he murmured pityingly, and with a few cheering words he roused her gently.

It is needless to describe the meeting between Ned and his old partner. Joe's eyes were quite moist as he grasped Ned's hand; it seemed as though he could not bear to relinquish it, and again and again he reiterated that to his last breath and last half-dollar Ned could count on his help.

"And you bet I knew it, Joe, or I shouldn't have tried you in this fix. But I don't want help for myself, it's for Rose—just a few days' rest. Excitement and worry have taken all the strength out of her. I guess she hadn't quite got over that accident when she started out. Rest, now, may pull her round; if she goes on, she'll give out altogether."

"Well, she shall have all the rest she wants right here, and we'll fix you too; you'll be safe enough here for a bit. Say! it's lucky you didn't turn up five minutes earlier, though! There was a mean son-of-a-gun, named Vasquez, here from town—smart as a steel trap he is, too. I tell you, you didn't want to meet him."

"I saw his horse here, and waited. Hold hard! look here, Joe! There's one thing I haven't told you." Ned paused for a moment before he blurted out, "I held a train up last night. Maybe you don't want to harbour train robbers."

"You did!—and you knew where I was, and knew I'd have given you the money you wanted! Ned— But I don't give a d——n if you held up all the country, you'd still be Ned Chase to me; and the only Ned Chase I know is the best friend I ever had."

"Kitty won't mind?"

"My Kitty!" laughed Joe, proudly. "Kitty's way is to help her friends when they need it, not when they don't. You go and bring Rose here and see."

And Joe was right; for never had way-worn, weary woman, a sweeter, kindlier greeting than Rose had from Kitty a few minutes later.

They had never actually met before; for unless trouble assailed them and she could be of service, Kitty held herself aloof from all of her own sex whose lives were not free from reproach. And though none could fix any definite discredit on Rose, her general recklessness, coupled with her calling as a piano girl, had warranted caution on the part of women like Kitty, who were not already acquainted with her. But now it was different, and Kitty took Rose by the hand and led her in, naturally and quietly, without question and without fuss, making her feel that here all the care and kindness which it was within one woman's power to bestow upon another was hers by right. And this without any effort to appear hospitable and good-natured, or even to make her guest realise that she was so.

Poor Rose! All that she cared for was rest. The excitement and physical strain of the last few days, coming upon the heels of illness and of a series of trying events, during years throughout which she had "lived upon her nerves," had quite prostrated her. For the time being all her energy and craving for excitement were gone. Had the fugitives not halted where they now were, her courage and the mental preoccupation of flight might still have sustained her for a little while longer. But once within the shelter of Kitty's house, the power of sustained effort was broken. All that Rose wanted now was rest, and obscurity, and safety, — the rest and safety of the grave, if it would only come.

Kitty shared her room with her. Ned and Joe slept in the open archway which connected the two ends of the house. Most of the following day was spent by the former in the little storeroom that opened into the corral behind. For, though few visitors came to the house, and those few could be seen from a distance approaching by the road either from the north or south, still it was wiser to run no risk of being seen.

To be sure, old Justo and his wife lived close at hand in their little *cajal* in the side of the sand hillock. But Justo was as true as steel and him they trusted, whilst his old wife never left her own "dug-out" unless called by Kitty to aid in some housework. Even had she seen the visitors, it would not have mattered much; for she was a trustworthy, taciturn old woman who had no gossips.

It at once became evident that days must elapse before Rose could be moved. She had absolutely no strength left. She at first was so ill as scarcely to notice what happened, and Ned simply dismissed all thought of the future from his mind. By the time Rose had regained strength enough to take an interest in things, news of their flight had permeated throughout the region, and they were safer concealed in Joe's house than they would have been upon the road. It was easy, therefore, to persuade Rose to remain where she was then until the state of her health should enable her to set out with some assurance of being able to stand the hardships of a journey.

Sweet for her was the rest of those long days! She looked back upon the fever of her past life with wonder and horror. Come what might, never again would she go back to such an existence. Strong influences were unconsciously at work, perhaps, to make this change in her, and constant intercourse with so true and sweet a woman as Kitty Johnstone no doubt counted for something.

During the day neither Rose nor Ned was to be seen about the ranch. But when day was done, they were free to issue forth and sit in those wonderful Mexican twilights — when the sky, quite cloudless save where a few golden reefs were burning low down on the horizon, was dyed with soft rainbow hues of colour, and all the air was steeped in a glow so deep and tender that it seemed to enfold them in its magic. Wonderful, too, was the silence, the perfect stillness of everything. All the earth seemed under its spell. It would have been solemn, even awe-inspiring, had it not been so tender. Yet it was a silence seen rather than heard. For through the peace that appeared to reign, nature's million voices might still be heard by any one who listened.

By common consent all reference to the events which had led Ned and Rose to their present pass was avoided in Kitty's presence. The others might have their dark hours — hours when the weight of the recent past and the gloom of the future seemed to be crushing all hope out of them. But knowledge of the past and apprehension as to the future were alike withheld from the blythe and cheerful Kitty.

CHAPTER XXII.

"Take me," said Kitty when, in answer to a question of hers one evening, Joe had replied that he was "only going to look at the young corn." "Take me," and she linked her arm in his and walked off with him.

"Joe."

"Look here! — and there! — and there again! — just the young tops nibbled off! Those gol-durned rabbits are getting away with more 'n their share of this corn."

"Yes, dear, it's very greedy of them. But Joe —"

"See here, Kitty, you want to starve that pack of dogs you've collected round the house so they'll get out and hunt some of these jack rabbits an' scare 'em off the ranch."

"Yes, Joe — all except Brit. We couldn't turn old Brit out to feed on jack rabbits, because he wouldn't catch one in a week — not even a little baby rabbit in arms, much less one of these great long-legged things that steal the corn."

"Well, I want Brit kept round the house, anyway. What was that you were going to say?"

"Why, Joe," and she got a little closer to him, "nothing — that is, nothing particular, only — Joe, *do* you think she cares for him?"

"Who cares for him?"

"Rose."

"What! for old Brit?"

"Brit! Rose and Ned I'm talking of!"

"Oh ——! Why — how sh'd I know, Kitty?"

"I thought you might have — judged."

"What'd I judge 'em for? It ain't none of my business."

Kitty cast at him that indescribable look of wonder mingled with pity which invariably fills a woman's eyes when the dead wall of man's absence of curiosity suddenly converts into a blind alley some bright path of speculation that she is following. It is useless to attempt explanation in such a case. "He" would never understand! And so evidently thought Kitty in the present instance, for she only answered naïvely:

"Why, no, Joe, I suppose it *wouldn't* matter to *you*, but other people's business does interest me sometimes — and Rose puzzles me. Joe, do you know, I think that hers is the saddest life I ever knew, because — oh, because I'm sure it might have been so different, so — well, beautiful and noble. I never knew a woman who was so entirely unselfish, or had such brave, sweet thoughts about what was right and good. There's something so gritty[1] about her, too; she just brings out all that's best in you; you feel as though you couldn't do anything mean or small while you are with her. And it's so strange, with all this, that she should have led the kind of life she has. Why is it?"

Joe shook his head.

"I guess it ain't — well, I guess I wouldn't go to figuring on her so close as all that while — while she's your guest, if I was you."

"But, Joe! of course I don't mean any harm. I don't want to pry into what doesn't concern me, only

[1] Plucky.

she *interests* me so, she's so different to most women. I feel like a child beside her. And I'm nearly as old as she is. It isn't that she knows such a lot, but — oh, you feel that she has felt such a lot. She stands such a way off you, and all by herself, you don't seem to be able to get to know her — her inner self. It isn't that she ever acts like she was hiding anything, — nothing of that sort, it's only that it seems there must be so much she could tell you if she chose."

" Well, I reckon that her life has been a pretty sad one."

" But so have other people's, some of them."

" Maybe, then, she feels more than other folks. She didn't have a square deal to start with, and she's been paying for her bad luck ever since," said Joe, chancing upon almost the same words once used by Colonel Dodge. " Most folks get shut of their grieving in short order, but I reckon she ain't built that way. She *feels* right along and, maybe, that's what's made her look on the general run of things — things that seems a heap to most folks — as no account ye see ; may be that's what's kind o' put her out o' your range as it were."

Conning in her mind what he said, Kitty merely nodded slowly.

" But say ! " she pleaded again directly, " *do* you believe she cares for Ned ? — poor Ned ! Joe, it makes me almost shudder when I touch him by accident. I try not to, but I can't help it. And I'm *so* afraid he'll notice it. He's so quiet, too, and still — so changed. But there's a look in his eyes that tells you he never forgets for a moment what has happened. His face just seems as though every hope and ambition in him had burnt right out. And yet with it all he looks so brave, so — I don't know; but you wouldn't dare to pity him. Joe, he worships the very ground she treads on, but I'm sure that he's never told her so, and never will now all this trouble's happened. *Do* you think she cares for him?"

"There couldn't no one tell that unless they was to ask her," replied Joe, in his matter-of-fact way. It was not his custom to speculate about other people's private affairs.

"Heavens, Joe!"

"Well, I meant that no one knew but herself."

"Oh, if it was any other woman, of course she wouldn't have done what she's done for Ned unless she did love him," pursued Kitty, reflectively. "But you can't tell anything about Rose. She might have done it just out of pure generosity. What has her life been, Joe? I mean what's the story of it?"

"Oh, I don't know; people talk so much that —"

"Yes, you do know, too! Don't prevaricate! Tell me all about it."

"Why —"

"Well? — go on!"

"Why, I believe, — they say, anyhow, that she run away from school and married Hannaford. And then afterwards she found out that he'd got another wife living."

"Oh, Joe! and she never thought — she never meant to do wrong?"

"I guess not."

"It does seem hard," and the tears stood in Kitty's soft eyes. "And afterwards?"

"Well, afterwards she just quit him, cold. But I reckon that what she'd done, or rather what he'd done, hurt her so badly 't she judged it was kinder impossible ever to recover herself, and so got reckless. And that's how she come to keep along with the life she was leading in mining camps and places."

"Poor Rose," murmured Kitty, compassionately.

They strolled back to the house where the mocking-bird, having spent most of the day in imitating the dogs and cats about the place, was pouring forth its own beautiful evensong at length. It was time for supper, and aided by Rose, Kitty set to work to place it on the table. The nondescript mongrels that enjoyed her hospitality were already gathered in an expectant semicircle before the house. In the centre of the right of way into the *portal* Brit sat on his haunches with his back to the supper table, gazing abroad in a lofty fashion that ignored the whole group of waifs and strays in front of him. He had been forbidden to fight them, and proper self-respect kept him from associating upon friendly terms with dogs of such evidently low lineage. Day was done; the afterglow of sunset endued everything with its tenderest hue, and in this golden setting — a homely picture, but somehow well in keeping with the scene, Ned and Joe stood watching the mules feed.

"Does Kitty still hold to her scheme of going back to the old country by and by?" asked Ned.

"You bet yer!" laughed Joe. "The durned little mule 'd sooner die than give up anything she'd set her mind on. We're sure going to England some day."

"*What* was that you called me? Joe! Joe!!!"

Kitty had come out to call them to supper and had caught the remark.

"*A durned little mule!* Well, I declare! A — a

m—ule! Aren't you a brute to me? Come, brute, come and get your supper. A mule! of all the disgraceful language I ever heard, that's the worst." And she ran off into the *portal* in delight to tell Rose.

Nor was it until the meal was nearly over that she forgave him.

"All right, I'll forgive him," she said at length, in answer to Rose's intercession; "but I won't take him to England now — no indeed," and she launched out into her plans with regard to the scheme in question.

"We're going, no doubt of it — that is, I am, not Joe. And we've got an old prospector out in the mountains now looking for a mine for us," she said, when they were seated under the blue, starlit skies outside, " — that is, *I*'ve got him, not Joe, it's to be my mine — mine mine — because I found the old prospector — picked him up in the road — and I'll give you half, Ned."

"Half the prospector?" laughed Joe.

"No, half the mine — Joe, you won't be in this, anyhow; you're too chipper and rebellious — besides you called me a durned little mule — "

"Oh, but you've forgiven him for that," interposed Rose, smiling.

"Yes, I said I'd forgive him, but I didn't say I'd *forget* it — It's to be a gold mine, Ned; I told him so."

"That was right, Kitty, you showed your foresight there — Joe wouldn't have thought of it. And you may just as well order a gold as a silver mine while you're about it," said Ned, gravely.

"That's what I thought and gold *is* worth more, isn't it? We'll give Rose some of it."

"Shan't we give poor Mr. Johnstone any — not even one little share?" she asked.

"No, not one. Ah, yes, poor old Joe shall have some! — *if he's good*, but he's getting very fractious. I think I feed him too well — or perhaps he's cutting his matrimonial teeth."

"That'll never do; can't allow that," said Ned. "We shall have to pull them as fast as they come."

"Joe, say!" she observed after a while, when the conversation had lapsed somewhat. "You were going out to the States to-morrow to bring in some hogs! — how about that? — have you changed your mind?"

"Why — there ain't no p'tic'lar hurry as I know of," rejoined Joe, slowly.

"No, but what I was thinking was, that if you've *got* to go, why not go while Ned and Rose are here? I shan't mind being left with them — I mean there won't be any need then for me to get some of the folks from the Custom House to come out and stay with me. Besides, if you went now, you might learn something — how things were in fact up in Wilbur."

"That's so," said Joe. "Ned, I guess Kitty's right. It 'd be a good scheme. You're safe enough here, as long as you keep out of sight, and you'd better stay on here a bit longer. Your horses are all right out in the hills along with old Cocktail. They'll never leave her. And if you should chance to want them, Justo knows just where they're ranging, and can fetch 'em in for you in no time. 'Sides, up to Wilbur I could learn what steps they've taken to follow you. I reckon Kitty's right. I'll pull out to-morrow. You stay here."

So it was settled after a little discussion, despite

the protests from Ned and Rose, and the following morning Joe harnessed the mules to his wagon and set out.

It was less than a hundred miles to Wilbur, even by the road; the mules were fat — synonymous on the frontier with being in good condition, — so he expected to arrive at his destination in a couple of days, and in four more to be back at the ranch again.

As for Kitty, her eyes grew moist as she stood waving her handkerchief until Joe's broad shoulders and old straw hat on the wagon seat were out of sight. Then she turned and went about her household work. Kitty was a born farmer's dame, industrious, fond of animals, and an excellent housewife. Single-hearted and innocent, simple yet sensible, always bright and cheerful, her dress was a good index of her character. For nothing could have been simpler than it was, and yet it always looked neat and tasteful; there was always some little bit of colour, some bow, some knot of ribbon about it which gave it an air of *chic* that the smartest clothes often lack. Her pretty figure, exquisite complexion, and winning manner did the rest. Decidedly Joe was a fortunate man;

> "For *Kitty* was a woman most complete
> In all her ways of loving."

Next to Joe, her pride was in her house. And she certainly had the knack of rendering it attractive and homelike at an infinitesimal expense. The Rancho de la Tortuga was wonderfully changed since her reign had begun there. Everything was spotlessly clean now. A rustic bench and a new flower bed graced the front of the house. She was training creepers over the latter here and there. Against the walls hung a cage of doves, and one containing her mocking-bird. Her cat and kittens, Brit and the other dogs, together with a rapidly multiplying colony of fowls, all helped to give the place a lived-in, comfortable air. And though the house was only a small one of *adobes*, Kitty was as happy in it as though it had been a palace. Joyously she sang as she went about her work, and all the world seemed so bright to her that she would not have changed places for an hour with any one.

Once or twice Rose noticed her check herself in full song, noticed her demeanour change, and tears suffuse her eyes.

"Why do you stop singing, Kitty?" she asked one day.

"I forget — I can't help it, Joe's so good to me, and I'm so happy. But it seems cruel to be like that when you and Ned are in such trouble."

"But, Kitty! *Don't* think of that, dear!" said Rose reproachfully; "you'll make me sorry to be here. Think what a pleasure it is to see any one really happy, and how much better it makes one think of the world. Sing — sing all day. I love to hear you."

Rose had begun to recover in a marked degree. It was not without cause that she had sometimes boasted of her constitution. Her exhaustion had been but a forewarning of what was in store for her if her mode of living had not changed. She was very quiet still, and often sat for hours motionless; but strength and colour were returning to her; she took more notice of what interested those about her, and in this little snatch of home life fell into her place quite naturally. A host of gentle and womanly traits were aroused in her that few who knew her simply as "Wild Rose" would have suspected, and many were the little winning services, evincing forethought or recollection, which she performed for those about her. There were times when she followed Kitty about the house as though loath to allow her out of sight, apparently as much interested in her frank and innocent nature, as in turn her own more complex one interested her hostess. Kitty was right when she had remarked how different her life might have been, passed under other influences.

Ned had set himself a hard task, but he never flinched from it, and Rose, though she said nothing, could not but notice what was passing; for she knew that he loved her, and realised how close the watch he kept over himself to spare her the slightest distress on this score. Great deeds and sacrifices are easier to accomplish than the constant trial of lesser ones is to overcome. To preserve uncomplaining calmness day after day when the mind is fraught with despair, filled moreover with the sleepless torture of a luckless love, might have tested constancy of the sternest fibre. Many a man would have yielded under the strain, have cast pride to the winds, and pleaded for his love and love's solace in such case. But Ned never faltered. He was true to himself and Rose. The only evidence of what it cost him was that, as Kitty had remarked, he had grown unnaturally quiet, and looked haggard and worn — years and years older than the Ned Chase of Dogtown.

Woman-like, Kitty longed to know the nature of the feeling which bound these two together, and sometimes she could not resist throwing out a little hint in that direction.

"I am very fond of him," said Rose once, frankly, in answer to one of those ingenuous lures, "but that is all. Tell me," and she looked full at the little housewife, with something strongly akin to moisture in her great, dark eyes, "do you think that lives like his and mine are fit to harbour love? Could you, in his place, ask for the love of any good woman? Could I, in mine, claim the respect of a man with any pride?" Her voice for a moment was hardly firm as she spoke. "Kitty, it would be impossible. I vowed long, long ago never to love again," and involuntarily her hands were pressed upon her bosom, with a gesture as of fear.

"But you might wake some day to find that love had come to you without your knowing it," protested Kitty, with dewy eyes, and in a sweet, low voice. "Let love stay if it comes to you, for love — ah, love is all the world."

An expression of sharp pain crossed Rose's features.

"No, no, I'd sooner die," she answered. "Could there be any more exquisite torture than for a woman whose past is like my past, and who thinks of love as I do, to really care for any one? Her life would be a burden of constant shame."

"Love loves to pardon," pleaded Kitty, gently.

"'Pardon'!" echoed Rose with flashing eyes, and there was something like a shiver in her voice. She paused whilst, as she gazed at Kitty, there came into that glance a something inexplicable, a half smile of sadness, half-absent expression of wonder. "Oh, yes, love loves to pardon faults committed against itself perhaps, but not those faults that went before its day. Love can more honestly forgive betrayal than the knowledge that it was not first." It was not the bitter retort of untamed pride that had risen to her lips at Kitty's words, but it served to cover its suppression. "I'm content," she added, after a pause, "to be with Ned like this, with nothing but friendship between us. I know what he suffers, and it wouldn't be good for him to be alone, he'd only grow more reckless. I give him something to think about other than the past, and I'm sure it strengthens the good in him; maybe it's good for both of us."

And Kitty kissed her gently, somewhat perplexed it is true; for in much of what Rose had said she scarcely followed her.

"Do you know," said Rose, one night, to Ned, "you've never told me anything about yourself, or how you came to be living in this 'wild and woolly' west — you weren't born here."

They were sitting in the soft starlight. Kitty had just gone indoors and left them alone. Ned had been smoking all the evening in comparative silence, whilst the conversation had been carried on by Rose and Kitty — to be more exact, whilst Kitty had talked, and Rose had punctuated her remarks with monosyllables or a word or two here and there.

"'Born here'?" echoed Ned, absently, and he paused whilst through his half-closed lids he seemed to be looking at something far away off in memory. "No, I wasn't born here." He laughed. "I was born a thousand years ago — in another life, another country; I was born some other person. Really it seems like that," and he turned towards her. "It seems sometimes so utterly impossible that the boy I recollect can ever have been me. We seem so distinct, so utterly disconnected, that it makes me stop and wonder whether I'm really awake,

or only dreaming after all when I think of those days.
Things that happened in the old life I remember like
things that I've read about; they don't seem to stir any
feelings in me; they don't appear the least like they were
real," and he laughed again, curtly. "Pshaw! What a
queer thing life is! What does it all mean, anyway?
No; I wasn't born here; I've only been out here about
six years." For a few moments he was silent. "I was
born in New York. My father was a Southerner, a rich
man, too, even after the war. He died when I was a
child, and left everything to my mother. You've seen
my brother?"

"I?"

"Yes; it was he who had the drawing-room in that
Pullman car."

"Ned, don't tell me that!"

"Why not? You needn't mind. I don't. He is the
cause, indirectly, of all that's happened to me. I guess
I was pretty wild as a youngster; I did heaps of foolish
things, but still — well, least said soonest mended. My
mother did it for the best. She trusted my brother completely, and he persuaded her when she died that it'd be
best to leave everything nominally to him — 'so that he
could take care of me and give me my share when I was
fit to be trusted with it,'" and Ned laughed sardonically. "My mother was just one of those sweet, innocent women, who seem born to be the prey of hypocrites
and rogues. She thought she was doing me a kindness.
Well, though it sort o' missed fire, thank Heaven I can
feel grateful to her for all she meant. I was away
at the time — in love, too — at least I thought so.
Eventually the girl I loved married my brother instead. Since then I've never seen either of them

until the other night, when we were on our way down here."

The short, pregnant sentences which finished the story died away, and Ned smoked on in silence.

"And he has made no effort to find you out?"

"No effort was necessary. He knew where I was. Friends of his have business in this country; I've met them often."

"He never even offered to restore what was left by your mother for you in his charge?"

"Not a cent of it — I wouldn't have taken it, anyhow. 'Taken it'! do you think I'd accept anything from him?" he said with bitter pride.

"Ah, Ned, you have been unfortunate," she murmured.

He laughed defiantly, and then as he gazed at the dark face bent earnestly towards him, shadowed and gentle, soft as the starlit night itself in its beauty, his own stern features relaxed.

"I wouldn't change my lot with any one on earth," he said simply.

CHAPTER XXIII.

But few persons ever came near the ranch, and of the approach of those few the dogs always gave timely warning, thus enabling Rose and Ned to secrete themselves before being seen. Vasquez called one day, but Kitty soon despatched him about his business. As already remarked, she disliked him, and, "upon a compelling occasion," her tongue could be sharp and brusque. Once Julian Padilla and Chata drove over from the Custom House to see whether there was anything that they could do for her during Joe's absence. Chata offered to stay and keep her company until his return, and to refuse the offer without hurting the girl's feelings tried all Kitty's tact. But she, laughingly, insisted that this time she had determined to be independent, and see whether she could not stay in the house by herself. Doubtless it would often be her fate to have to do so in the future, and she wished to be so prepared that, when the time came, she could do so with confidence.

Once, towards evening, Old-man Keck, the Mormon, stopped at the house on his way home. He had been "out in the hills with 'the boys,' gathering young colts to halter-break." Keck had done Joe and his wife so many kindly turns that he and Kitty were stanch friends, and they chatted pleasantly for a few minutes, although, as Joe was absent, Keck refused to get off his horse.

"I was hoping to see yer husband, Mrs. Johnstone," said he, at length; "I didn't know as he'd gone out to the States."

"Is there any message that I can give him for you?"

"Wal, it's like this," pursued the old man, after a moment's pause, and as he spoke he looked at her keenly, and glanced round him keenly also, "our folks hev lost a good many horses stolen lately, and they're a-looking for a feller name of 'Slick Pete.' We know as he sold two of 'em up in Silver, 'cause they was traced there with him, and we know as he come back down this way — we done got proof of that, too. Now ef our people gets a holt of him, it'll only be for that once. He'll never steal no more stock, you bet your life." There was a significance in Keck's tone which augured ill for the horse thief if ever he were caught. "Of course he ain't the only dead-beat o' that kind as is working the country, but we're on to their game, and 's I say, it'll be a cold day for any of 'em when we do catch 'em. Now, look at here, Mrs. Johnstone, we're good friends, and I guess we understand one another. You're new in this country; just let me give you a pinter. You don't want t' allow no strangers from the States as you don't know or as can't give mighty good account of themselves to come around and make use of yer, — stop over 't the house, and such like. There's a sight of white trash floating about this country as we've got to get shut of — and we're going to get shut of 'em too, and 's I say, you don't want to let yourself be imposed on, or b'come mixed up with them in any sort o' way."

Poor Kitty! for the moment she was frightened to death. Was he covertly alluding to Ned and Rose? It seemed more than likely. But Kitty was both plucky and loyal, and had all a woman's calm presence of mind in such cases. She still put a good face on the situation, determined at any rate not to betray her friends; and she answered unconcernedly that "It was some weeks since they had had any strangers call at the ranch at all."

"'Strangers'!" laughed Joe afterwards, when she told him of it.

"Well, Joe, Ned and Rose weren't 'strangers'— Ned wasn't, anyhow, and I said 'strangers,' not 'stranger,' so I was quite truthful, wasn't I?"

Joe laughed again as he kissed her. "Do you fool me like that?"

"I'm not going to give myself away," replied Kitty, smiling.

"Wal, so much the better," pursued Old-man Keck; "a lot of dog-gone, lazy whelps, beating their way through the country to see what they can steal, and loading themselves on to hard-working folks that gets their bread honestly! I ain't got no use for 'em, Mrs. Johnstone, no more, I guess, ain't you! If any genuine cowboy, or rancher, comes 'long 'tending to his own business, and wants a meal or a night's lodging, he can get the best I've got, but men as I can't size up and locate can just pass on. Don't you hev none of 'em make use of you. I allowed 's I'd just stop in and tell you this, 'cause the boys when they was hunting colts to-day seen a couple o' strange horses herdin' in 'long of that brown mare o' yourn. The brands don't b'long down here, and they's good-looking horses. In course they may be a couple of strays, but — well, I'd hate for your husband t' be imposed upon, and so's I say, I just allowed to give him a pinter 'bout how things stood. I know durned well as he wouldn't have no horse thief come around the ranch ef he knowed it, — he ain't that kind of a man, — but them fellers is pretty slick talkers some of 'em, and ye want to watch out for 'em."

Without any reflection on her hospitality, Kitty might be excused for feeling intensely relieved when her visitor took his departure. However, she had heard already about the Mormons' losses which he referred to, and before he left felt convinced that there was no covert meaning attached to his warning, and that he had no suspicion that the horses referred to had any connection with the train robbery, news of which had of course reached the country some time before. Still, considering that she had Rose and Ned concealed in the house, she was by no means anxious to prolong a conversation in which at any moment the event in question was liable to be mentioned.

It was the day on which Joe was expected to return, and Kitty and Rose were seated in the former's bedroom doing some needlework, when a chorus of barking as the dogs scurried off to meet some one approaching, took her out into the archway.

In a few moments she returned, with rather a fierce expression on her pretty face.

"It's that brute Vasquez coming again."

"Who is he, Kitty?"

"José Vasquez — a man who lives in Floretas. He's rich for these parts, and has a good deal of influence with the people, — some of 'em, — but he's a bad man, I reckon. He's always coming around, too, when Joe's out. And he looks and says things then that — well, I've had a mind to tell Joe of him more'n once, and I'd do it, too, too quick, only Joe'd break him right in half, and then maybe he'd make trouble for him with the natives."

"Shall I come out and stay with you while he's there?"

"No, no, you stay right here, and just tell Ned to keep out of sight. I'll go 'n' fetch old Justo's wife to stay around till he's gone," and Kitty darted off, out of the back of the house.

Rose heard her return presently with the old Mexican woman, and a few minutes later heard some one ride up to the house.

"*Buenas tardes, señora.* How we go the health, eh?"

"*Buenas tardes, señor.* I'm very busy," replied Kitty, shortly, making a great clatter with some plates that she had begun to wash.

"Beezy, *si?* Always de bizeness. And with what a grace, eh!—de white, white arms *tan bonita. Carambas!*"

"They're none of your business, anyhow!" retorted Kitty, with asperity. "*Adios;* you needn't trouble yourself to get down— *Hasta luego*— good-bye," and she turned her back on him.

"*Como?—Tan de priesa! Carai!* why you so hurry, eh?" laughed Don José, dismounting, and casting his reins over the snubbing post before the house. "*Con permisso, señora*— you no let to stay one *momentito?*" and he seated himself upon the low wall, which, save for the entrance, enclosed the otherwise open archway or *portal*. "*Con permisso*, I smok' one leetle *cigarro*, and then— oh, then I make you de pleasure to go— right 'vay, no?"

Kitty went on with her washing in silence. She was frightened to death lest Ned should come out and break her insolent visitor's head. But though Rose could hear everything that went on, and had determined to call him from the back room if it became in the least degree necessary, she had, as yet, told him no more than that there was a visitor in the portal.

Don José's bold eyes followed every movement of Kitty's persistently, but he was somewhat disconcerted by her brusque reception of him, and found it difficult to maintain a conversation.

"No is return *el Señor* Johnstone, is it not?" he inquired, after two or three failures to obtain any answer to his observations.

"You know that as well as I do," replied Kitty, angrily; "and when he isn't here, I'm not receiving any visitors, that's more; I've told you that before, and I want you to understand it."

"Ah? Zat is a custom of your *encantadora* — How you say dat? — charmings, eh? — of your charmings countrywoman?"

"It's my custom, anyway, and that's enough for me."

"*Esta bueno.* No have to quarrel for dat," he said, throwing away the end of his cigarette. And, rising, he lifted his broad *sombrero* gracefully, and held out his hand. "I have de honour to say you good-bye."

"Good-bye," returned Kitty, partly mollified by his final submission. "I guess I've been pretty rude to you, but when my husband's away I —— you cur!" she cried. "Help! Help."

For as soon as her fingers had touched his own, he had drawn her suddenly towards him, and was now trying to kiss her.

But a door flew open, and a hand was laid on Vasquez' collar. Simultaneously the Mexican was jerked backwards, releasing Kitty in his surprise, and as he did so the barrel of a six-shooter struck him with stunning force in the face, and stretched him on the clay floor.

He picked himself up slowly, staring blankly at the stranger, while the blood streamed profusely from his wounded face.

Ned, for he it was, of course, stood close to Vasquez, but he spoke not a word. He restrained himself with great effort, for he had taken life before, and the terrible lust to kill was on him now in full force. But he only pointed, with a hand that trembled uncontrollably, to Vasquez' horse. With his other hand he gripped his revolver with a grip that left his fist quite white and bloodless, and Vasquez' life hung by a thread.

"For God's sake, Ned! Ah, Ned, don't kill him! Ned! Ned!!" cried Kitty, in terror.

"Go!" gasped Ned, hoarsely. "God d——n you, go!— go!!" he shouted.

And Vasquez mounted in haste. It did not take him long to place half a mile between him and the house.

Ned wheeled short round, and went back into the storeroom.

But the look in his face had made a lasting impression on Kitty; the wild fury and thirst for blood that she had seen in it had been a revelation to her. Had he always been like this?— even in the old days in Dogtown when he had been like a brother to her? Were all men so?— had they all deep down in them such fearful passions as this?

"No, sweetheart," said Joe, when days afterwards she asked him about it; "and you bet Ned wasn't like that once, and wouldn't be now if he didn't count it a terrible thing to have killed those men. But that makes him reckless — aye, worse than that, just blind mad with the fate that druv him to it. Poor Ned!"

CHAPTER XXIV.

TRUE to his promise, Joe returned home that evening. Kitty, who had been watching his approach, met him as he descended from the wagon — Kitty looking so bright and beautiful and happy at the sight of him that, for the moment, at any rate, all the clouds vanished from his troubled face.

"Ah, Joe! the time is *so* long when you're away," she murmured, nestling in his strong arms.

"It's good to have me back?"

"Good? Ah, you don't know — you don't know how I love you!" and she kissed him tenderly again; "you're mine, only mine, and I'm all yours — yours with all my heart and soul! do you care? — are you happy to know it? — yes?"

"Happy? I'd like to see the man who'd better cause to be! Why, Kitty, haven't I got you!" and with his arm round her they moved towards the house. "Tell me what's happened since I've been gone — they're all right?"

She nodded.

"Anything else?" and Joe's honest glance searched her face, for there was that in her manner which made him a little uneasy.

She hesitated.

"Out with it, Kitty — I reckon it won't be any the worse for my knowing it."

"Why, Joe — that man Vasquez was here to-day —"

"And what'd Vasquez want around here?"

"I don't know, Joe — but I was very short with him, and told him to go, and — and as he was going he tried to kiss me."

"To do what?" thundered Joe. "D——n him! d——n him! d——n him! I'll kill him."

"No, no! — Joe! — Ah, Joe, for my sake, no more of that! — not you!" she entreated as she clung to him. "It would drive me mad; I couldn't bear to know that you had killed any one. Besides — listen, Joe! — Ned punished him, Ned almost killed him — he did, dear, really. Ah, Joe," and her voice sank lower as she pleaded with him, "if you love me — ever such a little — keep so that I can be near you without being afraid. You're all I have — my whole, whole world. Who could I turn to if I was afraid of you? Think of poor Ned, Joe — think! Don't let anything like that come between us and spoil all our happiness. I love you so — ah, so much, so much!"

And as he looked at the sweet, wet eyes and distressed face of his wife, the fiercer passions faded slowly from Joe's features, although there still remained a look of determination in them that boded ill for Vasquez.

"Maybe you're right," he said at length reluctantly, as he stooped to kiss her gently; "maybe you're right — God knows, poor Ned's made trouble enough killing those men — but I shall have something to say to Vasquez all the same when we meet — you bet! Are *they* inside?"

"Yes, Joe. What's the news! — is it good or bad?"

"Pretty bad," he answered, shaking his head.

"Poor things!" murmured Kitty, pityingly. "It does seem so hard when such a little would have altered their whole lives, that they should be ruined so utterly."

"It does that," rejoined Joe, as he turned to enter the house. "Call Justo, while I go in and speak to them, for they'll want to hear the news. Tell him to take these hogs out of the wagon and unhitch the mules."

"Well, Joe?"

"Well, Ned?"

"How is it?"

"Oh, I reckon it might have been worse, for they think you're away down below this; they don't have no idea that you're round here. But they're looking for you all the same. That son of a gun Hannaford's putting up most of the money, and he swears he'll get you if it costs him every dollar he's got."

Joe leant his arm against the door-post of the little storeroom in which Ned passed his days. Rose had joined them there, and soon Kitty came, too, and linked her arm in hers.

"The dirty dog!" muttered Ned. "I've given him his cowardly life twice."

Rose's eyes flashed, notwithstanding that she was listening to the news in a curiously impassive manner.

"Yes, he's putting up all the money they want, and he's got men looking out for you all over the country."

"Who gave you pointers?"

"I hunted up Dinkey, as you told me. They all reckon Dinkey such a durned fool, and think they're so smart 't they don't pay no 'tention to him. But you bet he's got as much *sabe* as any of 'em, and he keeps track of all there is to know. He told me everything they was up to, so I was able to go about my own business 'ithout appearing to take any stock in any of it."

"Did you see Hannaford?"

"No, sir! He knew I was in town, 'cause Dinkey heard him talking, but he kept away from me. He was right, too!" and Joe looked "ugly." "It seems they got after you pretty quick some of 'em, and trailed you quite a ways, too, before they lost your tracks. But they seen enough to tell 'em as you was heading south, and I reckon if you hadn't turned off west, and come up here, they'd be pretty close after you by this time. As it is, they're down below here looking for you. There's a posse gone over into Sonora, too; for a report come in that you'd crossed the Sierra, and been seen over on that big 'Cerillo' ranch. Of course they come sneaking round me, Al Whipple and a lot of 'em, to see what they could learn, — Hannaford sent 'em I guess, — but they didn't take nothing by that. I was pretty short with 'em and gave 'em to understand that I wasn't any spy of Hannaford's if they were; still I pulled out of Wilbur so quick that it's just possible there'll be some of 'em down here before long — 'sides, that dirty dog Vasquez has seen you, Kitty tells me — Ned, I'm almighty grateful to you for what you did about that — and you in hiding, too!"

"That's all right, Joe; don't bother over that. See here, what about now? I guess it's time to skin out of this —"

"Yes; if I was you, I'd quit."

"Send Justo out for the horses then, and tell him to bring them in as soon as it's dark."

Joe went to do as he requested, and then returned.

"I've been studying it over, Ned," he resumed, "and it looks like to me that, if you find you ain't able to get through down south, on account of them men watching out for you, your best plan'd be to strike north, and work back into the States. There's risk of course, but you don't have to go so far in the States to get out of sight as you do in this country. Down here you're marked all the time; everybody notices you."

Ned nodded.

"That's so — I've been thinking about that. I'll make a break to get through down south, if possible; but if that road's closed, why, I'll strike north, and get into the Chinacate range, and follow it back into the States. Folks are shy of those hills, because if ever an Apache gets off the reservation, that's where he stays. It'll be the last ground they'll search, and as the Apaches ain't out now they can't trouble us."

"Yes; it's a good scheme," said Joe. "Once you're in the States, too, there's plenty of folks'll help you, if you can get word to 'em. They told me that if you were in Dogtown now, the sheriff wouldn't dare meddle with you. The feeling's very strong there in your favour, and all-fired bitter against Hannaford. See here! there's another thing I was turning over in my mind, too, on the way down: Why shouldn't Miss Carlin stay right here? We can rig her out in some of old Juana's clothes — Justo's wife, you know — and with her head all covered up in one of them blue *rebosos* there ain't a soul on earth'd ever recognise her. She speaks Spanish, too, right like a native. I reckon she'd be safer here than in the hills. To be sure, if they come here, — as they're likely to, now that whelp Vasquez has seen you — for he's just smart enough to catch on to who you are, — they'll be apt to search pretty close. But I reckon we could send her off with old Juana somewheres."

Ned glanced at Rose, who had not spoken hitherto.

What passed in the minds of those two as they looked at one another, it would be hard to tell; the reasons and the impulses of feeling which swayed them for and against Joe's proposition were so numerous and some of them so complex. But out of the medley of them, Rose won her way without hesitation, as true hearts that trust themselves will always do.

"I'll go with you," she said, and she crossed the room to where Ned stood.

And why, none knew exactly, but there the question dropped entirely. Only into the minds of Joe and Kitty there entered at that moment a vague presentiment and sense of sorrow, and Joe's face looked very serious, whilst Kitty's blue eyes filled with tears.

Genuine emotion makes but scant display at parting. The horses were brought in and saddled. A few minutes later Joe and Kitty, Ned and Rose, stood by them under the shadow of the house.

"So long, Joe," said Ned; "you know how I feel about all you've done for me — no need to talk."

"That's all right, Ned. Wish I could have been more use to you. Mind! I'm here whenever you want me," and the small, sinewy palm of the one, the broad palm of the other, gripped one another firmly.

"God bless you, dear," whispered Kitty tearfully, kissing her speeding guest with infinite gentleness.

Rose shook her head doubtfully, and though she spoke no word, her faint smile and the long look of her great, sad eyes as she bent to return the kiss, imprinted her silent thanks indelibly on Kitty's memory.

A minute later they were gone, and Kitty, clinging to Joe's arm, stood with him listening almost in awe to the muffled sound on the sandy loam of their horses' hoofs, heard for some time in the perfect stillness of the night.

"God help them," she murmured earnestly.

"Yes — you bet they need it," said Joe, huskily.

Few men have ever had a more finished and complete thrashing than José Vasquez received next morning at Joe's hands.

Bent on administering the lesson, Joe rode into town and put his horse up in the Custom House *corral*. Then, with the butt-end of a broken whalebone buggy whip, the end of which he had wrapped in order to prevent it splitting, he went in search of his man. It was not necessary to go far. As he issued from the Custom House he found himself face to face with the Mexican. Joe was a man of few words when once he had determined to act. All that he said now was: "I was looking for you." And thereupon he took Vasquez by the collar, and began his task. Quick as thought, the Mexican drew his revolver. But in Joe's hands he was like a boy. The weapon was wrested from him easily and thrown aside. It was warm weather, and Vasquez' clothes were of white linen; the butt-end of the buggy whip was a severe instrument, and neither prayers nor cries availed him. Joe thrashed him until his own arms ached, by which time Don José was almost insensible. Nobody interfered to help him, because, except by the scum of the village, he was feared and hated. Even when, limp as a wet rag, he was cast aside, and for some minutes lay groaning upon the ground, no one offered to help him to rise. And though the immediate cause of Joe's quarrel with him was known only to the men concerned, the verdict in the village was none the less "*Esta bueno,*" wherever the tale of the thrashing was told.

CHAPTER XXV.

An evening or two later, as Joe sat smoking on the low wall that enclosed the *portal* while Kitty finished putting away the things after supper, a Mexican appeared trudging down the road that lay across the farm. For a moment or two Joe watched him before the dogs had discovered him. When they did, the whole pack, with Brit lumbering along in their rear, set off at score to hurl a noisy defiance at him. Brit, however, soon ceased to bark, and trotted up to him in friendly fashion.

"Who is it, Joe?" asked Kitty, abandoning her work for the moment, and coming forward to learn the cause of the disturbance.

Joe shook his head.

"— Looks kind o' familiar, too. Brit knows him, anyhow, so he's all right."

"I'll tell you, Joe!" exclaimed Kitty. "It's old Crispy."

"Justo's brother; that's so. I was bound I knew him somehow. Why, I'll be glad to see the old cuss again. Wonder what he's come for?"

"To tell us that he's found a rich mine, of course! Oh, Joe, won't it be good if he has!"

Joe smiled.

"More like he's come to ask for another grub-stake, or something — a few more *pesos*, I guess."

"Joe! Hush! Do let's be rich for a minute or two,

anyhow. *Como va, Don Crispin?* If I hadn't begun to think that you'd forgotten us entirely!"

Lucero took off his hat while he shook hands with her, and gave Joe the embrace of the country.

"Forget? *No señora, eso nunca!* No forget de true *amigos!*" and refusing the seat Kitty offered him, he deposited on the ground a handkerchief in which something was tied up, and sitting down on his heels opposite Joe, began to roll himself a cigarette, whilst they exchanged further greetings. Presently he exhaled a big cloud of smoke — slowly — luxuriously, and looking up, said:

"*Pues, señor, tengo una mina.* I find ze mine."

"You have, eh?"

"Gold, or silver, Crispy?" asked Kitty.

"Gold, *señora.*"

She clapped her hands delightedly.

"Joe! didn't I always tell you we'd get another?"

"Well, let's hope you're right, Kitty," returned her husband cheerily. "Got some samples there, haven't you?" and he nodded towards the handkerchief.

The old prospector unknotted and spread it open on the ground in silence, while Kitty bent over him, watching every movement of his horny fingers with interest. A small heap of ore samples was revealed. Don Crispin turned them over, and selecting two or three, handed them to Joe, whilst one — a small nugget of pure gold — he gave to Kitty. It was a curious contrast, the impassivity, bronze skin, and age of the one, the enthusiasm, fairness, and youth of the other.

"Look, Joe! look! pure gold!" she cried.

"Yes, but — free gold in lime — that's — that's something I never saw before," he rejoined perplexedly, turning the fragments of discoloured lime over in his hands, and studying them closely.

"*Yo tampoco* — I not see either," said Lucero; "but, you bet, is der."

"This light ain't very good; we'll have to wait till morning to see these properly. What is it you've got, anyhow — a vein or what — what's the formation?"

"On top is *pizarra* — what you call slate, no? — below is *porfido*."

"Porphyry?"

"*Si, señor.* And zis (indicating a fragment of the lime), zis form de *guia* — *de veta*."

"— The matrix — vein matter. Lime, eh?"

"*Si, señor.*"

"Well, it's a queer start to find free gold in it. And the vein, what's that like — is it a contact or fissure?"

"*Es 'contact,' si, señor.* De vein come between de *pizarra*, and de *porfido*, and ze dip is like zis," and he drew a line with his forefinger in the dust to indicate the pitch of the vein.

"How is it mineralised? Is it mineralised throughout, or only in stringers — *hilos*, don't you call them? — and pockets — what are pockets, Kitty?"

"*Bolzas.*"

"*Bolzas; eso es, señor!* — de gold come in *bolzas* and sometimes der is *hilo* dat cross de vein and break off against de *pizara*."

"You're liable to have to do a good deal of dead work then between strikes, and a fault in the contact — which might happen any place — 'd shut you out altogether."

Lucero lifted his shoulders with fatalistic resignation; there is something very Oriental about the older Mexican.

"*Es verdad* — true," he said. "I no say big mines for big company, but good for poor mans. Pay now — right from de top. When no pay — *pues, entonces lo dejaremos* — we leave. *Es posible encontrar* — find pocket *muy rico* — ver' rich. I think we do dat. Con ver' little ore like I find we do pretty well, no?"

At Joe's request, the prospector proceeded to give an account of his discovery. It seemed that gold had been found from time to time in the Rio de las Vueltas, but never in sufficient quantities to make placer-mining profitable there. It had occurred to Lucero to seek the source of this gold, which was evidently washed down from some formation higher up the river. In pursuance of this notion he had followed the stream back into the hills, washing for gold as he went, and shaping his course up those tributaries and *arroyos* in which he found colours of it. At length, he had encountered some fragments of gold-bearing float that afforded a clue to the formation in which the gold occurred, and, guided by these, had finally struck the contact ledge referred to. Here he had sunk an incline shaft of some depth to test his discovery, and reassured to a certain extent on this head, had cached the $700 or $800 worth of gold ore which he had extracted, whilst he himself returned to renew his stock of provisions, make a formal denouncement of the two claims required to cover the property, and request Joe to go out and examine it.

Joe hesitated. From Lucero's answers to the questions put to him, he gathered that the prospect was only about twenty-five miles off, but that the hills in which it was located were so broken that it was impossible to take a wagon into them; indeed, until a trail could be cleared, there were places where it was necessary to proceed on foot. It would be impossible therefore to take Kitty with them on a flying trip there, and after the fright she had recently received, he was extremely loath to leave her alone again.

But Kitty was fully determined that no favourable chance which fortune offered them should be missed owing to Joe's movements being hampered on her account. She offered, if need be, to go and spend the time that he was absent at the Custom House, but said that she would prefer to have one of the Padilla girls come out to the ranch to stay and keep her company. Julian Padilla could then send a *celador*, or customs frontier rider, there at night, and with old Justo to stay close to the house during the day she would be well protected until Joe's return. He would only be absent a couple of nights in any case, and so far as she was concerned there was not the slightest reason why he should not go. In short, she gave him no peace until it was settled thus.

During the next two days, therefore, Joe and Don Crispin made the necessary denouncements at the local government office in Floretas, and having completed such other preparations as the trip demanded, set out for the mine early one morning.

In Justo, Kitty was not by any means left with a merely nominal protector. The old fellow was absolutely fearless, extremely short-tempered, moreover, in any matter that concerned the interests of his master or mistress, to both of whom he was devoted. On one or two occasions when disputes had arisen between himself and neighbours who had attempted to steal things from the ranch, his indignation had been so great that only with difficulty had he been prevented from using his six-shooter. Joe trusted him entirely, and Justo was worthy of his confidence, for a big heart lay in his little wizen body; he was as stanch and plucky as a good watch-dog, and would have given his life in Kitty's defence unhesitatingly. Lucky was it for Vasquez that Justo had not seen him insult her, for he would have shot him for it without a second's hesitation. With him about the house, therefore, Kitty feared no intruder. Besides, she had Chata for company, her chief friend among the Padilla girls, and bright hopes with regard to the prospect that Joe had gone to see filled her mind to the exclusion of anything like fear.

Towards evening Padilla sent one of the Custom House guards on whom he could rely to sleep at the ranch with Justo, and the following evening drove out himself to spend the night there, bringing with him, as well as his guitar, a little present from his mother in the shape of some Mexican delicacy to add to their supper.

Pleasant are the hours spent under the starry skies of Mexico, when the soft air wakes to the music of the guitar, and songs of the south, full of gayety or passion, sadness or bold defiance, mingle with laughter in the mystery of those pearly shadows that lend night half its beauty. Padilla had a fine voice, and apparently an inexhaustible repertoire. Song after song he sang, Kitty and Chata joining with him in their refrains, and often all of them stopping to laugh gayly over some mistake of Kitty's in Spanish. In the midst of one of their pauses, the dogs that lay around them began to growl, and, rising one by one, trotted round to the back of the house. A chorus of furious barking followed almost immediately. But thinking that some prowling coyote or skunk was the cause of their excitement, none of the singers paid any attention to it until, suddenly, the report of a gun, fired in the same quarter, brought them all to their feet.

Padilla dropped his guitar, and drawing his six-shooter rushed through the house to the corral, the nearest way to the spot whence the sound had proceeded. But in a few minutes he returned laughing, with the explanation that hearing the dogs barking upon the sand hillocks at the back of the corral, Justo had gone out there to see what had disturbed them, and unable to discover anything had fired a buck-shot cartridge from the old gun that Joe had left with him, in order, if thieves chanced to be skulking about, to warn them that the place was protected.

Padilla looked graver, however, on the following morning when Justo drew him quietly aside before he left the ranch, and pointed out the tracks of some horses behind the hillocks, showed him where they had evidently been held waiting, and also the trail made by them in coming and going.

However, there seemed but little danger of the visit being repeated immediately, and Padilla was forced to return then to the Custom House where several wagons loaded with goods were awaiting dismissal. Promising, therefore, to send a man out at once to take his place until Joe returned that evening, and bidding Justo say nothing to alarm his mistress and her companion, he drove back to town.

Kitty and Chata, together, could accomplish as much housework as half a dozen hirelings; and laughing and chaffing, singing and talking as they went about their duties had set the house in order within a very short time after Padilla's departure.

With her big sunbonnet on Kitty now went out to the flower bed, and a little way along the banks of the *asequia*, or irrigating ditch, to pick a few flowers and grasses for decorating the rooms. She was returning when her quick eye espied some cattle trespassing upon a patch of corn that Joe had planted about half a mile from the house.

It had just begun to sprout, so that every mouthful that was taken of it destroyed a whole root. The amount of damage that a score of cattle could do under these circumstances was enormous. Woman-like, Kitty was a tremendous partisan, and the sight of "cows in the corn" that had cost Joe so much labour made her furious.

"Justo! Justo!! Justo!!!" she cried.

"*Senora?*"

The old man had been seated in the shadow of the house shelling some of last year's corn for the mules, but at the urgent tone of Kitty's voice he ran towards her.

"*Ganados hay en* — see! there! the brutes! — in the corn — *el maiz. Ande! ande!* drive 'em out. Quick! *Pronto!*"

Justo's anger needed no stirring on these occasions; it was greater even than Kitty's. He at once set off at a dog-trot to do as he was bidden, whilst Kitty herself returned indoors to Chata, who was deftly picking over a heap of *frijoles*, or beans on a towel on the kitchen table.

"Ouf!" laughed the Mexican girl, in mock alarm. "What a anger, to be sure! You tell to kill the cows, eh? — everyone? — and de li'le calves, too?"

Kitty laughed.

"Yes, I'm going to kill the whole herd myself if they come in Joe's corn," she said, sitting down to arrange her flowers in some little vases.

But before doing this she required some water, and rose again with the vases in her hand.

"You want de water? Is empty de pail; I no fill yet. Give me: I go," said Chata.

"No, no, I'll go. You finish those beans, or we shall never get them properly boiled to-day," and with the pail in her hand she went off to the well in the corral.

Chata continued to sort beans. A moment later she heard a little cry, as though Kitty had slipped or were startled. She looked up from her work, smiling, and as she did so a sharp, frightened scream rang out, and another and another.

"Chata! Chata! Help! Cha—"

The voice stopped, choked as it seemed in mid cry.

"*Por Dios! que es eso?*" cried Chata, rushing frantically towards the spot whence the screams had emanated.

She was just in time to see Kitty's form borne by two men through the corral gates, where a third scoundrel stood with drawn pistol and forbade Chata herself to move.

"*Por Dios! Por Dios!*" murmured poor Chata helplessly, as she stood there under cover of his pistol.

A couple of minutes later her guard left his post, and rapidly followed the others. Despite her fear Chata ran after them to the corral gates, and looking out saw the three men and Kitty on horseback moving rapidly away.

Justo had been purposely decoyed away in pursuit of the marauding cattle, and by the time he had learnt what had happened, the abductors of poor Kitty were a couple of miles away. And for the time Justo had no saddle animal at hand, nor any means of aiding his unfortunate mistress.

CHAPTER XXVI.

ENTIRELY in the power of her captors, gagged and strapped in her chair-like *albardon*, Kitty was in a sad plight. They had caught her at the well, one man who was already concealed in the corral when she had entered it having seized her whilst she was hoisting the bucket, and almost before she was even aware of his presence. Rushing through the corral gates, the others had come to his assistance immediately. To gag and bear her to the saddle, place her in it, firmly strap her there, and then urge the steady pony into a canter, was the work of a minute. The whole affair, in fact, passed so quickly that they were already some hundreds of yards away before Kitty recovered sufficiently from her surprise to realise her situation. Then, though unable to cry out, she tore madly at the bridle in the vain endeavour to stop her horse, and tried to unfasten the straps which secured her and to throw herself off even although the canter had become a gallop.

But the brutes she had to do with were good horsemen, and closing up beside her held her hands until they had gained some distance from the ranch, when Vasquez, dismounting, bound them behind her. Thenceforward she was helpless.

"Ah, the preety white arms that you no like to look at them your friends, eh! How strong they are! *Carai!* we must tie a leetle," he laughed, lifting his mask to reveal his face to her for a moment before remounting.

Not that this was any surprise to Kitty, for she had already recognised his voice in the orders he had given to the others. But the actual sight of him, his smile of infernal triumph and his look of still more to be dreaded admiration, brought home to her more vividly than ever the horror of her position.

In Vasquez' power entirely! And it would be a whole long day before Joe could so much as hear of her abduction! There were moments when the sickening fear that possessed her caused her pulses almost to stop, and a chill to strike slowly through her that froze the very springs of life! What was the Mexican going to do with her? Whither was she being taken? It was not long that she remained in ignorance of his intentions, and what she heard was that which she dreaded most.

"Ah, ha! *bonita! corazon de mi vida!* I have you, no?" cried Vasquez, mockingly, at her saddle bow. "Why cry you? No cry, *mi alma*. Am I not here?" and placing his hand beneath her chin, he turned her tear-stained face towards him. "Am I not here?—and I love you, I love you, I love you *mil veces mejor*—a thousand time better than that——, your husband! No cry, Keety! *Vas a ser mi querida*—my sweetheart, no? Ah, *vas a ver que tan*—you shall see how sweet de life in the Sierra! No can find us no one, no one!" and he laughed aloud, spurring his horse fiercely in the excess of his joy.

At the pace they were going the flat was soon crossed. They reached the foot hills and began the ascent. Here, after a little while, one of Kitty's captors drew rein and parted from them to return to town, whilst Vasquez and the other, removing their masks and the gag which had almost choked their luckless prisoner, proceeded more deliberately, although still at a good pace considering the broken nature of the ground.

Ah, that ride! It was one prolonged agony of terror, one enduring pang of despair for Kitty. On they went into those lonely mountain fastnesses, every step bearing her further from help, every step adding to the time that she must remain in Vasquez' power, even if her friends did learn where to follow and ultimately rescued her. What had she ever done that this crushing misery should suddenly fall upon her? And Joe! The thought of him, and the picture of what he would suffer, drove her almost frantic. There were moments when she was quite beside herself, delirious, when she called and screamed for "Joe," — Joe, at least a long day's journey off, — when she wrenched at her bonds until the skin was torn from her wrists and rendered raw wherever else they touched her. Sometimes she would grow calmer and beseech her captors to have pity on and release her, asking what she had ever done to them that they should treat her so; and then again she would become almost insane with passion, and threaten them with pursuit and the direst vengeance of both God and man.

It was all in vain. They only laughed at her. And she cried till no more tears were left her, and the great, dry sobs that shook her convulsively were wrung from her very heart.

She grew so weak at length that Vasquez in tardy compassion released her hands; and when he would have claimed a kiss for the service and she struck him in the face, only laughed and said significantly that she would have time enough to change her mood and atone for the blow.

But he was not always so unrevengeful.

Towards mid-day they halted for an hour. Kitty's captors unfastened the straps that bound her, and lifted her from the saddle. They offered her food, but she did not touch it. They themselves, however, were hungry, and eat and drank well, for a moment or two paying no attention to her.

It was folly — pure waste of effort and she knew it, only despair and the instinct to escape were too strong for her. She rose to her feet, and started to run down the trail they had followed — back towards home was all she thought about. Even had she escaped, she could never have found her way there through the intricate maze of cañons they had threaded; even had she escaped, she would only have done so to lose herself and starve. But that had been better a thousand times than to live in Vasquez' power. However, in less than a hundred yards he had caught her up, lifted her light figure in his arms like a child's, and was pressing her closely to him despite her struggles. And still he laughed as she fought with and struck him.

Not so when the time came for them to start again. Lifting her forcibly into the saddle he surprised and kissed her. She dashed her fist across his mouth and this time hurt him. Uttering a short, foul oath, he started back; his face grew livid to the very lips; then he said not another word while he finished refastening the straps about her. He was free now, and snatching the quirt which hung to the pommel of his saddle, he turned on her with the cry of a wild beast and lashed her with the cruel weapon till her piteous shrieks frightened even himself.

"—!—!—!" he reiterated in fury. "Ah, you do not know José Vasquez! You shall learn him! I am your master now!—you hear?—your master? You shall learn to come like a dog that I embrace you."

But Kitty reaped from the barbarous incident at least this one advantage, that throughout the rest of the afternoon his rage did not abate, so that although from time to time he would shower on her the foulest abuse that the Spanish language and the resources of a foul mind were able to furnish, he did not touch her.

Their ride was continued now without interruption, turning and twisting among the labyrinth of valleys, and *arroyos*, and cañons that intersected the shattered country, until an experienced woodsman would have found difficulty in retracing his steps if unacquainted with the route, whilst Kitty would have found it impossible. Whenever it was possible also, they followed the water up the little streams that fed the valleys, and took such other means as were available for concealing their tracks.

Towards evening they began a long ascent, and it was already late at night when they reached a group of houses far up on a giant ridge. Into one of these Vasquez thrust Kitty.

"*Me veras mas tarde*," he said as he fastened the door outside.

* * * * * * * *

In their endeavour to traverse the country south of

Floretas, Rose and Ned had found themselves subject to perpetual danger. The news of Ned's escape and of the train robbery appeared to have reached everywhere. Even when they themselves were not looked upon with suspicion, they still were apt to hear garbled versions of their own story under discussion. Few things are more curious than the way in which news travels, even in the mountainous and sparsely populated parts of Mexico. Wherever you arrive, you find that your business, all that you have done, together with a good deal that you may have said during the last hundred miles of your journey, is public property. The whole country seemed to be warned against these two, and in less than as many days they had two or three narrow escapes of being detained by village *Presidentes* or *Jefis* of districts whilst messengers were sent to communicate with some one of the posses that were scouring the country. Nevertheless they held on their way with the intention, when, if ever, they should reach Barranca del Oro, of striking west across the Sierra towards the seaport of Guaymas.

To obtain food for themselves and horses they had turned off the road and entered the village of San Diego, which lay in a small valley further back in the hills than ran their direct route. It was about the middle of the afternoon; during the long morning the heat had been excessive, and here, surrounded by bare hills of porphyry decomposed and white upon the surface, the sun's rays seemed to focus and accumulate. In the little store, to which the first villager they met had directed them, they had easily obtained a substantial meal for themselves together with corn for their animals; and now, whilst the latter were feasting on a large heap of *tasoli* in the corral, they themselves were lounging in the deep verandah before the house. Here, no one displayed the least curiosity about them; it was a relief from the strain to which they were usually subjected.

The village was one of those sleepy hollows, common enough in Mexico, which lie off the road to anywhere. There were not even any mines in its immediate neighbourhood; had there been, the inhabitants would certainly have been too lazy to work them. As it was they kept a few animals, and scratched the narrow strip of rich soil along the river-bottom close at hand on which to plant the scanty crops that satisfied their wants; that any one should do more than this would have seemed to them folly. They played hip-ball occasionally, also cards for small stakes; very frequently they got drunk on home-brewed *mescal*. Occasionally one rose up and killed another; after which he was confined in the dilapidated jail for a time. If he tried to escape and was seen doing so, he was shot in the act; if not, when interest in the matter had gradually subsided, he drifted back into society again. The settlement was said to be very old. Possibly the hot springs near it had been the original cause of its foundation. But with the expulsion of the Spaniards the use of these had lapsed — lapsed so entirely that it was no longer known what virtue the medicinal properties that the springs were said to contain possessed.

Like most Mexican villages, San Diego had a certain charm about it. Age, dirt, and laziness are often picturesque, and the age and laziness were there even if, so far as could be seen through the long, low, narrow windows, the houses within looked tolerably cleanly. The village consisted of a single *plaza* in the form of a parallelogram of long low buildings with very deep, brick-paved verandahs or *portals* before them, the slanting, red-tiled roofs of which were upheld by massive octagon pillars of thin burnt brick. Here and there between the houses and in the corners of the *plaza*, were fine pomegranate trees, their deep-green foliage aflame with exquisite blossom. Near one end of the *plaza* stood the church, its low, massive bell-tower surmounted by a dome. It looked older even than the village; for it had probably not been whitewashed for fifty years, and time had peeled even the cement almost entirely off its walls and buttresses. A few complacent-looking sheep lay chewing the cud in its shade, goats and a stray donkey or two hobbled about outside the verandahs, picking up scraps of refuse; but there was not a human being in sight, if one or two sleeping forms in the depths of the verandahs be excepted. San Diego was yet engaged in its rigid observance of the *siesta*.

It was the intention of Rose and Ned to set out again as soon as evening approached, taking advantage of the moonlight to travel by night, a course by which they would not only escape a good deal of notice, but spare their animals the distress of forced marching under a hot sun. They were still discussing the project when a Mexican rode into the farther end of the *plaza* and stopped at one of the houses there. Time passed and the circumstance had been forgotten by the fugitives, when they saw the same man crossing the square on foot towards them.

He entered the *portal* where they were seated, his big spurs ringing as he moved, but otherwise in a curiously quiet manner — a manner that at first sight seemed almost deprecating. This impression quickly vanished, however, in view of the grave deliberation of his actions, the steady glance of his eyes which looked before their owner spoke, and slowly took in everything without betraying the slightest change of expression meanwhile. They were rather unusual eyes — large, extremely sad, and of a very light but brilliant grey, which contrasted oddly with their black pupils and very long, curved lashes of the same hue. His face was thin and melancholy, rather delicate, not handsome; but he had a slow, wistful smile that was very winning. For the rest, he had a brutal mouth, and in person was small, slight, and almost insignificant. He was armed, but that was natural in a Mexican, and he had a soft, agreeable voice that was well calculated to disarm others.

"*Buenas dias, Cabelleros,*" said he, bowing with the natural grace so often noticeable in his countrymen; and despite the coolness of the reception which met him, he seated himself.

He did not say much — apparently he had no great command of conversation. But this did not seem to embarrass him; he said enough to prevent the pauses becoming too prolonged, and in the intervals he studied Rose and Ned, — not impertinently, his glance was too grave for that; besides, when it met theirs he smiled the pleasant wistful smile that seemed natural to him.

However, finally he appeared to realise that he was bearing the burden of conversation almost entirely, and with a laugh was evidently about to make some remark to that effect, when he checked himself and producing a specimen of ore from his pocket, said to Ned:

"*Vd. esta minero, señor,* do me the favour to tell me what that is?"

How did he know that Chase was a miner? — or was it merely a chance shot? Ned looked the speaker full in the eyes as he took the specimen, nor did he withdraw his glance at once even when he held the latter in his hand.

"Tell him this blackish stuff looks like tellurium," he said to Rose, after examining it carefully for a moment or two. Although he understood a smattering of Spanish, he did not speak it much, and Rose always interpreted for him. "It might be very rich in gold, but you can't tell that till you assay it. He'd better get it assayed. If he wants to work that ore, he'll have to roast it before milling it — and roast it very carefully, too, for the gold will be easily volatilised."

"Ah!" ejaculated the Mexican, in a tone of satisfied doubt, and he muttered some comment that ended with a curse between his teeth. "A thousand thanks," he said then aloud. "Señores, I think that you have not great confidence in me," he proceeded with a smile. "As you please, but you have not why to fear me. We are of the same fur (*Somos del mismo pelo*), as it seems. Heraclio Ponce — at your orders," and he bowed gravely as he introduced himself.

The name he mentioned was that of one of the best-known bandits at the time in Mexico. A considerable price was offered for him, dead or alive, by the government, and he was believed occasionally to frequent the district in which the fugitives were now. Report credited him with having committed acts of barbarous cruelty, but he was also known to have performed some that displayed a spirit akin to chivalry.

In a grave and almost fascinating manner he proceeded to tell them that he knew all about them, that he had even fallen in with one of the posses in pursuit of them and had travelled with those gentlemen in the direction of San Diego. The reason that they had not arrived together was because, their horses being stale whilst his own was fresh, he had parted company with them at mid-day and come on by himself. They might, however, be confidently expected to arrive in half an hour or so. It appeared that one member of the posse was a miner by profession, and Don Heraclio had asked his opinion of the specimen which he had shown to Ned. The individual in question had declared it to be worthless, but had afterwards offered to go later on with him and "see if the vein were worth anything."

"Your countrymen often have the fault that they think all others are fools," said Don Heraclio, and he smiled sweetly. "If you had tried to deceive me, I would not have warned you, but now it is different. If you permit me to say to you, in my conception you will do better to go to north, and return to the United States. Here in this *pueblacita* no one knows you, as I think. Below, every one is warned, and they have not better to do than look for you. I know my people. If you go south you will surely be taken — or killed, for what is offered for you. It is not for you as it is for me. The government wants to seize me, but the people are my friends. You see!" and he waved his hand negligently towards the sleeping village, wherein it certainly did not appear as though any one were troubling much about the bandit. "They no molest me. If you wait here half an hour, you will see your compatriots enter by that road" — he indicated the one by which he himself had arrived. "Wait, if you like, but always have your horses saddled and ready. You will still be able to escape, because, as I have told you, theirs are tired out. Perhaps a shot or two — but that does not matter for you," and he looked with frank appreciation in Ned's strong face.

From time to time as he had talked his eyes had rested gravely upon Rose, and though with instinctive politeness he said nothing to indicate that he penetrated the secret of her disguise, he undoubtedly did so.

"*Vamos! un tragito, Cabelleros*, and I am going to retire!" he concluded. "Carlos! The favour to bring the *mescalito*."

The owner of the house to whom he had called appeared with a bottle of *mescal* and some glasses. He filled and handed theirs to them, then, filling his own, drank courteously to their healths.

Whatever might be the case at other times, in his present mood there certainly was an odd charm about this red-handed ruffian with his sad eyes and wistful smile, his quiet, almost gentle manners. With regard to the advice he gave, Ned would have settled the matter promptly had he been alone; for certainly no danger would ever have turned him from his road in his present temper. But Rose was with him.

He glanced at her and said abruptly: "You're a good judge of character; what do you say?"

"Trust him," she answered unhesitatingly.

Don Heraclio bowed to her at the words.

"Ah! you understand English, then?"

"No, *señor* — here and there a word or two, no more, but the eye reads something of all the idioms. You are going to return?"

"Yes," replied Ned, curtly; "what can you tell us about the trails?"

The bandit gave him all the information that he was able to retain, and a few minutes later he and Rose were on the road again.

"Look, Ned! look!" said Rose, whilst they were still mounting the pass which led from the San Diego valley. "He was right; that must be the posse."

Along the road indicated by Ponce, just where it wound up the slope betwixt the river and the village, a body of six horsemen were approaching. They were but little more than dots in the distance, but it was easy enough to distinguish that they did not wear Mexican *sombreros!*

CHAPTER XXVII.

"ABANDONED long ago!—a big mine too, once, to judge from all these ruins."

"How long do you suppose it is since it was worked?" Ned shook his head.

"Look at the trees growing inside those *arrastras!* that'll give you some idea. It's probably an old Spanish mine," and he glanced round him where he sat in the saddle amidst the ruins of an old *Hacienda de Beneficio* of the primitive works in use among the former conquerors of Mexico.

"Why shouldn't we camp here?" suggested Rose, who had pulled her horse up beside him.

He surveyed the scene again doubtfully.

"Not much grass just here—and I don't *see* the water."

"There must be water somewhere, or there wouldn't be all these old *arrastras* here."

"You can't always tell. Some of these old Spanish mines haven't a drop of water now, and you can't see where the old fellows used to get it—made dams, I reckon, and caught it. No doubt there's a choked-up spring somewhere," remarked Ned surveying the neighbourhood again,—"and there's probably grass higher up the cañon. Let's look round here."

They dismounted, and were glancing through the ruins when an exclamation from her companion called

Rose's attention. One of the houses had the appearance of having been roughly repaired within recent years. It was the only one in the group possessing a door or roof. They entered it. Inside were a few Mexican *ollas*, a *matate*, and some cooking utensils. A charred log lay in one corner of the room, above which there was an opening in the roof to permit smoke to escape. But of that they most stood in need, provisions, no sign appeared.

"Kind o' looks," observed Ned, considering the room and its contents, "as though this place was used occasionally — not regularly, for the ground outside's not worn enough. I should like to find the owner's larder."

"He wouldn't leave his provisions in the house, even if he kept any here," remarked Rose.

"No — a Mexican wouldn't carry them far off, though," rejoined Ned. "Let's look a little further."

The other buildings much resembled this one; they were all small-roomed houses, littered inside with the débris of the partly destroyed stone walls. Here and there trees had grown up within them, or they were choked with brush. In one some still live brush partly buried by heavy stones attracted Ned's attention. The stones lay heaped and scattered as though they had fallen from the walls above. But the walls happened to be in tolerably good condition, and it was evident that the stones could not have dropped from them. Ned's suspicions were aroused; he set to work to clear the ground, and in a quarter of an hour had discovered a smugglers' cache containing several packages of manufactured goods from the United States. But with the exception of a sack half full of corn, nothing in the shape of provisions was found. Their stock of *gordas*[1] and dried meat, procured at San Diego, was a slender supply with which to make the long mountain journey that lay betwixt them and the first point in New Mexico where it would be safe for them to leave the hills. However, the corn alone was a treasure trove. It would be invaluable for their horses, and they could crush it between stones, soak it in water, and make of it rough cakes for themselves. As for meat, deer were occasionally to be seen: Ned was a fine shot and he still had Quandt's rifle with him.

"A smugglers' cache undoubtedly," he declared, desisting finally from his search. "Well, it shows that we're on the right trail, anyhow — Ponce said that it was the smugglers' highway from the States. Come, let's go and look for water, and find a good place to camp."

He rose from the ground with the sack of corn on his shoulder, and, returning with Rose to their horses, threw it across his saddle. Proceeding from the *hacienda*, by a little disused trail up the steep cañon, they soon found that a thread of water trickling through the boulders had made in places small pools, near one of which they came to a hollow carpeted knee-high with grass, — an excellent spot for a camp.

Both they and their animals bore the marks of travel. Ned was in worse case than Rose; for, unless utterly wearied out and unable to fight sleep any longer, he did not allow her to take any share in the night watching without which it was not safe for them to camp. Whilst, therefore, he appeared haggard and worn, she, if a little fine-drawn owing to poor fare and hard work, looked the picture of health. The sun could not

---

[1] A corn cake made with lard.

injure her complexion; it only made its clear, warm tinge glow more richly than ever. And now that she was removed from all contact with society, and in constant touch with nature, she had dropped her frontier slang and mannerisms, and was scarcely to be identified with the "Wild Rose" of the Mint Saloon.

Some influence seemed to have stolen into her life that had softened her. Moreover, she felt that, although in one sense unconscious of the fact himself, Ned wanted her; that she was necessary to him and that her influence kept him from the last step towards that fatal plunge in sentiment which would convert him from a man still within shelter of the excuse of misfortune, into a wanton criminal entirely beyond that plea. She knew that her presence softened him and she allowed herself to hope that if they ever escaped, she could win him from the abyss into which he had fallen, to a condition worthier his qualities.

She was in better spirits than was Ned; for she had the consciousness of unselfish aims and hopefulness for the future, whilst the iron of recent events had entered too deeply into Ned's soul not to leave its marks upon his character as well as his visage. As a rule, he was silent — silent often for hours together with a gestureless silence matched only by the passionless expression of his face. But sometimes at early dawn, after the lonely watches of night, Rose had seen in his eyes that which belied all the impassiveness of his demeanour during the daytime. He felt and suffered horribly. There were intervals, it was true, when he was gay, even uproarious. But those moods came upon him as summer wind storms come — the storms that rise so suddenly and seem so unnatural and weird, because their hot breath is untempered by a drop of rain. At such times, too, a steely nature that was not truly his — as yet — glittered occasionally in a look, a word, or gesture through his more normal self; and but that he had Rose's safety to care for, he would have courted danger then and tempted bloodshed; he would have followed the very men who were hunting him, mocked at and eluded, dared and played with them, with a cold-blooded recklessness as devoid of excitement as it would have been of fear. It was little wonder that the hard lines of repression about his brows and lips had begun to settle there, that his eyes glittered restlessly except when they met Rose's. Even then they had not the frank, free look of former days, — the look of the man who knows that his life bears scrutiny.

What Ned suffered at present, — the pangs of wounded pride, the knowledge that his whole life was blasted, — Rose had suffered too, and possibly even more than this. If the outward and visible signs of this suffering were less marked now than formerly, it was not because she had become insensible to her position, but only because she had become accustomed to the pain. She had buried ambition and hope so long ago that she had come to realise that she had nothing to look forward to, nothing to wish in life except to be rid of it. Thus, though Ned had his dark hours, and his fits of mad gayety, she was always the same. The beautiful, colourless face, with its great eyes that seemed to know everything, its sensuous lines, yet its fearless and proud expression, was always tranquil.

It was but little they talked, as a rule; the bond of mutual confidence and sympathy between them was too complete to call for utterance from either. They understood each other perfectly.

Through the *mesquite* bush, and *madroños*, and scattered *maguays*, they had climbed the rough trail from the *hacienda* in silence. A sea of hills lay behind them, here bare as skeletons, there covered with green-velvet robe of pines; and all strangely beautiful now in deep tones of atmospheric colouring, save where the higher points had caught faint lights from the setting sun. Down in the great valley whence rose the hill on which they were, and in numberless other gorges that were visible, the first blue veils and films of evening — scarce as yet shadows of darkness — had begun to grow. Aloft the vast expanse of heaven was filled with small silvery clouds — clouds beyond clouds, in exquisite shades of frosted grey. And here and there amidst them was a rosy stain reflected, a ruddy shred afloat in some open space, alone, like a ship at sea. Light and colour faded swiftly. For a minute or so all was pale. Then purple obscurity filled the valleys with mystery, leaving only the crests of the massed ridges sharply outlined against the afterglow in the sky. And lo! the stars were there; a silver moon hung in a field of blue; the hills had come forth again like ghosts; and it was night.

It was night. Overcome by drowsiness, Ned had fallen asleep after their frugal supper. Rose, glad to take her turn as sentinel without controversy for once, sat with the ends of the lariats in her hands, changing her place occasionally in order to allow the horses to reach fresh pasture.

The cañon they were camped in was but a notch in the great hillside, and they were too near the mouth of it for her view of the expanse of country before and below her to be much impeded. In the exaggerating effect of moon-lit night a whole world seemed outspread there — disguised in a silvery veil of mystery, sunk in a spell of perfect stillness, dreaming an enchanted dream of peace. Once the baying of a grey wolf away to the right, echoed down the valley; occasionally a fox barked nearer at hand; and once, from far below, Rose heard the fitful chorus of a pack of coyotes as it passed. Otherwise, except for the intermittent cry of the dwarf owl, the *cocové*, the fitful movements, and monotonous crunch-crunch of their feeding horses, all was still.

With her arms on her knees, her hands before her loosely grasping the lariats, Rose sat on the ground, a *zarape* thrown over her shoulders. A flood of moonlight streamed into the little opening where she was, revealing her curiously impassive yet tear-stained face. Long enough it was since she had wept for herself; but something in the silence and beauty of the night made her do so now. Her endeavour to help Ned, while it had strengthened and made her happier in one way, had weakened and made her more unhappy in another. For it had awakened in her a host of impulses and feelings which she had thought were dead. Moreover, although it afforded her an opportunity to do brave work of a kind in unison with all her truer and more womanly instincts, it aroused in her an ever-present sense of the failure of her own life, a constant regret for what she felt a kinder fortune might have made that life. From such musings it was but a little journey in thought back to the days in her Californian home, when she had commanded every luxury, had lived in an atmosphere of adulation, ruling alike with her merest whim a strong but unwise father, and an indulgent but selfish mother. And as she compared her position then with what it now was, despite her tears, a low laugh of mockery broke from her. But she checked it on her lips, for at that moment her eye caught the glimmer of a light below her — at the mouth of the little cañon; it could only be among the houses of the old *hacienda*.

Quick as thought she stole towards Ned and awoke him.

"Hush! There's a light down below!"

Ned was alert in an instant.

"Where? Ah! in the *hacienda!*" and he muttered an oath between his teeth, as he realised the trap they were in, for they could not get their horses out of the cañon without going back through the *hacienda;* while, if they stayed where they were, their tracks would be seen on the morrow by the new-comers.

The light below was growing; it was evidently a camp-fire newly started.

"Stay here," said Ned, "while I go and reconnoitre," and he stole away down the cañon.

Drawing near the ruins, he left the trail and dropped into the bed of the watercourse, from the edge of which, where it passed the *hacienda*, a good view was to be obtained of the fire. Here he saw two Mexicans engaged in cooking — an occupation that required the disposal of a good deal of stimulant, judging from the frequent recourse each had to a bottle that lay upon the ground between them. Evidently they were not men whose arrival needed cause Ned any great anxiety, and he would have returned sooner to reassure Rose on this score, had it not been that the sight of *three* horses browsing in the background puzzled him. Where was the third man? For some time he continued to watch in the hope of solving this point, but finally concluding that the third horse must be a pack-animal, probably brought to convey away a load of smuggled goods, he made his way back to their camp.

"If they're smugglers, they'll find out that we've discovered their cache — and have taken their corn."

"So much the better; we can pay them for it. We'll go down there directly."

"Yes, but — Good God! what's that?"

A woman's scream — and again and again it burst forth agonisingly in the perfect stillness.

"Help! help! help! — help! — help!"

"God d——n them!" exclaimed Ned, fiercely; "they've got a white woman there!"

Back down the glen he rushed without another thought or word, followed closely by Rose. No concealment now! Straight as was possible he went through the intervening ruins to the place whence the sounds originated.

The woman was still screaming in broken, exhausted tones that were piteous to hear, and as Ned drew near he caught the undertone of a man's voice cursing her brutally in Spanish.

In another moment the buildings that hid them were passed, and in the open space near the fire he saw a woman struggling — weakly enough now — to resist a man who was forcing her back into the house.

The noise they made had allowed Ned to approach unheard. He was upon Vasquez — for it was he, before the latter saw him, and but for the woman the Mexican held he would have killed him then and there. Vasquez felt the hand upon him, and turning, grappled with the new-comer like a tiger. Hitherto his companion had remained seated by the fire, paying more attention to the bottle than to Kitty and her captor. But suddenly he realised that they were not alone, that there were others upon the scene; he saw the writhing forms of Ned and Vasquez, saw Rose approaching, and supposing in his drink-heated imagination that they had been followed and overtaken, sprang panic-stricken to his feet, fired his revolver into the group, and fled.

Ned felt his antagonist's form stiffen suddenly, his muscles become like steel — for one second — and then as suddenly relax. The teeth that had been fastened in his shoulder parted. Vasquez became a dead weight in his arms, and as they instinctively opened, fell in a heap at his feet.

"Ned! Ned! it's Kitty!" cried Rose's voice at that moment.

"Good God, Kitty! how do you come here?"

And half hysterically, laughing and crying by turns with joy, Kitty told the tale of her abduction.

"And, oh, Ned, when Joe gets back to the ranch tonight and finds me gone, what will he do? — what *will* he do?"

"That 'll be all right, Kitty!" replied Ned, cheerily. "His trouble won't count for anything by comparison with what he'll feel when he gets you back again all safe and sound."

Vasquez was stone-dead. The bullet fired at random by his confederate had struck him below the shoulder-blade and probably penetrated his heart. Ned carried the inert form into the house which the dead man had intended should be Kitty's prison. Then he proceeded methodically to rifle the Mexican's saddle-bags, taking therefrom whatever was likely to be of use to Rose and himself.

When he returned to the fire where the two women had remained seated, Kitty was just finishing the recital of the events in her long day of misery.

"— I broke from him; fortunately the door was not fastened and I rushed out. He caught me again, and then — and then — I don't remember, till suddenly he let go of me, and I found that some one was helping me and I was saved — saved! Ah! Rose! do you know, I feel as if I could just sit and say, 'Thank God! Thank God! Thank God!' all the rest of my life. All those words that have to do with pain and suffering have a new meaning for me from to-day," and the big, bright tears stood in Kitty's eyes again.

But the way in which she had welcomed Rose, only a little while before, when the latter had come to her door weary and ill, had not been a whit more kindly than was the manner in which Rose now strove to comfort her. And as it grew upon her that she actually had escaped, and that she really was with friends, her courage began to return.

"Kitty," said Ned, presently, "I'll bet you haven't had anything to eat all day."

"Eat!" and Kitty laughed hysterically. "How could I eat, Ned?"

"Well, I'll have something ready for you in two minutes. And then the best thing you can do will be to try and get a little rest before daybreak, for you've got a long journey before you — not but what we'll get you home all right."

"*You're* not going to take me?"

"Of course we are, dear," said Rose.

"You bet!—take you pretty close home, anyhow—close enough."

"But if anything happened to you and Rose—"

"Look here, Kitty, it's no good talking. I know, Rose—if I didn't take you she would. Don't say another word about it; it's settled."

"—Beyond all question," added Rose. "Ah, Kitty, don't think worse of us than you can help!"

Before daybreak Ned had everything ready for them to start, but Kitty had just fallen into a fitful slumber; so they gave her a little respite, for she was sadly in need of rest. However, she awoke uncalled a few minutes later, and it was yet twilight when they set out.

Towards noon they met Keck, Bell, and a couple of younger Mormons, together with a half-breed Indian permanently employed at the colony to trail lost horses and cattle, and who, as luck would have it, had chanced to be with Keck's party when the latter met Justo going into town to carry the news of Kitty's abduction.

The Mormons had been engaged in rounding up a band of steers which they had sold, but on learning the news had immediately started in pursuit of Vasquez. The care which he had taken to conceal his tracks whenever opportunity offered, and the fact that night had checked their progress, had prevented their coming up with him. But the half-breed was an unerring tracker, and sooner or later they must have overtaken the Mexican.

Ned gave Kitty into Old-man Keck's charge, merely explaining that he and his "partner" were "prospectors," who had fallen in with Vasquez by chance, and seeing that he had an unwilling captive with him, had released her. To tell the truth, the old man looked a little suspiciously at the strangers, but whatever he thought he kept to himself; for at all events they had done a great service to neighbours of his for whom, in his rough fashion, he had a considerable regard.

"Wal, I hope you killed the son-of-a-gun, anyhow," he said with fervour.

"Why, no," replied Ned, "I didn't; but it so happened that his own partner got to blazing about in the dark, and put a bullet in him."

Keck laughed as though it were a good joke. "His own partner done it, eh? That's a new one on me, sure!"

CHAPTER XXVIII.

THE long days spent alone with Rose in the mountains were to Ned a strange experience of the bitterness and sweetness of life. On the one hand he, an obstinately proud and sensitive man, found himself a fugitive from justice, branded a murderer, and what, according to his southern ideas, was almost worse, a thief. On the other hand there was with him a woman whose lightest touch thrilled him with joy. Daily her exquisite face won more completely on him, daily the picture in his imagination of what "might have been" under happier circumstances became more mockingly enchanting. But at the same time there was a nobility and purity, stanchness and strength in her beauty and her constant bearing, which called forth all that was best in his own nature and made him feel that, even had his love not been irksome to her before, it would be an insult now. The power of self-control grows with use, and in time Ned's task became easier in the sense of self-respect that in his present unfortunate circumstances he had sad need of.

Feeling fairly safe in the Chinacate mountains, where they now were, Ned and Rose were moving northward comparatively slowly. Every day gained in time would, they knew, relax the interest concerning them in the States; and this once stale, they would have a far better chance of being able to conceal their identity when forced eventually to leave the mountains in New Mexico, than if they were to do so sooner.

It was about eight o'clock in the morning; they were leisurely descending a trail which led into a deep but narrow cañon. The way was rough and steep almost beyond belief; the wildness of the scenery exceeded description. To reach the summit of the opposite ascent would take at least three or four hours of hard climbing, yet as the crow flies it was but little more than a quarter of a mile from them. Ned led the way on foot — as indeed to spare their horses he had covered most of their journey lately, vowing that he did so simply because he found it easier work to walk than to cling to the saddle in such broken country. His horse, well trained by this time, followed him like a dog. Rose brought up the rear. There was a workman-like aspect about the couple and their belongings, a look of self-reliance and endurance, that was very marked. Neither horses nor riders carried an ounce of superfluous flesh, yet all moved with an ease and sureness that betokened plenty of reserve strength. Attached to Ned's saddle were their few utensils, — tin cups, an *olla*, and a canteen. Its saddle-bags were fairly distended, and the remainder of their corn was balanced loosely across it in the sack. Ropes of jerked venison hung in festoons from the pommel; for Ned had killed a black-tail deer a day or two before, and had dried a good deal of the meat.

"So that's what you'd do if you were a queen, eh?" he said, half laughingly, pursuing some conversation that they had drifted into.

"That's what I'd do. Pride may be one of the deadly sins, but much of the virtue we do see is due to it, while charity does more harm, speaking generally, than avarice. For charity — gifts that there is no hope of ever repaying — must sap the spirit of independence. And what is a nation without pride or independence. The strongholds of a nation are its people's hearts."

"Everything in your philosophy depends on self — personal effort, self-control — "

"Everything," she answered, with a flush of unwonted colour in her cheeks and full, soft lips. "True freedom lies in self-control, true happiness in your own heart. The heart is the only real alchemist," and she smiled softly; "some hearts turn everything to gold."

Ned strode on down the rugged trail in silence, but her smile seemed to have found a reflection in his eyes, and for a little while the set sternness of his habitual expression vanished.

"Looks like a good mineral country, all this," he said presently, glancing with the eye of a prospector over the mineral-stained cliffs and hills of the opposite ascent; "that hill 'paints' like gold," and he pointed to a rich red spur that dipped precipitously down into the valley bottom.

"Which?" asked Rose, drawing as closely to where he had paused as the narrow trail permitted.

He pointed it out to her.

"And, see!" he added, "that line of rock running uphill — looks like a big snake in the distance; if that isn't the outcrop of some vein, I don't know one!" He resumed his walk, often glancing towards the spur in question as they descended lower and lower into the valley, and remarking, "A likely hill — durned likely — good colour — lots of iron there, and an iron cap is a good sign. Bird's-eye porphyry, too," and he glanced around him again at the formation. "The best mines in the Sierra Madre are found in bird's-eye porphyry."

There are few stronger passions than that which possesses the miner. A genuine prospector would stop at the gates of heaven to examine a ledge.

"Let's go a little way up the cañon and look at those croppings," said Ned, when they had reached the bottom at length. "If they *are* croppings, and not some big porphyry dike, they're phenomenal."

"Let's go," returned Rose, smiling; "we might find a big mine."

"It would be just like my luck to do that," he observed bitterly.

They were watering their horses at the stream, and he had stooped to fill her canteen.

"You don't believe in luck?" he said, looking up at her.

She shook her head. "We make our own luck."

Through the profuse vegetation of ferns and creeping plants and brilliant flowers, through *cacti* and waving *otates*, beneath spreading *higueras*, *hilatis*, and maples, past *mimosas* with their lace-like foliage, and mighty boulders, gaunt and bare, amidst which flashed fleet humming-birds and fluttered gorgeous butterflies, they picked their way towards the spur they had noticed. Here and there they lingered gathering *pitahayas*, — the luscious fruit of the candelabra-like cactus of that name.

They had reached the neighbourhood of the croppings when Ned stopped and pointed silently.

"What is it?"

"Don't you see? — the vein breaks right across the river — you can trace it there up the opposite hill. Eight or ten feet broad if it's an inch! — and a true fissure! See here! — here it is right in the river-bed."

It was as he said. The vein was clearly traceable to the water's edge and distinguishable beneath the crystal ripples. Betwixt porphyry walls the decomposed and discoloured quartz, of which it consisted, showed distinctly for a couple of hundred feet or more in the hill on the opposite side of the river they had just crossed.

"The same lode," muttered Ned, turning from it to glance again at the croppings he had first noticed.

He threw the bridle of his horse over the pommel of Rose's saddle, and walked towards the partly dry bed of the river, where the vein was most easily examined, stooping to knock some pieces off it with a loose stone, as he drew nearer and nearer to the water's edge. There by the constant action of the current the quartz was worn and washed clean, and in places he saw the free gold flashing like jewelry in it.

All the eagerness had faded out of his face; it had grown dark and gloomy. He was silent; he did not move. Rose called to him once, but he did not hear her.

"My luck!" he murmured finally, as he stood up, "my cursed, damnable luck! A year ago this would have changed my whole life! Ah!" and he looked up at the serene, blue heavens above, with a gesture of impotent passion that yet had something pathetic in it.

Rose's voice was raised again calling to him. He turned to go, but, pausing, stooped again to break off a fragment of quartz in which the richness of his discovery was splendidly displayed, and washing it once in the sunny waters, rejoined her with it in his hand.

Rose glanced at it with interest. Coarse gold was scattered throughout it; one of the nuggets was as broad as a ten-cent piece.

"Ned!" she exclaimed in astonishment, "what a magnificient specimen!"

"Yes — and a true fissure in bird's-eye porphyry! No superficial vein that 'll give out in a hundred feet! You could go down on that — that's a *mine!* — the sort of prospect a man sees once in a lifetime, and most men never. Look how that vein runs! look at the breadth of it! look at the wood and the water power! look how it could be tunnelled! There's millions there!" and he threw out his arm with a passionate gesture. Then a little short laugh broke from him, and shrugging his shoulders slowly he muttered: "Well, life's a queer business."

"Do you care so much?" asked Rose, looking him full in the eyes.

And as he met her glance, a dark veil seemed to be drawn suddenly from before his face, it's expression changed so completely. "Care? No, I only thought I did. What is there in a gold mine, after all!" and he laughed the clear, frank laugh, not heard since the old days at Dogtown.

She handed him back the specimen, and he was on the point of casting it away when she checked him.

"Stop! Don't throw it away, you may be able to send Joe Johnstone here; it may do them some good even if you can't use it."

"That's so, you're right. It's just like you to think

of it. I would give anything to do Joe and poor little Kitty a turn. There's a couple you can bet on."

"Yes, truer friends than they are not met often."

"Once in a way they are, though. I know one," and he glanced at her brightly.

"Go on," she laughed; "we've got that long hill to climb yet."

Soon after noon they reached a little upland valley which ran at right angles to the cañon, filled with pines and cedars, interspersed here and there with the *encina roble* — whose broad leaves change their dark green for a beautiful red-lacquer tone before they fall; and the lovely *madroño* — that weird, antidiluvian-looking tree with its trunk of frosted silver, its snake-like, fleshy arms of coral and amber hue, its emerald foliage.

Having tethered their horses to graze, they chose a shady spot for their midday camp, commanding a view of the trail by which they had descended the opposite side of the valley.

"Are you going to light a fire?" asked Rose, seeing that Ned had begun to collect a few sticks.

"Why not? If pursuers have trailed us thus far, they'll trail us farther, whether they see the smoke or not. Besides, there won't be much smoke with this dry wood — and as they can't get across the cañon under three or four hours, we've always got a start of them even after they come in sight."

With some of the corn, soaked over night, which they had taken from the smugglers' cache Ned made a couple of rough cakes, and while they were cooking in the embers, he took some of the dried venison, brayed it between two stones until it was like picked hemp, and with a little of the venison lard which he had melted and preserved, warmed it in their frying pan. *Pitahayas* and water completed their frugal meal.

It was afternoon. The soft voice of the *Coa*, the jewel-plumaged queen of the Sierra birds, was calling not far off. From a distance came the melancholy, monotonous cry of a dove; two blue *urruaches* were chuckling garrulously in a big oak tree; a chipmunk was playing hide-and-seek on a fallen cedar trunk near at hand, whilst a couple of pretty grey squirrels reconnoitred the strangers curiously from the offing. In the blue above a hawk sailed lazily near the summit of a ridge on the right, whose fringe of dark green pines stood out beautifully against a bank of silver clouds. Down below, the cañon was choked with rich waves of colouring formed by the luxuriant undergrowth and trees. Beneath the oaks and cedars round their camp the myriad splashes of winnowed sunlight, mingled with the shadows of foliage, lay on the sward like scattered coinage of bright gold and discoloured silver. And with here and there a breathless pause, rising and falling in waves of sound, the restless wind swept on with that subdued, expectant, far-away roar peculiar to the forest.

Neither Rose nor Ned had spoken for a long while. Her face was thoughtful — serious even, and yet there was in it an expression, a light almost of exaltation. Nothing could have been more beautiful than its exquisite softness in that moment.

"Do you know I believe that nothing dies in this world unless — unless it has touched evil," she said softly, breaking the silence between them.

Lying at full length on the ground, with his chin resting on the palm of his hand, he had been watching the opposite trail lazily.

"Death's no less sure," he answered, turning his face towards where she was seated.

"I think, for instance," she pursued, without noticing the cynicism, "that a love that is true — a love that is never sullied by selfishness or passion — that is used only to forward the nobler aims which love reveals to us, and resist the temptations to which it is subject will never die. It will live on and be resumed again and again in later lives, helping and strengthening always those that feel it, so that gradually they win and are won by each other towards the way that leads to final happiness. There must be some rest, some goal to end all the trials and sufferings here — don't you think so?"

Whether her fanciful suggestion drew any serious assent from him or not, his iron-grey eyes were full of musing softness as he answered:

"It's a beautiful thought, at any rate."

"And don't you think that what is beautiful in thought is generally true?"

She had turned and was gazing across the valley before them, her clean-cut profile outlined against the fallen cedar trunk whereon the chipmunk played.

"Think!" he echoed passionately. "I think with you — with all you say! You are like a religion to me."

She was silent, and sat there quite motionless for a little.

"You think these are dreams — a woman's fancies," she resumed; "well, perhaps so. But you don't know what a woman's fancies mean to her. If she hadn't them, what would she do! — weak in purpose and in character as she is — impulsive, quick to feel and act — most that she does quite unpremeditated, it would be bad indeed for her if she had not something to fall back on when a breach of the accepted law has made an outcast of her," and she turned and looked at him in a way that seemed to trust him with her whole history. "But a woman has ideals and fancies of her own — trivial enough sometimes perhaps, but which she clings to and which preserve her power for good long after she has grown indifferent to the judgment of the world. Many a woman whom the world thinks utterly reckless has at heart certain tests and faiths that she wouldn't be false to to save her life."

Was what she had said a warning to Ned not to mistake the motives which had led her to accompany him in his flight? or was it merely the natural cry of a woman with whom the world had dealt hardly?

There was a long silence between them. Leaning back against the oak beneath which she sat, her hands locked round one knee, Wild Rose sat gazing straight in front of her. Her *sombrero* was tilted over her eyes, and it was difficult to see whether she was watching the trail, or only buried in thought. Her cheeks were pale, and the expression of her mouth almost harsh. Ned had not stirred. From time to time he glanced at her in silence, whilst every mood that crossed his mind was reflected in the thin face and haggard eyes that betrayed his perpetual unrest. Despite its recklessness and determination, it was a face that could no longer be looked upon without compassion.

At length a sigh, almost of relief, escaped his companion.

"There they are!" she said simply.

The remark was so quiet and so irrelevant that, at first, he fancied she must be thinking aloud. But following her glance, he saw that it was fixed upon the opposite side of the valley, and discovered at once to what she was alluding.

The figures of some men on horseback — Americans — were coming through the pines near the far edge of the cañon.

"Get back among the trees; they haven't seen us yet!" he exclaimed, and the ruthless look of a hunted man whose life was at stake, and who had his enemies at his mercy, came into his stern face. "We have them now!"

He knew, and she knew, too, that if he waited until they were half-way down the cliffs they had to descend, their escape would be impossible; he would be able to pick off every man of them at his leisure.

Their eyes met for a second, and then Rose stole back to where their horses were picketed, to wait for him.

For a few moments Ned crouched there on the ground watching the party file over the edge of the cañon. His hands, meanwhile, were unconsciously fingering the rifle he held, and his face revealed the bitter conflict that was taking place within him.

Rose watched him from a little distance. The men passed out of her sight, but Ned could still see them and had not stirred. Suddenly he rose and came hurriedly towards her.

"Let's go," he said hoarsely. As he spoke she sheathed the pistol she had drawn. He noticed the act.

"What were you going to do with that?" he asked with a strange look in his eyes.

She shrugged her shoulders.

"If you had fired at those men in cold blood, I should have — left you," she answered coldly.

A few moments later they were pushing forward at a pace that defied pursuit.

CHAPTER XXIX.

It was early morning. At the foot of the hills near the summit of which Rose and Ned had bivouacked lay a small mining village. Beyond it the yellow plains, like a field of cloth of gold in the sunlight, stretched out towards Indian Peak and Painted Mountains in the East. The fugitives had come out of the Sierra at length.

On first discovering that they were followed, they had struck west in order to deceive their pursuers as to their objective point, winding and turning among the hills, and using every stratagem to obliterate their trail, and put their enemies at fault. Not until after some days — during part of which time even they themselves had lost their bearings — did they turn their faces fairly eastward again.

That their wanderings had brought them some distance north of the Mexican frontier line they knew well enough, but the exact point they had reached was a matter of doubt to them. Until this was settled they would willingly have avoided venturing into any village; but their necessities had become imperative. Not only were their horses entirely worn out, but for several days game had been scarce, and their supply of dried meat was exhausted. Before proceeding further they had to obtain remounts and procure provisions. It was their intention then, if possible, to gain some point on the Mid-Southern and Oceanic Route, there turn their horses adrift and take the train, proceeding eventually across country into Canada.

"I'll go down alone and reconnoitre," said Ned, after some discussion as to their best course of action and conjectures as to the name of the village below them. "If I'm not back in a couple of hours, you can ride down and join me as though you had merely dropped behind; that is, unless you chance to hear shots. And then — Ah, Rose, it was a bad day for you when you met me!" he said sadly.

She shook her head, ignoring his last remark.

"Ned, it's useless to try to shield me from danger," said she, with a winsome smile. "We're so situated that you can't do it without leaving me in a worse fix than ever. Besides, what do I care for danger! — you know that. Fate is fate. We'll take our chances together as we have done right along. The boldest course is the safest course now. Let's ride down together naturally — just as though we had come through the hills from Arizona."

"We look too 'tough' for that; it's evident we've come off a hard trip."

"But I don't look any 'tougher' than you do," she returned with a smile, as she began to coil her horse's lariat preparatory to mounting.

"Hold hard! I've got a notion that this place is Bedrock, where Doc Stovall has his mine. That's the point I've been steering for, anyhow; and if we've struck it, we're all right. Doc 'll help us. But we mustn't give ourselves away unnecessarily. It's well known that there are two of us in the hills. If one goes into town alone, it will be less likely to excite suspicion than if we both go."

She smiled, for she did not believe a word of it. "Take me," was all she said, but she said it in a way that she had never spoken to him before.

He hesitated, but finally refused again.

"Better not," said he. He knew only too well that their long journey in the Sierra had given them a way-worn, ragged appearance liable at any moment to excite a curiosity that might prove very dangerous. "Better not; it will be safer for me to go alone."

"Well, I'll wait for you here then. Good-bye," and they shook hands hurriedly as though each was afraid to linger over it.

But there was something in her voice that rang in his ears all the way as he rode down the hill — "Good-bye — good-bye;" something that he had never heard in it before — something that awoke a feeling of strange, fierce joy in him.

Trailing her lariat behind her, Rose moved off, leading her horse, and sat down at some little distance from the road — sat quite still, shading her eyes with one hand, whilst she watched the figure riding away from her through the yellow grass and the dark green live-oaks scattered here and there. A strange light shone in the girl's eyes, for all that they were shaded from the sun — a light which now flashed eagerly and now smouldered with infinite softness as Ned went on, sometimes lost to sight for a moment behind the oaks, and sometimes clearly marked against the yellow plains below.

At one point the trail passed close to some rough lumber buildings that sheltered the hoisting works over the shaft of a mine. An engineer stood loading his pipe at a window.

"What's the name of this burg?" shouted Ned, pulling up for a moment, and pointing to the cluster of *adobes* and board houses below them.

"Wyman," came the answer.

"'Wyman,'" muttered Ned, as he rode on. "Further south than I thought we were. D——n the luck! we ought to be fifty miles north of this."

As he neared the village, two miners going uphill to their work, passed him on the road, and eyed him curiously. It must be confessed that his appearance was calculated to excite, at any rate, some passing attention. Unlike Rose, who was scarcely touched by the sun, he sunburned very easily, and his face had become almost as dark as an Indian's. Handsome enough he looked still with his level brows and straight features, keen eyes, and the little pointed beard that he had grown of late; but his reckless and haggard face, the skeleton condition of his horse, and his weather-stained and ragged clothes, spoke of rough travel and prolonged sojourn in the hills. Ned looked a "hard case" and the miners noticed it; they even turned and glanced after him when he had passed.

"Ef a man wuz lookin' fur trouble, I reckon he could find it right thar," said one of them, dryly.

"You bet yer! I'd go around that duck like I'd go around a mud hole. He's tough," rejoined his companion.

A woman was drawing water from a well close to the first house in the village. If you have a question to ask on the road, always put it to a woman. She is quicker to seize your meaning than a man, and readier to impart information. To tell all she knows, in fact, is the one impulse stronger in a woman than curiosity. Curiosity comes first with a man. Ned asked her if there were any store in the village.

She directed him to the only one it possessed — at the end of the village, and thanking her he rode on before she had time to question him.

Stopping at the frame house she had indicated, he fastened his bridle to the rail for that purpose in front of it, and entered.

Sacks of flour and corn were stacked along the wall on either side of the doorway; a rough board counter ran the length of the room; behind, shelves partitioned off and reaching to the ceiling, were filled with canned goods and bottles, bales of calico and cotton stuffs, together with all the thousand and one articles that go to make the stock in trade of the one store in a village. No one was present when Ned entered, but the sound of his footsteps brought a young man out of the inner room.

At the sight of Ned he stopped short in the doorway.

"Ned! — by gosh! I never reckoned to see *you!*"

Ned was silent.

"D——n it! shake, old boy," cried the other, gladly. "——! but you're looking hard!"

Ned looked at the hand extended towards him and then back at the speaker's smiling face.

"Jimmy Hannigan," said he, "if you're going to sell me out, I don't want to shake hands with you."

"Why, g'long, Ned!" returned the storekeeper, reproachfully. "What's gone with you? When'd you ever know me to go back on a fellow? I know the fix you're in, but that's none of my business. I ain't forgotten the time you stood by me when I was 'tending bar over to Lone Mountain. If you hadn't shoved in and clumped Cherokee Bill over the head when them fellows was on to me, I wouldn't be here now, would I?

Well, then, shake and don't think I'd go 'n' sell you out. No, sir! What 'll you drink?" He pushed a glass towards him.

Jimmy Hannigan was an Irishman of about thirty, a smart, good-looking, and industrious fellow with a wife and a couple of pretty children. He had been a bartender, but had been induced by his wife, a New England girl, to leave the business — fortunately too, as it happened for him, for he was now making money rapidly in the store he had set up at Wyman. Prosperous and naturally warm-hearted, happy in his family ties and fortunate in other respects, he was far more disposed to aid than side against any one, and in the present instance, as already mentioned, he was under an obligation that he had not forgotten.

Ned saw that he could trust him, and did so. In a few words he stated his position and necessities.

"Well, we can fix you," said Hannigan. "Can't get you no horses right here, but there's an old fellow, name of Burke, has a little ranch 'bout eight miles up the river — lives there all alone — a queer old stiff — comes in here 'casionally to get his mail and bill of goods, but don't never speak to anybody. Money talks, though — and gets an answer from him every time. If you've got any dough, you can get all the horses you want from him, and if you're short of money, why you can get it right here. As to provisions, only say what you want, that's my business now. Jimmy Hannigan don't forget his friends, no, sir. Is that your horse outside?"

"Yes — you might give him a little corn — not too much, for he isn't used to it."

"All right; bring him around to the corral at the

back— Hold hard! Whoa! Who's them fellows stopping here? They're new to me. Say! get in behind here — quick! You don't want to see any strangers. Ruthy!" said he hurriedly to a sweet-faced, delicate-looking woman in the inner room into which he had thrust Ned, "this gentleman saved my life once. He wants to lie low for a bit, while some strangers are in the store."

"Leave the door ajar," whispered Ned as he went out.

From where he was Ned heard the new-comers enter the store; he heard the whiskey called for, and the toast, "Here's how," uttered in a chorus of voices.

"Led's hid her anoder lick," said some one then.

And Ned's air of impatience vanished. He became at once keenly alert. He knew the voice.

"Led's hid her anoder lick! Oh, Pink! you best ged in here right 'vays, or you geds left."

"I'll go you!" cried some one outside, and the next moment he, too, entered and joined them.

They asked for some breakfast. To provide meals was part of Hannigan's business; he could hardly refuse them therefore without its seeming strange, besides he saw a way while they were eating to get Ned and his horse away.

In his hurried visit to the back room to tell his wife to prepare what they asked for, he arranged for Ned to slip out of the back of the house as soon as the meal was ready, and while they were eating inside to come round to the front of the house and get his horse.

"Do you know who they are?"

Ned nodded.

"Looks durned like a sheriff's posse."

"After me," replied Ned, laconically.

"Well, listen all you can and lie low. They ain't taking any chances, you bet! — ain't even left their rifles outside."

"Is that your horse?" asked one of the posse when Jimmy returned to the store.

"What horse?" said Jimmy.

"That there one hitched outside along with ours."

"Oh, that! — no. Belongs to a fellow in from one of the ranches round," Ned heard Jimmy reply, unconcernedly.

Apparently his interrogator began to look about him for the individual in question, for Hannigan added: "He ain't here, he's gone down town somewheres."

"Durned if it don't look in pretty poor fix for a ranch horse, all the same," resumed the first speaker, suspiciously; "looks a sight more like it 'd come off a journey."

"That's what," coincided another, who had gone to the door to look at Ned's nag.

"You bed! — and a preedy, gol-durned hart journey, too," observed the owner of the voice that Ned had recognised. "Say, young feller, whose is dat horse, enyvay?"

"Don't I tell you! — belongs to some fellow working out on Tim Townley's ranch," responded Hannigan.

"And he's gone up town, vat?"

"— Few minutes before you come in; gone to sell a beef to some of the miners."

"Vell, I joost like to see dat feller, enyvays."

"You can do that, too, if you wait for a bit."

"You bed, I vait."

"He'll be back here before you're through breakfast."

The speaker went outside, followed by one of the others. Evidently some consultation took place there between them, for presently he returned and said to Jimmy:

"Young man, I joost god to look tro' dis house."

"There don't anybody search my house without my leave," returned Hannigan, sharply.

"Der don't, eh?"

"No, sir, you bet there don't."

"Vell, I show you de varrant firs'. And den you don't better mek us no trouble, percause ve're too many for you, and I mins pizness. My name vas Quandt, der sheriff von Placer County, and I bin come here in de execution of mine duty. Here vas de varrant — see? — vat gif me all de power vas necessary to search vere I tinks prober for de man I vant. You joost 'low me to pass, please —"

Had they not all been so interested in seeing whether the storekeeper would persist in "standing off" Quandt some of them might have heard a sound outside as though a man had stumbled and fallen.

A pistol shot, however, brought them all to attention.

Simultaneously there was a stampede among their horses.

They rushed outside. Here one of their number lay, stunned, upon the ground, while with cut reins flying loose, three of their horses were going in all directions. Ned himself mounted on one, and, leading the other of their remaining two, was galloping down the road which led through the village.

Recognising Quandt's voice, he had realised immediately that he had fallen in with a sheriff's posse in pursuit of himself. Unwilling to make his escape unmounted, he had waited a little upon events, but as soon as he had found the course they were taking, he had sallied out by the back door and stolen round to the front of the house, determined to act at once. As he turned the corner, he found himself face to face with one of Quandt's men; fortunately the latter did not recognise him. The situation required nerve and decision. Ned was determined to get his remounts. A shot would have spoilt all. He passed on, therefore, as though bent on entering the store. As he came abreast of his man, he wheeled suddenly, drawing his pistol at the same time, and struck him a stunning blow on the head with it. His knife was ready, and with it he slashed through the reins of three of the horses, thus setting them loose. Releasing the other two, he sprang into the saddle of one of them, fired a single shot to scatter those that were loose, and galloped off with the one he was leading.

But he was by no means out of danger, and he knew it. The men behind him could handle their rifles, and had not parted with them.

"Whit — whit — whe—ew!" flew the bullets past him. One struck his hat and tore it off him, leaving a scalp wound behind. To hasten the remount he was leading for Rose, he fired his own pistol in the air. And then! — a regular volley was heard behind him; he felt the horse he rode leap wildly forward; the reins of the other were torn from his grasp, and he knew no more.

Up on the hillside Rose sat with her gaze fixed on the village. She could see it distinctly over the tops of the live-oaks away down below her. She saw Ned, doll-size in the distance, enter it, ride down the straggling street, and stop at Hannigan's store. And full of a deep light and tenderness that lent them an even more exquisite beauty than ever, she kept her eyes riveted on the little house.

Lured by fresh grass, her horse drew the lariat from her hand. She did not notice it. A jack-rabbit hobbled by and then stopped a dozen yards off to sit up and look at her for a moment or two. The motionless figure in the Mexican *vaquero's* dress did not see him. Once Rose dashed her hand across her eyes, and then looked again at once.

Suddenly she uttered a short sharp cry and started up. Her face was deathly pale, her eyes dilated; she looked the picture of intense alarm. Quandt's party was dismounting before the house that Ned had entered. Fixed as her attention had been on the house itself, she had not seen them approaching.

"Who are they?" And her hands were clasped together, and pressed against her cheek in an attitude of the tensest distress. "Who are they?" she cried aloud.

The sound of her own voice awoke her. She glanced around. Dragging his lariat after him, her horse was quietly grazing a few yards off. She sprang towards him and mounted in haste. The life was ebbing back into her cheeks, her teeth clenched fiercely, and as she urged on her weary horse at his best pace, she mechanically pulled in and coiled up the rope which trailed behind her.

"On, on!" — perhaps Ned was in danger. She had had some presentiment of this. "On, on! get on, poor brute! Ah, I can't help it! — you must!" and stumbling, sliding, tripping as he went, the tired and half-starved horse was urged down the steep descent.

Still it was slow work; and her heart was beating — ah, so madly! her brain calling up pictures that wrung every nerve in her with agony.

She had reached the foot of the hill now, and was cantering heavily across the flat, the condition of her horse rendering a gallop out of the question. But the village was close at hand, and "thank Heaven! She had heard no shot fired."

Hark! What was that! Her thanks had been uttered too soon. The first report, that of Ned's pistol fired to stampede the horses, had reached her.

"On, on!" and her face was white to the very lips; great tears were in her eyes.

Another shot and another! — shots following each other in quick succession, a dozen of them!

And Ned was alone against them!

She reached the village, passed the first house, turned a corner, and saw him galloping down the street towards her, hampered with a led horse,— the horse he was bringing for her.

The bullets ricochetted and whizzed past her, but she never heeded them. She saw Ned fire his pistol in the air. Across the road behind him she beheld a string of men, with wreaths of smoke among them, and all were firing. Suddenly she saw Ned's horse leap forward and crash down upon the ground. Ned struggled up, stumbled, half rose again, and then fell forward, motionless.

A moment later she was beside him and his head was in her arms.

"Ned! Ned! Speak, Ned! — speak! — speak to me! Ah!!" she cried in awful terror. And then she felt him stir, saw his eyes open, and her laughter rang out in delirious joy. "Thank God! Ah, ha, ha, ha! thank God! thank God!"

But strong hands seized her and held her, handcuffed and disarmed her. And long before Ned had thoroughly recovered consciousness, he was handcuffed and disarmed also.

CHAPTER XXX.

The excitement in Wilbur when Ned and Rose were brought back there was immense. Even before the events in which they had recently figured had occurred, both had been well known; both, in fact, had by this time attained that pitch of notoriety when the public has made the person of interest stand sponsor for any and all the tramp anecdotes and fatherless stories of the countryside. Notoriety is more nearly synonymous with popularity in America than in most other countries. In the present instance the prisoners had undoubtedly enjoyed a good deal of popularity that was genuine enough in its way; and it must be admitted that their recent adventures had not, at any rate, fatally injured this prestige. In the case of Rose, on the contrary, the courage and adroitness that she had shown in effecting Ned's escape had increased popular feeling in her favour.

Upon arriving at Wilbur, Chase was confined again in the jail; Rose, however, was placed under guard in a private house, where she was supplied with clothes befitting her sex. Had any effort been made to release her, it would probably have been successful; for she was not only carelessly watched, but was allowed to receive visits from whomsoever she pleased.

On the day succeeding her arrival Dinkey came to see her. After her departure he had returned to

Dogtown, where he had obtained regular work as driver of the stage-cart which carried the mail between that point and White Pine, a small camp distant some twenty miles in the hills. Altogether, whether owing to the effect produced in him by his intimacy with Rose, or from other causes, he had taken a new departure, although it would have been difficult for him as yet to have induced anybody to believe it. During his absence in Wilbur a substitute was doing his work for him. But business and reformation counted for nothing with Dinkey by comparison with his devotion to Wild Rose. The moment he had heard of her capture, he had set out to rejoin her. If he should eventually lose his post by so doing, why he should lose it, and, as he himself said, "that's all there was to it."

A few days later Joe Johnstone arrived in town with Kitty. Intelligence of Ned's recapture having travelled to Floretas with the mysterious rapidity such news usually commands, they had come at once to see whether it were possible for them to help him in any way. With this object in view they had brought with them the first instalment of ore from the mine; only about a ton and a half, it is true, but worth over $2000, half of which, according to their contract with Crispin Lucero, was their own. It was their intention to employ the money in Ned's defence. At the same time they were able unostentatiously to provide many little comforts for Rose, to whom during her stay at Floretas Kitty had become very much attached.

Some days elapsed before Joe could prevail upon Quandt to allow him to visit the prisoner. But whatever the sheriff's faults might be, they certainly were not small ones. He did not bear malice. In his eyes Ned had only done what was perfectly natural in endeavouring to escape; if anything, his daring had rather increased the sheriff's respect for him. That Quandt should himself have suffered in pocket and reputation by it was unfortunate; but he acknowledged that this was his own fault entirely.

"Wal, I 'low you to see him," said he finally to Joe, "putt only upon von condition: dat I 'bin present vile you are mit ihm."

To this Joe readily enough assented, since under no other conditions was he likely to gain the permission at all.

He found Ned perfectly quiet and self-contained, his manner not affording the slightest indication of his actual feelings. Indeed he seemed averse from discussing his own position, or anything concerning his defence, dwelling, instead, on the subject of Joe's affairs, and subsequently referring to the time he had spent in the mountains with Rose.

"Quandt, how came you to be at Wyman?" he asked.

"Vy, it vas like dis: ve's looking for you down in olt Mexico — ve hearn of you pelow Floretas, and ve follert you nort'. In Floretas ve fell in mit some Mormon poys vat say you bin stopping over mit Mr. Johnstone here. It sim dot de sem poys actually seen you demselves in der hills, but dey don't knows den who you vas — not until aftervarts. Dey tell vere to strike you' trail and von dem also ve get a half-breet Indian, a fine trailer, and follert on de trail goin' nort'. By'm bye you strook vest, and fin'ly ve lose de trail altogeder, and can't find it no more. So I send de trailer 'crost de mountains to warn Cap Cook — de sem vat het a posse vatching de foot hills ofer in Sonora — and I come op de foot hills on de oder side."

"Then yours was the party we saw once in the mountains?"

"I reckon. Vhere you seen us?"

"Why, just before our trail struck west — close by a deep cañon; we lit a fire on the north side of it" — Ned was speaking very slowly and distinctly now, looking at Joe as he spoke — "and we saw you coming up south of the cañon in the afternoon."

"De hell you say!"

Ned nodded.

"Vell, dot's vat de trailer say — dot you seen us, sure! Ve seen vhere you mek de fire, und von der on he say von your tracks dot you vas going fast, like you bin scairt."

"Say, Quandt! don't you know I could have killed every man of you if I'd waited until you got half-way down that cañon — just lay behind a rock on the other side of it, and picked you off, one by one."

"Dot's a fact; I reckon dot's so, sure," rejoined Quandt, after a moment's reflection. "Vy you don't do dat, eh?"

"You bet it occurred to me; but — Christ! it wasn't even sport — worse than jack-rabbit shooting," he responded scornfully.

The sheriff laughed. "Vell, I bin glad you feel dot vay; you sure got de drop on us."

"So you remember that cañon, eh?" pursued Ned, presently, glancing aside at Joe in a way that commanded his attention.

"You pet your life, I remember it!—de hell of a cañon, vat? It took us de rest von de day to ged 'crost it."

"Who was the trailer you say you had along?"

"Joost some mens vat de Mormons employ to trail der cattle—he work der right along—Copper Nick, I tink dey call 'im."

"Copper Nick? Do you know him, Joe?"

"Why, yes. Copper Nick? Know him well, he's the best trailer in the country."

Ned laughed curtly.

"It don't take good men to get away with you when you're out of luck; any fool can do it then. But if you know the fellow, you tell him I've got a job for him. Don't forget!—as soon as I get out of this I've got a job for Copper Nick," and he changed the conversation.

They talked for half an hour longer on indifferent subjects, but as Joe was leaving Ned ransacked his saddle-bags (which he had been allowed to retain) and produced therefrom the specimen he had taken from the gold lead in the cañon.

"See here, Joe! you say that mine of yours won't hold out?"

"No, it's a ter'ble broken vein, liable to give out any time."

"Well, here's a sample that I took from a vein we found in the hills that's the biggest thing on record. It'll pay from the start, too. When your mine peters out, you go in there and work it."

"Gosh! she's a dandy, ain't she!" exclaimed Joe, admiringly, turning the specimen over in his fingers. "Whereabouts is it?"

"If Quandt weren't here, I'd tell you, and tell you

how to get there. But Quandt 'd send one of his deputies out right away to denounce it. I know Quandty. You ask Rose; she knows all about it. You've got to thank her for it, anyway. I shouldn't have thought to put you on to it, if she hadn't remembered you. All I've got to say, Joe, is, if you make a strike there — and you bet your life you'll do it! — do what's right by *her*. As for me, I guess Quandt isn't going to let me go again just yet — eh, Quandty?"

"Ve try not, enyvay," rejoined the sheriff, modestly.

The moment Joe inquired of Rose about the mine, and she began to describe the situation of it to him, he saw the drift of Ned's conversation before Quandt in the jail, and understood that all he had to do in order to find the prospect was to get Copper Nick to guide him over the trail until he reached the cañon near which the remains of Ned's fire had been found.

Although Rose and Ned were prisoners, their position was by no means desperate. The action of the law in the West is neither swift nor sure. It would be idle to cite instances in which the perpetrators even of the most unprovoked and dastardly murders, proven though these have been to the hilt, have escaped the penalty of their crimes altogether, or with merely nominal terms of imprisonment. The miscarriages of justice, due whether to corrupt judges, corruption, timidity, or perverted ideas of right and wrong on the part of jurymen, are too generally known to admit of the slightest question. Timidity, by the way, plays a far greater part in such cases than might be supposed. Many a man who, for fear of revenge on the part of the accused or his associates, would suppress condemning evidence or vote for an acquittal, would join gladly with a mob in the work of lynching the very prisoner he would otherwise have helped to escape. It matters little how inexcusable the crime may be; if the murderer escape lynching and be provided with money, he is sadly out of luck if he be executed, or even severely punished. The majority of trials for murder in the West are scarcely more serious than trials upon the stage.

Much depends upon the temper of public feeling in relation to the victim and in relation to the slayer. In the present case Ned Chase had undoubtedly been a popular man; on the other hand, Dutton was quite the reverse, whilst Frost, whose rôle as an officer of the law ("d'être tué pour gagner sa vie") was a well-paid one, was not in general estimation entitled to a great deal of sympathy. Moreover, in both cases Ned had stood an equal chance with the men he had slain — justifiable homicide, therefore, many people called the deeds. Towards Dutton he was regarded as having behaved with great forbearance, and towards Frost with admirable chivalry. The sympathy of the locality was with him, therefore, and a harsh sentence could never have been secured by fair means. As regarded the train robbery, the railway company upon whose line it had occurred had rendered itself so generally detested by its short-sighted policy of grasping exaction, that any indictment in connection with it was foredoomed to miscarry. Besides, the vital necessity that Ned had for the money, together with the decision and smartness displayed in the robbery, would have counted for something with a Western jury. As concerned Rose, regarding her actions in the light of devotion to her lover — and no one now for an instant doubted but that Ned stood in that position to her, — it is certain that she would have escaped with a very light penalty.

But the fact had to be taken into consideration in Ned's case, that he had a ruthless and pertinacious enemy who, by fair means or foul, was determined that he should die, and was willing to spend a considerable sum in gratifying his animosity. This enemy, of course, was Hannaford.

At first he cautiously sounded the jurymen who nominally had Ned's fate in their hands. But though he found sundry of them ready enough to be bribed into falling in with his object, they demanded a far more than ordinary price for their votes — it was one thing, the least scrupulous recognised, to be bribed to let a man off, another to be bought to deprive a man of life, even by the machinery of the law. Moreover, a strong undercurrent of sympathy with the prisoner was distinguishable amongst them all, which made it very doubtful whether, even when bought, they would "stay bought." If money were brought to bear on them by the other side, Hannaford felt that this would be extremely improbable. Also there might be appeals, changes of venue, a score of delays on as many pretexts, with the prospect of uncertainty always as the ultimate issue of the affair. After considerable hesitation, therefore, Hannaford decided to adopt surer and speedier methods.

Among the riffraff of a frontier town there are always to be found men unscrupulous enough for anything. From among such "toughs" Hannaford selected a few suitable agents, whom he commissioned to foster in the ranks of their associates, a quasi-feeling of public indignation against Chase. This was not difficult to manage. A few bribes, a good deal of drink, and a little prompting, raised an outcry for Ned's life among them in a very short time. Threats of lynching began to be heard. To be sure, no one of any weight paid the slightest attention to them; nevertheless matters, in reality, soon assumed a very ugly aspect. It was at this juncture that Dinkey came to Joe one night.

"Joe, do you know what them ———— are talking of doing?" he asked in a voice of mingled rage and emotion.

"No; what?"

"They're talking of lynching Ned!"

"Oh, pshaw!"

"I tell you it ain't 'pshaw'; it's the God's truth; they mean business. You know the sort of whelps — the sort of —— bloodthirsty wolves some of them fellows are when they're started, and Cherokee Jim and Smiley's heading 'em. This ain't no child's play; you know the reputation them fellows bears."

Joe knew it well. They were two of the worst men in the territory.

"The hell!" he muttered significantly.

"Lord knows what's got into *them* to take a hand in a thing of this kind. They ain't looking for no 'law 'n' order,' as a rule. There's something behind it — Hannaford's putting up money, I guess, on'y you can't prove it on him. What's to be done?"

"Warn Quandt, right away."

"I ain't so d——d sure of Quandt. Quandt's to be bought if Hannaford's a mind to buy him — and pay his price. There ain't no 'mediate danger, anyway. They can't do nothing 'fore to-morrow night; they ain't laid their plans yet. D'ye know what I think's the best we can do?"

"What's that?"

"Why, for you to strike right out for Dogtown — go to-night — and bring down a whole raft of them boys to set Ned and Miss Carlin free. I'd go myself, but they wouldn't pay 'tention to me like they would to you; they might want to put it off a day and take their time coming, and I tell you there's no time to lose. *You* can handle 'em. They'll do what *you* say. And they'll come! The sympathy of the whole camp's with Ned — to say nothing of Miss Carlin. I've been looking for 'em to come down and take 'em out b'fore this."

"I'll go," said Joe. "Get me a horse. Can I make it?"

"Yes — if you travel. It's fifty-one miles, using that cut-off 'cross the hills above Daws, and the other little cut-off beyond Willow Springs. You can do it on horseback and get here again easy if you don't waste time in Dogtown. D'ye know the road?"

"Every inch of it — you cross Moccasin Creek, and pass Brigg's ranch and the Box Cañon."

"You've got it. Get ready then. I'll go 'n' fetch y' a horse, and a dandy too, if I have to steal him."

"That'll be all right. I'm good for all he's worth — and the owner shall fix the price."

Joe re-entered the house, and without exactly telling Kitty what was toward, explained to her that he would be away until the following evening on business in Ned's interest, at the same time recommending her, if possible, to conceal his absence.

In a few minutes' time Dinkey came quietly down the street with the horse.

"It's Al Higgins' grey — the best traveller in town," said he. "Al don't know as it's gone — I just took it out of the corral, but I'll explain it to him to-morrow."

Joe mounted.

"How long can you give me to get back?"

"The sooner you're back after dusk the better, though it ain't likely as that crowd'll get ginned up 'fore midnight; it takes a flood of whiskey to move 'em."

"All right. I shall be there before sun-up, and we'll be back before evening. You get around and see Quandt."

"I'm goin', right now; but I know Quandt and don't you reckon him."

In a few minutes more Joe was out on the prairie, steering for the pass below Hooded Peak. And all night long he rode — over broad, silent plains mysterious with the soft refulgence of the wonderful starlight in those clear skies, by dim valleys and dark cañons which echoed his lightest breath, across slumbering hills, with crests clearly cut against the blue, through stretches of pine timber, shadow-haunted and still as death; the muffled beat of his horse's hoofs on the carpet of fallen quills the only sound that woke the charmed silence, his only companions thoughts now surging up in fierce imaginary combat, now scheming with a clearness and coolness that seemed unnatural. Suddenly a loose rock, as he rode down into a dry riverbottom, gave horse and rider a stunning fall. And when the latter, badly shaken, pulled himself together and regained the saddle, it was to find his horse with a strained shoulder — dead lame and still seventeen miles from Dogtown!

CHAPTER XXXI.

MEANWHILE Dinkey derived but little satisfaction from his visit to Quandt. The sheriff refused to credit, or rather professed entirely to discredit, the possibility that there could be any serious movement on foot for lynching Ned. He admitted that a few "dive loafers might be talking through their hats," but said that that afforded no indication of public feeling, and he declared the idea that Ned's life was in danger to be ridiculous. There was far more likely to be an attempt to release than to lynch him.

It was useless to press the matter. Quandt listened to all that Dinkey told him, but remained incredulous — so stubbornly so that Dinkey came away convinced that, if not already bought by Hannaford, he was at least keeping his hands free in order to be able to listen to proposals should they be made to him.

In deference to Dinkey's warnings, or possibly merely with a view to proving afterwards that he had not quite disregarded them, he placed an extra deputy in the jail and gave orders for one to remain on guard with him that night.

Soon after noon next day, he himself left the jail and walked down to dinner at the hotel at the railway "depot." As it was here that Hannaford stayed when in Wilbur, there was nothing surprising in the fact that Quandt had not long been seated at table when he was casually joined by him.

"You got my note then?" said Hannaford in an undertone, after they had exchanged greetings.

The sheriff nodded.

"You vant to speak mit me, vat? — I reckon it's joost to varn me dot de poys vas allowin' to lynch Ned Chase to-night; but I hearn all about dot."

"The hell they are!" rejoined Hannaford, an indescribable look passing between himself and his companion.

"Yes, sir, dat's what! But dot don't goes, all dot nonzense. I puts a tozen teputies in de jail, vell armt, und de poys don't stand no show mit dere lynchin'."

"Of course not."

"Dey ged it ride vhere de chicken god de axe — in de neck — if dey come foolin' rount mine jail. I bin quide ready for dem."

"That's right, Quandty," and Hannaford curled his long, fair moustache, and looked superbly indifferent and cheerful.

The topic was dropped whilst they discussed other matters. Towards the close of the meal Hannaford said: "And how's the mine?"

"De prospec' out in dem *Caballo* Hills? Tings is going liddle bit slow mit dat prospec'. I ton't hev de money ride now to tevelop it — not on no pizness scale, dot is."

"You don't say! If you wanted money to work it, why didn't you come to me? I could always let you have a thousand."

"Ride here in der hand?" and Quandt glanced keenly at his companion.

"Right here — right now."

"Vell — vell, dot's all ride 'nough, but de on'y ting is

dot tousand tollers don' go, Mr. Hennafort — mit tree tousand ve mide do som' tevelopments."

Mr. "Hennafort" looked rather blank. Three thousand dollars was a larger sum than he had contemplated parting with to Quandt. He hesitated.

"Two thousand, Quandt — one thousand down and —"

Quandt took out his watch and looked at it, then glanced at Hannaford with all the contempt of a strong nature for a weak one. "Vell, I goin' op town," he said, cutting the other short.

"Stop! all right; you shall have it."

"Ged de money den, ride now, pecause if not, I hev mine breparations to make, and vonce de're med dey can't pe change' bek."

"I've got most of it here, but I'll have to go up to the bank and cash a cheque for the balance. Stay round here for a few minutes till I get back," and Hannaford left the hotel.

In a little while he returned and took Quandt with him to his room. Scarcely a word was uttered on either side. The American paid the money, the stolid North German as he took it counted it without hesitation or mistake. No evidence of the transaction passed between them.

"You'll hear from me about midnight, or maybe a little earlier," was all that Hannaford said as the other was leaving.

Quandt nodded. "Vhenever you're ready;" and perfectly unmoved, save that he was smoking a long, black, and very bad cigar at a rather greater rate than usual, and that there was an unconscious glimmer of gratified avarice in his little beady eyes, the sheriff left the hotel.

Throughout the day Dinkey hung about anxiously in the neighbourhood of the jail. What he saw there was not calculated to allay his fears concerning Ned's security. He noticed Quandt go down to the hotel to dinner, then Hannaford come hurriedly up-town to the bank, and retrace his steps in the same fashion. Shortly afterwards he observed Quandt reappear, looking anything but ill-pleased with himself. Twice he remarked Cherokee Bill and Smiley sauntering past, pausing occasionally as they did so, to study the jail and its approaches. As evening drew nearer, he became aware that others were doing the same. But that which most of all troubled him was the fact that a teamster had recognised Joe some distance on his journey, evidently hastening on some important errand, and had brought the news into town where the carpenters and joiners of gossip, putting two and two together, had arrived at a conclusion very nearly right as to the nature of his business. In the ordinary course of events Ned would have been safe until late at night, but the belief that Joe had gone to Dogtown for help was apt to lead to an attack being made upon the jail comparatively early in the evening. In which case if Joe were not very punctual, as Dinkey expressed it to himself, "Ned was a gone goose."

He made another appeal to Quandt, but the sheriff laughed at and refused to listen to him any further. "If der bin anyting on foot, I hearn von it, not? And I don't hear notings. You bin *loco*, Dinkey; der pris'ner's all ride," he said.

"G——d d——n you!" exclaimed Dinkey, finally, his anger getting the better of him. "I believe you've done sold him to Hannaford, and that's why you won't take proper measures to protect him."

Quandt drew his pistol deliberately before he spoke, his small eyes glittering evilly as he did so.

"If you efer dare to say anoder word like dat, I shoot you dead, ride in you' tracks! You —— —! ——!" he hissed between clenched teeth. "Ged out, I say, von dis! Don't led me seen you' face rount here no more! De hell of a dead-beat loafer, trying to teach me mine pizness! — and meking dot kind of a talk! Ged out von here! ged out, I say!"

Dinkey went; for though he valued his life but little, it would have been foolish to have thrown it away while there was still a chance that he might be of some use.

In vain he strove to interest others in the matter. No one listened to him seriously. For the first time he fully realised how low he stood in the social scale, what a thoroughly "no account" creature he was in the eyes of his fellow-men. And for the first time his degradation stung him — stung him so that, with trembling lips, he swore a solemn oath to change his life, and "get even" with all those who scorned him now. And he kept his oath.

Evening approached; dusk deepened and passed swiftly; night had come.

There were indications of activity amongst Ned's enemies which led Dinkey to suppose that the contemplated outrage would not be postponed very late. But as yet there was no sign of Joe, nor of any one from Dogtown. Every minute seemed an hour to Dinkey now — every hour a lifetime, in the state of nervous excitement into which he had worked himself.

It was eight o'clock. He loafed into the little "Cow-camp" Saloon, a haunt of some of the "toughest citizens" in and about town. The place was crowded; for Cherokee Bill was there treating any and all who chose to drink, an alternative in favour of which there seemed to be the utmost unanimity. Smiley was marshalling forces in another saloon.

"Get in here, Dinkey! What's your pizen?" cried Cherokee, a black-browed, black-eyed half-breed of villainous countenance. "——! you'll do to come along; we can ring you in with the rest!"

"You bet you can, if there's any free drinks hanging to it! What's the game?"

"We're going to do up that ——— Ned Chase!—— him! I've had it in for him these two years and more. See?" and he showed a scar on his temple. "He done that, up to Lone Mountain. But I'll play even with him to-night, sure. The boys 'll begin to bunch up here soon; you come with us."

"Why, you bet I'll come! if there's any sport on hand I'm a full partner. What time d'ye open?"

"Somewheres round nine."

"Count me in then."

But as soon he could do so without attracting notice, Dinkey "counted himself out," and slipped away from the house.

Once in the open air he paused to collect himself. Matters were evidently fast approaching a crisis. Joe's non-arrival was only to be accounted for by the supposition that something had happened to delay him on the road; for Dinkey knew the feeling of the Dogtown miners too well to doubt that, thus urgently summoned, they would have come at once to Ned's assistance. What could he do to delay Ned's falling into the hands of Cherokee's mob — or even to give him a chance of defending himself? Any death was preferable to hanging. For a few minutes the loafer stood still in the starlight, his face furrowed with lines of the cruelest perplexity. Slowly it cleared; his expression grew set and stern, — an expression different from any that he had worn for years. An idea had occurred to him, and, wild though it was, he meant to act on it. He went rapidly up-town to borrow a spare six-shooter, which he thrust in the band of his trousers, concealing the handle of it beneath his waistcoat. Then he returned to the saloon, where, simulating partial drunkenness and an eagerness in the project in hand second only to Cherokee's own, he was soon foremost among those who clamoured for Ned's death.

Quandt and a deputy named Chick Wilson were playing cribbage to while away their watch. The latter individual was a deputy sheriff only in virtue of a temporary appointment. By profession he was a "tin-horn gambler." His adversary, therefore, had to watch him very closely in order to avoid being cheated. But Quandt, as he had been known to say himself when whiskey had opened the pores of his heart and the choked valves of his veracity, was "a bit of a sure-thing man himself," so the contest was not one-sided.

He invariably directed Chick's attention to the fact when the latter chanced to deal himself a card too many, or "held out" a five for subsequent use. Chick, upon his side, was quite as attentive in correcting Quandt when he happened to score wrongly. But each did this without any ill-bred feeling or prejudice, indeed in a spirit of perfect courtesy; for each felt that it might occur to any gentleman, even to himself, to make those trivial mistakes in the excitement of a close game and a natural anxiety to win it.

They had just finished the last hand of a very close game, — so close, in fact, that Quandt had only just won it by playing a "last card." But in order to retain this "last card" in his hand, he had omitted to play it during the first round of "thirty-one," calling it instead a "go" at twenty-seven, and thus obliging Chick to follow on and uselessly sacrifice a deuce and an ace. The card that Quandt had withheld was a tray. Chick, in justice to himself, was gently breaking the fact of this little irregularity to Quandt, whilst Quandt, by revision of the cards, was being reluctantly convinced of it, when, with a loud crash, the street door was burst open.

"Hands up!" cried some masked men, rushing into the room over the fallen fir pole which had been used as a ram, and levelling their revolvers at the cribbage players.

Ordinarily Quandt's own six-shooter would have been out before he was fairly covered, and the first few men to enter would have fallen to it. But to-night he was a little slow.

It would evidently have been madness to have attempted any resistance after they were once under fire. Quandt consequently raised his hands above his head. Chick had already done so.

"We want your prisoner, and we mean to have him," said one of the intruders. "Where's the keys?"

"Don't you petter find dem? — sims like you vas running dis show," growled Quandt, sarcastically.

He knew the class of men that he was dealing with, and it vexed his professional pride to be "run" by such scum. The room was half full of them now. Outside a large crowd was collected, the front rows of faces pressing round the door being illuminated by the lamp within.

But little time was lost in following Quandt's sneering suggestion, one man in particular displaying marked activity in searching his pockets. He it was who eventually secured the keys. There was a rush for the inner door. He opened it, and together with Cherokee Bill burst into the room beyond. Simultaneously a shot was heard in the dark, and a voice rang out, clear and firm:

"Stand back, boys! The first man in here dies!"

The rush forward was converted into a surging and struggling retreat, the attack into something very like a stampede.

Dinkey — for he it was who had entered with Cherokee Bill, took advantage of the momentary pause to unlock Ned's irons and hand him a revolver and some cartridges, briefly explaining the situation to him at the same time. He then bent over Cherokee's prostrate form to take his six-shooter away from him. As he did so, the man attempted to rise.

"You ain't dead yet then?" remarked Dinkey, sardonically.

"Not by a d——d sight!" muttered the half-conscious ruffian.

"By ——, you soon will be then, if you don't lie still, you —— hired murderer!"

The outer room was cleared now, but outside for several minutes a Babel of voices were heard shouting all manner of suggestions and advice.

At length the crowd seemed to scatter round the building; a regular fusillade was commenced through the doors and windows. But Ned and Dinkey kept well under cover, and the only person injured by this was Cherokee Bill, who received another bullet before Ned was able to draw him under cover. The shooting, however, was so evidently a waste of cartridges that it was soon discontinued. A long pause ensued. Finally the ominous silence was broken by the dull thud-thud of iron striking against the foundations of the prison walls in three or four directions. To Ned, as a miner, the sound was perfectly familiar.

"Dinkey, do you know what they're doing?" he asked presently.

"Yes, and I don't give a d——n!" replied Dinkey, doggedly. "Let 'em blow us up; they'll blow their own man up with us."

"He's dead. I guess they know that. See here! I'm going out."

"What for?"

"They're determined to have me, anyhow; but there's no reason why they should get you, too."

"What in —— do I care!"

"I care, though," replied Ned, quietly.

At this moment they heard some one order silence outside, and a voice from near the street door shouted: "Say! you men inside there! we've mined the walls of your room and we're going to put the charges in. If Ned Chase don't come out right away, we'll blow you to hell."

"Blow and be d——d!" bellowed Dinkey, tauntingly.

"Boys, I'll come," cried Ned; "but on one condition."

"Give it a name — and speak quick!"

"That you let my partner go."

"D——n your partner! We don't want him, but we mean to have you if we wreck the town getting you."

"Good-bye, Dinkey," said Ned, and they gripped each other's hands. "No, it's no use talking. I'm going. Stay where you are till — till we're gone — and say 'good-bye' to Rose for me."

Without another word he stepped calmly into the outer room and threw down his pistol. A moment later a score of hands seized him, and he was forced out into the street, when, like jackals hungry for prey, every one strove to reach him.

"Where to?" was the cry.

"The 'deepot'! the 'deepot'! — a telegraph post! Let's hang him high!" came from a score of throats.

The "deepot" (depot or railway station) was but a couple of hundred yards away. Bearing Ned, hemmed in in the midst of them, the rabble tramped towards the first telegraph post in sight there. A baggage truck borrowed from the platform was placed immediately beneath it, and while one more active than the rest began to climb the tall pine spar, bearing with him one end of the rope, Ned was thrust up on to the truck, where he was made to stand, a masked guard on either hand of him armed with drawn revolvers.

"If you've got anything to say, you'd best say it, right now," said one of these. "Shut your mouths boys! The man's going to speak to yer!"

The sovereign mob took up the cry until each dirty member of it had repeated the order, when silence ensued.

It is trying enough to confront a hostile crowd in any circumstances; to confront one with the prospect of shameful and immediate death to follow, must be as severe a test of physical courage as a man can undergo. Ned, however, bore it unmoved. No trace of emotion in his face betrayed the bitterness of soul that in his position he naturally felt. He was bareheaded and alone, quite friendless and defenceless among the throng; his shirt had been torn from his back, and the blood was trickling from blows that he had received upon the head. But still he stood there with a dignity that betokened perfect self-reliance. His grey eyes met his enemies tranquilly; never a twitch stirred his level brows or calm mouth. They were about to kill him, but they could not extract a sign of fear from him. Blood tells, say what they will, and whatever his faults Ned Chase was a gentleman by birth, whilst the coyote crowd that howled around him were only whiskey-sodden mongrels.

Above him rose the tall spar, and half-way up it was the man who carried the rope. The sea of faces before him fronted the lights of the station, and in their glare were as pallid as death. Ned glanced down on the crowd for a moment in silence before he spoke.

"Gentlemen," said he then, and as he uttered the word there was a smile of mockery on his lips, "let me congratulate you. It's no great honour to be Hannaford's hired hangmen, but no doubt he pays you well, and it's certainly all you're fit for — "

A cry of rage went up from his hearers as they caught the words, and a volley of foul abuse was hurled at the speaker.

"Hang him! hang him! hang him! hang the —— —!" they yelled.

The climber had reached the top of the telegraph post now, and was pulling the rope up after him, to pass it over the arm which carried the insulators. The end of it as it descended, swinging to and fro, lightly struck Ned's bare head, making him glance up.

It was seized, and a slip noose made with it by one of Ned's guards, who placed it over his head and drew it close. Then, pinioning his arms, the guards sprang from the truck; for they, too, were anxious to aid in hoisting him.

"Stand clear to move the truck! stand clear!" The packed herd of men were jostling one another to make room for this purpose, when, in the pause of voices that ensued, the reverberation of many hoofs swept up on the wind was heard and then was lost again. It recurred immediately. This time it was nearer — in the very main street of Wilbur! — coming towards the station!

"Hark! hark! What's that? Troops! Soldiers, by ——!"

Horsemen they certainly were, evidently in strong force.

No houses intervened now to muffle the clatter of galloping, and as with growing thunder its turmoil roared down the broad road that led towards the station, a panic seized the jackal mob that held Ned prisoner. On came the horsemen, nearer and nearer; they reached the station yard, poured out into its open ground, and with a yell of blasphemy charged straight at the scattering crowd on the other side of it.

The would-be executioners fled like hares. In the twinkling of an eye they had scattered and were hidden among the station buildings.

For a moment or two Ned stood quite alone under the telegraph post.

Then a new crowd surrounded him. A score of friendly faces were crushed together about him, a forest of eager hands was outstretched to help him. His bonds were cut, the noose was removed, and a cheer went up from the Dogtown miners that rent the starlit sky.

"Christ, Ned! but it was a close call!"

"Two minutes more 'd have done it."

"Joe's horse broke down, or we'd have been here sooner."

"That's what! But Joe fetched us, all the same."

"Done it afoot, by gosh!"

"Hurrah! hurrah for Joe!"

"Hurrah for Ned!"

"Where's the whiskey?"

"Give the boy a drink."

"Hell! fill him full, — let's all get full, and fire their blasted town."

Nor was it without argument that wiser counsels prevailed, for "the boys were hot" against Wilbur. However, before midnight the whole party, including Ned and Rose, had left the town, most of them scattering in all directions in order that Ned's own trail might not be discovered.

CHAPTER XXXII.

ABOUT two miles off the road, in the wildest part of the hills between Dogtown and White-pine, was a deserted claim, which had been taken up by an old Dutchman in the early days of Dogtown's prosperity, and by him named the Last Chance. Whether the title had been selected with any view to ultimate events, none had ever heard its owner declare, but, at any rate, after working there alone for fourteen months without discovering ore of any value, after exhausting his last dollar and eating his last crust, the old fellow had shot himself in the bottom of the incline shaft. The circumstance had had its touch of pathos. For the man was sober, steady, and industrious; in the rare instances when he had come in contact with his neighbours he had won their good-will by his kindly manner and evident generosity; there were plenty of men who would willingly have helped him or given him credit had they known his straits. Whether however, withheld by personal pride from soliciting assistance, whether restrained by bitter experience, or in sheer weariness of life, he had sought no aid; but having come to the end of his own resources, he had laid down his burden and gone his way alone, without seeking the attention or sympathy of any one.

The superstition prevalent among miners that blood shed on a claim brings luck, had induced others to carry on work on the same prospect after the death of its first owner. But their success being no greater than his, finally it had been abandoned altogether.

A more secluded spot could scarcely have been imagined. Not another cabin was to be found within ten miles of the one which stood here. No cattle ranged there, consequently no cowboys ever came that way. Even prospectors had deserted the neighbourhood; for it was now a well-ascertained fact that, despite its favourable appearance, it was barren in so far as mineral was concerned. Altogether it would have been difficult to select a better hiding-place than it afforded, and it was here that Ned and Rose took up their temporary abode. For them it possessed the special advantage that, lying as already remarked within two miles of the Dogtown and White-pine road, which was traversed every day by Dinkey with the stage-cart, they were able there to receive small supplies of provisions, together with constant intelligence concerning the measures taken to discover their whereabouts.

There was nothing either striking or beautiful in the scenery about their retreat. It was monotonous, almost commonplace — pointless hills clad with juniper trees and *mesquite* brush. But there is a condition of mind in which fine scenery ceases to stimulate, and the overtaxed imagination turns from it in weariness to welcome the repose of monotony. In such a mood were Rose and Ned. After the wear and tear, both mental and physical, of all they had gone through lately, the life they were leading at the Last Chance claim was an intense relief to them. Virtually, they no longer needed to trouble about the present or immediate future, since stanch friends in Dogtown who were watching events for them, had undertaken in the meantime to warn them of any impending danger, as well as convey them out of the country when this could be done with safety.

Ah, those long, quiet days! Sometimes Ned forgot the past entirely, and was happy. He had become in a measure used to curb the passionate impulses of his heart, used to the discipline which kept him from pleading his love to Rose, grown accustomed to regard it as hopeless. That she cared for him in some way of her own he could not doubt, but that she would ever care for him after the fashion of the world, that his lips would ever touch hers and find them athirst with a longing like his own, he had ceased to dream, even in his most imaginative moments.

Thinking over their past in his own mind as he often did, knowing her story also and the almost quixotic chivalry of her nature, he had framed ideas that to some extent explained her position. With her, he realised the matter was not merely one of pride, but of feeling that, since she had not the right to command the chivalrous consideration and devotion without which love would have no charm for her, she would not accept them as gifts. But she had felt the degradation which love can bring, and Chase knew that, even should she ever love again, she would avoid all that had gone before, and seek in love only its noblest and purest inspiration, only that which would elevate it above the ordinary loves of men and women.

The bond which united these two was one of the most enchanting friendship, guaranteed by mutual confidence and self-respect, by a firm conviction of each other's honesty and strength of purpose. And though Ned's love for Rose struck deeper roots in him than ever in those quiet days — for daily he grew to appreciate more thoroughly the beauty of her character, and feel more fully the charm of intercourse with her, yet daily he found it easier to preserve even in thought the relations which she had silently established between them.

She let him know her as she really was now. The armour of defiance, with which most people who have any true feelings to disguise hide them from the world, was laid aside. The acquired tone, and speech, and manner of the frontier was abandoned. To him, she was no longer "Wild Rose," but the Rose that she herself knew — frank and simple, generous and tender-hearted, full of brave thoughts and noble impulses, sweet, womanly traits and enchantments. Her manner to Ned seemed to say: "If I cannot love you as you wish, if I cannot be yours after the fashion of the world, at least I can surrender myself to you in spirit." He needed not to be told that no one had ever known her as he knew her; her every word and action bore that truth innate in it.

How quickly the time sped with them! Seated together upon the rough log seat outside their little cabin, they found the hours fly like minutes. There Rose told Ned all her thoughts, recalled all that could interest him in her past, or drew him to talk of his. There was a wonderful charm in her conversation. Without ever failing of that reserve the absence of which is so fatal, it had a frankness that was delightful. It was interesting rather than amusing, seldom witty, though sometimes she would play with a fancy as a woman might play with a bonnet — turning it, twisting it, trimming it, trying on it the effect of a flower, a feather of thought, brightly coloured or sad, playful or strong, deep or light as air. But if a question really stirred her, she affected no lightness or indifference, but frankly displayed her seriousness, speaking so simply, and with such straightforward honesty and feeling, that, right or wrong, her views always carried some weight with them.

She made Ned forget the past in her company. His dark hours only came now when he was alone. With her he would sometimes launch into glowing schemes of the life he meant to lead, the success he meant to achieve in South America, if ever he reached there.

"But I talk as though you would be with me," he said, pausing once in mid-flight, and gazing earnestly at the exquisite face beside him. "Shall you — afterwards, I mean, when we get away from here?"

She was silent for a long while, and something in her restrained him from speaking again, until he saw that her eyes were full of tears.

"What is it, Rose? — tell me," he said gently.

"I don't know, — only when I think about the future it doesn't seem real — it all seems to slip away from me when I try to build in it; I can't build as you do," and as she gazed at him with wet eyes she shook her head slowly.

He laughed. "Then let me build for both; it will only be for one, after all," he added more softly.

"If one could only claim a little grace from Time, — it's so inexorable," and still as she looked at him she shook her head faintly.

Suddenly she rose in a paroxysm of weeping and turned to go indoors. He would have followed to try to soothe her, but with a vehement gesture she stopped him.

It was an hour or more before she returned. Ned

had brought his horse up to the house to be saddled; for it was time for him to go to meet Dinkey, and this he durst not neglect. Their safety — her safety — might depend on it.

He was "saddling up" when she came out of the house. She looked pale; her eyelids were heavy, too, but her face now was quite emotionless.

"You're going to meet Dinkey?" she said inquiringly.

"Yes — if there are no passengers with him. I must go and watch for the cart, anyhow; he may have some news."

"Poor Dinkey! he has been such a good friend to us!" she said, and she moved across and stroked the horse's muzzle absently with her cold hand.

"You bet he has! Do you know, Dinkey's turned over quite a new leaf, — says he's done with drink and will never touch morphine again."

"Really!" and her face lit up with pleasure for a moment. "Ah, you don't know how glad I am! Tell him — tell him *from me* to be brave and conquer all that."

"I'll tell him," laughed Ned, "and that'll settle it. If *you* told him to, he'd try and conquer the world."

He swung himself into the saddle, and baring his head with a charm of manner that, despite the rough life he had led, had always distinguished him with women, stooped to touch her hand.

She gave it to him, and their eyes met for a second.

"Good-bye — come back soon," she faltered.

"Soon as I can," he answered almost gruffly; for the sight of her unwonted emotion distressed him, and he scarcely dare trust his own voice.

He turned and waved his hand as he rode down the slope, and she nodded to him once.

But long after he was out of sight the arrowy figure of the girl stood where he had left her, outlined in the light of the setting sun. In her humid eyes there was a gaze of exquisite tenderness, and her lovely lips — love's altars that would never know love's service — quivered uncontrollably. She shivered, and, turning, seated herself on the bench outside the door, and leaning back her head against the rough pine logs of the house, closed her eyes, like one tired out with emotion.

A *cenzontli* was singing beautifully in a *mesquite* bush a little way down in the hollow before her. She knew the bird; he sang there every night, and every morning she rewarded him by placing some crumbs near his haunt. Slowly the slumbrous hum in undertone of insect life awakening grew in contrast with the vivid melody of the lone bird's song. The lurid fires of sunset waxed soft, — softer and still inexpressibly softer, till the sun himself was lost behind one of the surrounding hills, and only an intense afterglow of roseate gold lingered above where he had sunk. The heavens were swiftly entering into the fairest tints of that great heritage of colour which evening brings, and the solemn stillness that usually attends the passing of day already reigned.

Suddenly Rose became conscious that she was not alone.

She started up, her cheeks all blanched; for, like a bird of ill-omen, Hannaford was beside her. Wrapped in her own thoughts, she had not heard him approach, and he had prepared for some such surprise as this by wearing moccasins, in order that he might steal upon her unobserved.

He laughed sardonically.

"It's no use hiding, Rosy! Fate's against you! I guess fate gave you to me long ago, and— Stop!" he interrupted, checking her motion to escape and holding her, "you're not going to get away. Hear me out. I've come to save you this time."

"From whom?"

"From the men who're on Ned Chase's track."

"To save us — *you!*"

"I didn't say anything about 'us'. Chase can go to hell!" he answered, sullenly, stung by her tone.

"Ah!" and she turned aside, trying in vain to release herself from the grasp he kept on her.

The ironical tone of her brief exclamation added fuel to his anger.

"You fool! You cursed fool!" he cried, swinging her round until she faced him again. "Will you never learn sense? Will you never learn, by God, that you can play with me too long?"

She did not deign to answer.

"You've got your last chance now — go slow! If you say 'no' this time, you say it for good and all."

She only strove, still vainly, to release herself. For a moment there was silence, then:

"Ah!" she exclaimed suddenly in a voice of loathing. "Are you blind? Cannot you *see* that if you came to me with death in one hand, and all the world with your filthy worship in the other, I'd die before I'd listen to you?"

"And, by God, that's how I come," he answered in a low, trembling voice. "You think you love that train-robbing, murdering whelp —"

Passion lent her strength at last; she wrenched herself free and faced him without fear or thought of fear in her mind.

"And if I do love him?"

Hannaford's face grew livid, but he still contrived to maintain some control over himself. "Say '*did* love him' in future; it'll come nearer being true," he sneered.

"What do you mean?"

"Just this; that you'll never see him again alive."

A gasp of terror escaped her. She gazed at him like one fascinated.

"You'll never see him again alive — nor I, nor any one," he continued in rising tones. "He's cornered — do you hear? — he's ambushed! — down where he reckoned to meet the stage; and, by God, by this time he's so full of lead that a horse couldn't carry him."

"Ah, my God!" she gasped again and again, chokingly, and her hands clasped each side of her face convulsively.

For a moment both stood there quite motionless, she staring blindly before her.

"No!" she exclaimed triumphantly, then — but in her voice there was a piteous ring of wildness — "No! it's a lie! it's a lie! it's just like you to tell a cruel lie like that."

"Is it? You wait and see. So you do love him, eh?" sneered Hannaford again.

"With all my heart and soul, with all the strength I have, I love him."

"Take it back," he thundered, the last vestige of his self-control vanishing in a burst of fury.

"Never!"

"Take it back, or by the living God I'll kill you!

Take it back!" he cried, beside himself now in the madness of his jealousy. "Take it back!"

"Never! I love him with all my life."

"Then die!—— you! die, you ——!" and, snatching his six-shooter from its sheath, he fired.

Even as the noise of the shot passed away he caught the sound of hoofs galloping rapidly towards him. "——! he's escaped!" he exclaimed. And a violent trembling shook his limbs; for with all the fear of a coward he feared Ned Chase, and he knew that if he had escaped, no power on earth could save him.

He fled — without looking back, or scarcely whither he went — fled through the bushes and the *taskate* like a frightened animal.

On came the horseman, galloping swiftly — and on, and on, and up the slope towards the hut. The light of the golden afterglow was beginning to wane; evening was speeding rapidly away.

"Rose! Rose!" cried a voice, sharply and excitedly. "Where are you, Rose? Quick! We're discovered! Rose! Where are you? Ah——!!" and a long, awful cry of anguish rang hoarsely through the intense stillness.

Ned had found her. In his hurry in the dusk he had stumbled and almost fallen over her prostrate form.

He stooped to raise her head, and held her in his arms. Under the influence of his presence she rallied a little, but she was terribly weak.

"Who has done this?"

She made a little motion with her head to silence all such useless questions.

"Hush! No — stay here — no one can help me now." As she spoke her arms stole round his neck and encircled it, and with her little remaining strength she drew his face down beside hers and nestled close to it. "Ned," she whispered, "Ned, I love you — Ah, Ned, I love you, I love you with all my heart and soul. I've loved you always," and she kissed him lingeringly again and again. " It's worth while to die to tell you this. I couldn't have told you — if I'd lived. I — I used to hope — at first — you wouldn't care for me, but afterwards — I was glad — so glad. We're both the better for it, dear — Did you think me cruel? — Ah, Ned, it was as hard for me as you! I loved you so dearly — so dearly." She was silent for a moment or two, and when she spoke again her whispers were lower still. " Go now! — yes, yes, go — live for my sake — don't let them — Ah! Ah, Ned! help! help me!" she cried in tones of piteous distress, her slender figure growing almost rigid in his arms with the spasm that racked it.

It passed. A sigh of utter exhaustion escaped her. Her hands strove feebly to guide his face to hers once more. He bent to meet her lips, and all the love and tenderness of which womanhood is capable seemed to dwell in their sweet kiss.

"Ned — tell me you love me — " she whispered almost inaudibly.

And the smile on her lips never changed again.

For a few moments only the sound of Ned's convulsive sobs broke the stillness. But a sort of darkness came over him. Unconsciously he laid reverently on the ground the form of the woman he had loved so well and staggered up, groping blindly before him as though the twilight were thick night, whilst deep-drawn gasps for breath broke from him at intervals in the silence.

Suddenly the movement of his hands ceased; for a brief second he stood there motionless, then reeled, threw up his arms, and pitched heavily forward.

The ambush had proved successful, after all. He had ridden fairly into it, and more than one bullet had wounded him mortally.

* * * * * * * *

"Both dead?" exclaimed voices an hour later.

"Looks like it."

"And who in hell killed the girl?"

"She killed herself," said Hannaford. Before the action could be noticed, he had taken occasion to remove Ned's pistol from its scabbard and had dropped it beside her. "She killed herself after he died. I saw her do it with his pistol."

THE END.

www.ingramcontent.com/pod-product-compliance
Lightning Source LLC
Chambersburg PA
CBHW030343230426
43664CB00007BA/510